Mohammed and Charlemagne

MOHAMMED

AND

CHARLEMAGNE

by HENRI PIRENNE

MERIDIAN BOOKS *New York* 1957

Henri Pirenne

Born and educated in Belgium, Henri Pirenne (1862-1935) first lectured at the University of Liège. From 1886 to 1930 he was professor of history at the University of Ghent. He was the first president of the Union Académique Internationale (1920-23), and received many foreign academic honors. Noted for his works on medieval cities and social conditions, his *Histoire de Belgique* in seven volumes revolutionized current conceptions of Belgian history and nationality by showing how the Flemings and the Walloons were drawn together by a community of tradition and economic interest. This edition of *Mohammed and Charlemagne* was translated by Bernard Miall from the French of the tenth edition published by Librarie Félix Alcan, Paris, and Nouvelle Société d'Editions Brussels.

Meridian Books Edition published February 1957
First printing January 1957

Reprinted by arrangement with
W. W. Norton & Company, Inc.

First published 1939 by W. W. Norton & Company, Inc.

Library of Congress Catalog Card Number: 57-6675

Manufactured in the United States of America

CONTENTS

PREFACE

WHEN my father was taken ill, on May 28th, 1935—it was the day on which his eldest son, Henri-Edouard, died—he left on his table the three hundred pages of the manuscript of *Mohammed and Charlemagne*, which he had completed on May 4th.

This was the crowning achievement of his last years of work. The problem of the end of Antiquity and the beginning of the Middle Ages had always preoccupied him. Before the War, in his lectures on the History of the Middle Ages, he drew attention to the profound traces which the institutions of the late Roman Empire had left upon those of the Frankish epoch. But it was during his captivity in Germany, when, as a prisoner in the camp of Holzminden, he organized, for the many Russian students who shared his fate, a course of lectures on the economic history of Europe, that the solution of this capital problem seems to have dawned upon him. And during his exile in the village of Kreuzburg, in Thuringia, while he was writing his *History of Europe*, he emphasized, for the first time, the close relation that existed between the conquests of Islam and the formation of the mediaeval Occident.

The *History of Europe*, which he did not live to complete, was published only after his death. At that time no one was aware of the subject of the present volume.

My father, however, returning again and again to his study of the available sources, had never ceased to examine this problem, which was the great scientific interest of the last twenty years of his life.

In 1922 he published in the *Revue belge de Philologie et d'Histoire* a short article entitled "Mahomet et Charlemagne," which contained a statement of his thesis. He then expounded it before the International Historical Congress—which met in Brussels in 1923 and in Oslo in 1928; it was also the subject of a course of public lectures delivered in the University of Brussels in 1931–1932, and of other lectures given in the following Universities: Lille (1921),

9

New York (Columbia College 1922), Cambridge (1924), Montpellier (1929), Algiers (1931), and Cairo (1934); and also in Rome, at the Institute historique Belge (1933).

Further, while the present history was in preparation, he wrote a number of papers dealing with various details: "Mérovingians et Carolingiens" (*Revue belge de Philologie et d'Histoire*, II, 1923), "Le commerce du papyrus dans la Gaule mérovingienne" (*Comptes rendus de l'Académie des Inscriptions et Belles Lettres*, Paris, 1928), "L'instruction des marchands au Moyen Age" (*Annales d'Histoire économique et sociale*, I, 1929), "Le trésor des rois mérovingiens" (*Festschrift til Halvdan Koht*, Oslo, 1933), "De l'état de l'instruction des laïques à l'époque mérovingienne "(*Revue Bénédictine*, 1934). And he expounded his theory in the first chapters of his "Villes du Moyen Age" (1927), as explaining the economic and social evolution of the centuries following on the fall of Rome.

The volume which my father completed on May 4th, 1935, is therefore the climax of many years of research. But although it contains all the author's ideas, it would not, had he lived, have been given to the public in its present form.

It was my father's custom to write all his books a second time. In the first version he put the book together regardless of form; it was in some respects a rough draft. A second version, which was not a mere revision of the first, but an entirely new text, gave the work that objective and deliberately reticent form behind which he chose to conceal his own personality.

This first draft was written for himself; urged on by the ideas which he was in haste to express, it often happened that he did not complete the construction of a sentence, so that it thus assumed a schematic aspect, or he ended it with an irregular stroke of the pen, comprehensible to all those who have heard how often, when speaking, he dropped the last few words of a sentence, in his impatience to pursue an idea that outstripped his speech.

The references were indicated in a summary fashion, and sometimes my father even contented himself with indicating one of his files.

It was therefore necessary, before the work could be offered to the public, to undertake a certain amount of revision—as little as possible—in respect of its form, to complete the references, and to collate the texts which were cited in the latter.

Wherever the text was complete I have treated it with scrupulous respect. I have ventured to revise it only where it appeared to be unfinished, and in this case I have restricted myself, making use of my father's own notes, to adding the few words which were needed to make them comprehensible.

The revision and completion of the references was a more delicate matter. In order to do this effectively my mother and I appealed to one of my father's most valued pupils, M. F. Vercauteren, Associate of the Fonds Nationale de la Recherche Scientifique, and professor in the Université Coloniale of Antwerp. The studies to which he has devoted himself have made him one of the most erudite authorities on the historical sources and the scientific literature of the early Middle Ages. He granted our request with the greatest alacrity, and devoted several months to the work of collating all the texts which have been cited in this volume, and in verifying and completing the references. I take this opportunity of expressing our warmest and sincerest thanks.

Just as it stands, in its first draft, this last work of my father's pen contains his most vital, boldest, and most recent ideas, on which his mind was actively engaged upon the eve of his death. It is with confidence that we offer them to the public, dedicating them to all those who loved him, and who, now that he is no more, have paid such unanimous homage, not only to the work which finds its conclusion in the publication of this book, but also to the man; and they will doubtless feel that he lives again in these pages, the last he was to write.

JACQUES PIRENNE

NOTE

IN January 1937 Mme. Henri Pirenne and M. Jacques Pirenne brought to my notice the manuscript of a posthumous work of my late master, asking me to assist in its revision with a view to its publication. The text with which I had to deal was complete, but it was a first draft. It had, however, been slightly revised, as regards its form only, by M. Jacques Pirenne.

Before all, Henri Pirenne's ideas had to be loyally respected. I have therefore refrained from making any alterations or suppressions or additions which would in any way have modified the thesis expounded by this eminent historian, even though there were passages which seemed to me debatable. In these pages, therefore, the reader will find a work which is strictly personal to Henri Pirenne.

At the same time, however, I had to verify the material accuracy of a certain number of facts, dates, and quotations. The footnotes and bibliographical references indispensable in a work of this character were very often given only in the germ; these I felt I could revise and develop in conformity with the requirements of contemporary scholarship. In some cases I have even thought it desirable to cite one or more additional texts in support of the views expressed by my eminent master.

For more than twelve years it was my great privilege to work under the guidance and with the assistance of Henri Pirenne: and I think I may say that I was fully conversant with the ideas and the theories which he held as regards the subject of the present volume, in respect of which he had already undertaken a great deal of preparatory work. Destiny unhappily decreed that he was not to offer to the public a completed work, fresh from his own pen. It goes without saying that I have not entertained the presumptuous ambition of giving to the work those finishing touches of which he alone would have been capable, and to which he would have brought an objective care, a conscientious scholarship

13

as great as the ardour and enthusiasm with which he applied himself to its first writing.

Above all, I do not forget that if there are those who were kind enough to consider that I had some qualifications for undertaking this work, I owe them, before all, to Henri Pirenne himself, to his teaching and his example. I have felt that I was performing a pious duty in enabling the thought of the master to bring us, even from beyond the tomb, the benefit of his profound learning, his synthetic vision and his incomparable talent.

F. VERCAUTEREN

Part One

WESTERN EUROPE BEFORE ISLAM

THE CONTINUATION OF THE MEDITERRANEAN CIVILIZATION IN THE WEST AFTER THE GERMANIC INVASIONS

1. *"Romania" before the Germans*

Of all the features of that wonderful human structure, the Roman Empire,[1] the most striking, and also the most essential, was its Mediterranean character. Although in the East it was Greek, and in the West, Latin, its Mediterranean character gave it a unity which impressed itself upon the provinces as a whole. The inland sea, in the full sense of the term *Mare nostrum*, was the vehicle of ideas, and religions, and merchandise.[2] The provinces of the North—Belgium, Britain, Germany, Raetia, Noricum, Pannonia—were merely outlying ramparts against barbarism. Life was concentrated on the shores of the great lake. Without it Rome could not have been supplied with African wheat. It was more beneficent than ever now that it could be navigated in perfect security, since piracy had long disappeared. On the roads that led thither from all the provinces the traffic of these provinces converged upon the sea. As one travelled away from it civilization became more rarefied. The last great city of the North was Lyons. Trèves owed its greatness only to its rank of temporary capital. All the other cities of importance—Carthage, Alexandria, Naples, Antioch—were on or near the sea.

---

[1] The term *Romania*, denoting all the countries conquered by Rome, made its appearance in the 4th century. EUG. ALBERTINI, *L'Empire romain*, in the collection PEUPLES ET CIVILISATION, published under the editorship of L. HALPHEN and PH. SAGNAC, vol. iv, Paris, 1929, p. 388. Cf. A. GRENIER's review of HOLLAND ROSE, *The Mediterranean in the Ancient World*, 2nd ed., 1934, REVUE HISTORIQUE, vol. 173, 1934, p. 194.

[2] It was undoubtedly the Mediterranean that prevented the dyarchy following the reign of Theodosius from giving rise to two Empires.

This Mediterranean character of "Romania" became even more marked after the 4th century, for Constantinople, the new capital, was before all a maritime city. It was opposed to Rome, which was merely a consumer-city, by virtue of the fact that it was a great emporium, a manufacturing city, and an important naval base. The more active the Orient, the greater its hegemony; Syria was the terminus of the routes by which the Empire was in communication with India and China, while by way of the Black Sea it was in touch with the North.

The West depended on Constantinople for manufactured articles and *objets de luxe*.

The Empire took no account of Asia, Africa and Europe. Even though there were different civilizations, the foundation was everywhere the same. The same manners, the same customs, the same religions were found upon these coasts, which had formerly known civilizations as different as the Egyptian, the Tyrian and the Carthaginian.

The maritime traffic of the Mediterranean was concentrated in the East.[1] The Syrians, or those who were known as such, were the pilots and traders of the Eastern Seas. It was in their bottoms that papyrus, spices, ivory, and wines of quality found their way even to Britain. Precious fabrics were brought from Egypt, and also herbs for the ascetics.[2] There were colonies of Syrians everywhere. The port of Marseilles was half Greek.

As well as these Syrians, the Jews were to be found in all the cities, living in small communities. They were sailors, brokers, bankers, whose influence was as essential in the economic life of

[1] This supremacy of the Orient, from the 3rd century (but it existed even earlier) is emphasized by BRATIANU, in his article: *La distribution de l'or et les raisons économiques de la division de l'Empire romain*, ISTROS, in the REVUE ROUMAINE D'ARCHÉOLOGIE ET D'HISTOIRE ANCIENNE, Vol. I, 1934, Part II. Here we see the beginning of the separation of Occident and Orient which was completed by Islam. Cf. also PAULOVA's essay on *L'Islam et la civilisation méditerranéenne*, in the VESTNIK CESKE AKADEMIE TCHEQUE (MEMOIRS OF THE CZECH ACADEMY), Prague, 1934.

[2] P. PERDRIZET, *Scété et Landevenec*, in MELANGES N. JORGA, Paris, 1933, p. 745.

the time as was the Oriental influence which made itself felt at the same period in the art and the religious thought of the period. Asceticism came to the West from the East by sea, as the worship of Mithra and Christianity had come.

Without Ostia, Rome is unimaginable. And if, on the other side of Italy, Ravenna had become the residence of the Emperors *in partibus occidentis*, it was because of the attraction of Constantinople.

Thanks to the Mediterranean, then, the Empire constituted, in the most obvious fashion, an economic unity. It was one great territory, with tolls but no custom houses. And it enjoyed the enormous advantage of a common monetary unit, the gold *solidus* of Constantine, containing 4·55 grammes of fine gold, which was current everywhere.[1]

We know that since the reign of Diocletian there had been a general economic decline. But it seems that in the 4th century there was a recovery and a more active circulation of money.

In order to provide for the security of this Empire surrounded by Barbarians the frontier guard of the Legions had long sufficed: on the edge of the Sahara, on the Euphrates, the Danube, and the Rhine. But behind the dyke the waters were rising. In the 3rd century, owing partly to civil disturbances, there were cracks in the dyke, and then breaches. From all directions there was an irruption of Franks, Alamans and Goths, who ravaged Gaul, Rhaetia, Pannonia and Thrace, advancing even as far as Spain.

They were swept back by the Illyrian Emperors, and the frontier was re-established. But on the German side of the Empire the *limes* no longer sufficed; a deep defensive front was necessary. The cities of the interior were fortified: those cities that were the nerve-centres of the Empire, Rome and Constantinople, became two model fortresses.

And there was no longer any question of closing the Empire to the Barbarians. The population was diminishing; the soldier had become a mercenary. The Barbarians were needed, as soldiers, and as agricultural labourers. They asked nothing better than to enter

[1] ALBERTINI, *op. cit.*, p. 365.

the service of Rome. Thus the Empire, on its frontiers, became Germanized in respect of blood; but not otherwise, for all who entered the Empire became Romanized.[1] All these Germans who entered the Empire did so to serve it and to enjoy its advantages. They felt for it all the respect of the Barbarian for civilization. No sooner did they enter it than they adopted its language, and also its religion: that is to say, Christianity, after the 4th century; and in becoming Christians, in losing their national gods, and frequenting the same churches, they gradually merged into the population of the Empire.

Before long almost the entire army was composed of Barbarians; and many of them, like the Vandal, Stilicho, the Goth, Gainas, and the Suevian, Ricimer, achieved fame as soldiers of the Empire.[2]

2. The Invasions

As we know, in the course of the 5th century the Roman Empire lost its Western territories to the Germanic Barbarians.

This was not the first time that the Empire had been attacked by the Germans. The menace was of long standing, and it was to guard against it that the military frontier Rhine–Danube *limes* had been established. It had sufficed to defend the Empire until the 3rd century; but after the first great assault of the Barbarians it had been necessary to abandon the old comfortable confidence and to adopt a defensive attitude, reforming the army by reducing the size of its units in order to render them more mobile; and finally it consisted almost entirely of Barbarian mercenaries.[3]

---

[1] However, in 370 or 375 (?) a law of Valentinian and Valens prohibited marriages between *Provintiales* and *Gentiles*, under penalty of death (*Code Theod.*, III, 14, I). Cf. F. LOT, *Les Invasions germaniques*, Paris, 1935 (Bibl. hist.), p. 168.

[2] ALBERTINI, *op. cit.*, p. 412; F. LOT, PFISTER AND GANSHOF, *Histoire du Moyen Age*, Vol. I, pp. 79–90, in L'HISTOIRE GENERALE published under the direction of G. GLOTZ. Even under Theodosius, Arbogast was "master of the soldiers." Cf. LOT, *ibid.*, p. 22.

[3] ALBERTINI, *op. cit.*, p. 332.

Thanks to these measures, the Empire continued to defend itself for two hundred years.

What was the cause of its final failure?

It had its fortresses, against which the Barbarians were powerless, its strategic routes, a military art whose tradition was many centuries old, a consummate diplomacy which understood how division might be created among the enemies of the Empire, or how they might be bought—and this was one of the essential features of the Empire's resistance—and further, its aggressors were incapable of agreeing among themselves. Above all, the Empire had the Mediterranean, and we shall see what an advantage this gave it, even down to the time when the Vandals established themselves in Carthage.

I know, of course, that the difference between the armaments of the Empire and those of the Barbarians was not what it would be today; nevertheless, the Romans enjoyed an impressive superiority over peoples without a commissariat and without regular discipline. The Barbarians, no doubt, were superior in numbers, but they did not know how to revictual their forces. Think of the Visigoths, dying of starvation in Aquitaine, after living on the country, and Alaric in Italy!

As against its advantages, we must remember that the Empire was obliged to keep armies in being on the frontiers of Africa and Asia while it had to face its enemies in Europe. Further, it had to deal with civil disturbances; there were many usurpers, who did not hesitate to enter into understandings with the Barbarians; there were Court intrigues, which set up a Rufinus in opposition to a Stilicho; while the populations of the Empire were passive, and incapable of resistance; without civic spirit, they despised the Barbarians, but were ready to submit to their yoke. Consequently the defence could not count upon moral resistance, whether among the troops or in the rear. Fortunately, there were no moral forces on the side of the aggressor either. There was nothing to provoke the Germans against the Empire: no religious motives, no racial hatred, and still less any sort of political consideration. Far from hating the Empire, they admired it. All they wanted was to settle down in the Empire and enjoy its advantages. And their kings aspired to the attainment of Roman dignities. There was nothing comparable to the contrast between the Musulmans and the Christians of a later date. The paganism of the Barbarians did not inspire them with hatred of the Roman gods, nor did it excite their hostility toward the one God of the Christians. About the middle of the 4th century a Goth, Ulfila, who had been converted to Arianism in Byzantium, introduced the new religion among his compatriots on the Dnieper, and they in turn propagated the faith among other Germans, Vandals and Burgundians.[1] Heretics without knowing it, their Christianity nevertheless brought them closer to the Romans.

On the other hand, these Germans of the East had had some initiation into the ways of civilization. On descending to the shores of the Black Sea the Goths had come into contact with the ancient Graeco-Oriental culture of the Greeks and Sarmatians of the Crimea; and there they learnt to practise the production of the florid goldsmith's art which they afterwards made known throughout Europe under the style of *Ars Barbarica*.

By sea they were in communication with the Bosphorus, where in the year 330 Constantinople, the great new city, had been founded on the site of the Greek Byzantium (May 11th, 330).[2] It was from Constantinople that Christianity had come to them with Ulfila, and we may be sure that Ulfila was not the only one of their number to be attracted by the brilliant capital of the Empire. In the natural course of events they were bound to feel the influence of the great city beyond the Black Sea, just as the Varangians were to feel it at a later date.

The Barbarians did not spontaneously hurl themselves upon the Empire. They were pushed forward by the flood of the Hunnish advance, which in this way caused the whole series of invasions. For the first time Europe was to feel, across the immense gap of

[1] L. HALPHEN, *Les Barbares*, in PEUPLES ET CIVILISATIONS, vol. V, 1926, p. 74.
[2] ALBERTINI, *op. cit.*, p. 359.

the Sarmatic Plain, the repercussion of the clashes between the populations of Farthest Asia.

The arrival of the Huns flung the Goths against the Empire. It seems that their method of fighting, perhaps their appearance, and their nomadism, which seemed so terrible to a sedentary population, rendered them invincible.[1]

The defeated Ostrogoths were flung against Pannonia, and the Visigoths fled across the Danube. This was in the autumn of 376. The Romans had to let them pass. How many were they?[2] It is impossible to say precisely. L. Schmidt imagines that there were 40,000, of whom 8,000 were warriors.[3]

They crossed the frontier with their dukes, like a nation, with the consent of the Emperor, who acknowledged them as allies, subject to the obligation of furnishing recruits to the Roman army.

This was something quite new, and it was a happening of extreme importance. With the Ostrogoths a foreign body had entered into the Empire. They retained their rights of nationality. They were not divided up, but were left in a compact group. The arrangements were hastily made; no territory was assigned to them; and finding themselves in a sterile mountainous region, they revolted no later than the following year (377). What they coveted was access to the Mediterranean, and they began to march toward the sea.

On August 9th, 378, at Andrinople, the Emperor Valens was defeated and slain. The whole of Thrace was pillaged, excepting the cities, which the Barbarians could not take. They penetrated as far as Constantinople, which resisted them, as it was afterwards to resist the Arabs.

Without the possession of Constantinople, the Germans were able to establish themselves upon the coast, thereby reaching the vital centre of the Empire. But Theodosius drove them away from

[1] Some excellent remarks upon nomadism will be found in E. F. GAUTIER'S *Genseric, roi des Vandales*, 1932, *in fine.*

[2] F. DAHN, *Die Könige der Germanen*, vol. VI, 1871, p. 50.

[3] L. SCHMIDT, *Geschichte der deutschen Stämme bis zum Ausgang der Völkerwanderung. Die Ostgermanen*, 2nd ed., Munich, 1934, pp. 400-403.

it. In 382, having defeated them, he established them in Moesia. But they still constituted a nation. During the war, doubtless for military reasons, they replaced their dukes by a king: Alaric. It was very natural that he should have wished to extend his territory, and to attempt the capture of Constantinople, which fascinated him. But we must not regard this endeavour, as L. Schmidt has done, on the authority of Isidore of Seville (!),[1] as an attempt to set up a national Germanic kingdom in the East. Although their numbers had been considerably increased by fresh arrivals from beyond the Danube, the Germanic character of the Goths was already greatly diminished by the addition of the slaves and adventurers who had come to join them.

The Empire had taken no precautions against them, if we except the law of Valentinian and Valens, introduced in 370 or 375, which prohibited marriage between Romans and Barbarians under penalty of death. But in preventing their assimilation by the Roman population this perpetuated their condition of a foreign body within the Empire, and probably did something towards inducing them to undertake fresh adventures.

Finding the way open before them, the Goths ravaged Greece, Athens and the Peloponnesus. Stilicho, sailing for the East, fought them and drove them back into Epirus. However, they remained within the Empire, and Arcadius authorized them to settle, still as allies, in Illyria; and hoping, no doubt, to make him submissive to the authority of the Emperor, he invested Alaric with the title of *Magister militum per Illyricum*.[2] By this means the Goths were at all events safely removed from Constantinople, but they were near Italy, which had not yet been ravaged, and they launched an attack upon it in 401. Stilicho defeated them at Pollenza and at Verona, and drove them back in 402. According to L. Schmidt, Alaric invaded Italy in order to realize his "world plans." This is to imagine that with the 100,000 men whom Schmidt attributes to him he conceived the idea of replacing the Roman by a Germanic Empire.

[1] L. SCHMIDT, *op. cit.*, p. 426. [2] L. HALPHEN, *op. cit.*, p. 16.

In reality, Alaric was a condottiere who was greedy for gain. He was so free from convictions of any sort that he hired himself to Stilicho, for 4,000 librae of gold, in order to fight Arcadius, with whom he had a treaty of alliance.

Stilicho was assassinated at a convenient moment for Alaric. With an army enlarged by a great proportion of Stilicho's troops, he marched upon Italy once more in 408.[1] In Alaric the Barbarian was becoming metamorphosed into an intriguing Roman soldier. In 409, as Honorius refused to treat with him, he caused the senator, Priscus Attalus,[2] to be proclaimed Emperor, whereupon Priscus promoted him to the superior rank of *Magister utriusque militiae praesentialis*. Then, hoping to become reconciled with Honorius, Alaric betrayed his creature. But Honorius had no intention of becoming a second Attalus. Thereupon Alaric proceeded to pillage Rome, having taken the city by surprise; and when he left it he took with him Galla Placidia, the Emperor's sister. Was it his intention to turn back and attack Ravenna? On the contrary. He marched into Southern Italy, which had not yet been pillaged, intending to cross over to Africa, the granary of Rome, and the most prosperous of the Western provinces. And as it marched his army ravaged the country, in order to obtain food. Alaric was not destined to reach Africa; he died at the end of the year 410. His burial in the bed of the Busento was that of an epic hero.[3]

His brother-in-law Ataulf, who succeeded to him, turned back to the North. After some months of pillage he marched upon Gaul, where the usurper Jovinus had just assumed power. He was determined at all costs to obtain a Roman title. Having quarrelled

---

[1] Alaric would have preferred to stay where he was, but he could not; he needed the authorization of the Emperor, and the latter took good care not to allow the Barbarians to take possession of Italy, just as in the East they were not allowed to take possession of Thrace.

[2] F. LOT, PFISTER and GANSHOF, *Histoire du Moyen Age* (Collection GLOTZ), vol. I, p. 35.

[3] See C. DAWSON, *The Making of Europe* (New York), 1932, French translation, *Les origines de l'Europe* (Paris, 1934), p. 110.

with Jovinus, who was killed in 413,[1] and dismissed by Honorius, who remained immovable, he married the beautiful Placidia at Narbonne in 414, which made him the Emperor's brother-in-law. It was then that he is said to have made the famous declaration recorded by Orosius:[2] "To begin with I ardently desired to efface the very name of the Romans and to transform the Roman Empire into a Gothic Empire. *Romania*, as it is vulgarly called, would have become *Gothia*; Ataulf would have replaced Caesar Augustus. But long experience taught me that the unruly barbarism of the Goths was incompatible with the laws. Now, without laws there is no State (*republica*). I therefore decided rather to aspire to the glory of restoring the fame of Rome in all its integrity, and of increasing it by means of the Gothic strength. I hope to go down to posterity as the restorer of Rome, since it is not possible that I should be its supplanter."[3]

In so saying he was making advances to Honorius. But the Emperor, still immovable, refused to treat with a German who, from his headquarters at Narbonne, might attempt to dominate the Mediterranean.

Thereupon Ataulf, unable to confer the Imperial dignity upon

---

[1] F. LOT, PFISTER and GANSHOF, *Histoire du Moyen Age* (Collection GLOTZ), vol. I, p. 43.

[2] OROSIUS, *Adversus Paganos*, VII, 43, ed. K. ZANGEMEISTER, 1882, p. 560. L. SCHMIDT, *op. cit.*, p. 453, attributes to Ataulf the idea of an "Anti-Roman, national Gothic Policy." E. STEIN, *Geschichte des Spätrömischen Reiches*, vol. I, 1928, p. 403, says nothing of this; but he observes that after his marriage Ataulf's policy was friendly to Rome.

[3] F. LOT, PFISTER and GANSHOF, *Histoire du Moyen Age*, vol. I, p. 44. It was undoubtedly upon this famous declaration that L. SCHMIDT based his theory of Ataulf's "Germanism." But even though Ataulf thought of replacing the Roman by a "Gothic" Empire he did not assert that this State would be Germanic in spirit; it would, as a matter of fact, have been a Roman Empire in which Ataulf and the Goths would have exercised the power of government. That he did not create such an Empire was due to the fact that he had realized that the Goths were incapable of obeying the laws: that is to say, the Roman laws. He then decided to place the strength of his people at the service of the Empire, which proves that he did not entertain the idea of destroying "Romania."

himself, once more declared Attalus the Emperor of the West, in order to reconstruct the Empire with him.

However, the unfortunate Goth was compelled to continue his raids, for he was starving. Honorius having blockaded the coast, he marched into Spain, intending, perhaps, to make his way into Africa, and in 415 he died, assassinated by one of his men, recommending his brother Wallia to remain loyal to Rome.

Finding that he too was being starved in Spain, owing to the blockade of the ports, Wallia attempted to cross over into Africa, but was driven back by a tempest. The West, at this moment, was in a desperate condition. In 406 the Huns, who were still advancing, drove before them—this time across the Rhine—the Vandals, Alains, Suevi and Burgundi, who, jostling the Franks and Alamans, moved southwards across Gaul until they reached the Mediterranean and Spain. In order to resist them, the Emperor appealed to Wallia. Driven by necessity, he consented to help the Empire; and having received 600,000 measures of corn[1] from Rome, he turned back to stem the flood of the Barbarians, who, like his Visigoths, were trying to make their way to Africa.

In 418 the Emperor authorized the Visigoths to establish themselves in Aquitania Secunda, conferring upon Wallia, as formerly upon Alaric, the title of ally.

Stabilized between the Loire and the Garonne, on the Atlantic coast, and shut off from the Mediterranean, which they no longer menaced, the Goths had at last obtained the territory which they had never ceased to demand.[2]

This time they were treated like a Roman army, and the logistic regulations of the Roman army were applied to them.[3] But this

[1] E. STEIN, op. cit., p. 404.

[2] At first the allies were confined to infertile provinces: the Visigoths to Moesia, and later to Aquitania Secunda, the Burgundi to Savoy, and the Ostrogoths to Pannonia. One can understand that they wished to escape from these provinces.

[3] According to H. BRUNNER, Deutsche Rechtsgeschichte (Leipzig, 2nd ed., 1906), vol. I, p. 67, the regulations of the tercia were not applied to the Goths until a later date. For the regulations concerning distribution, see E. STEIN, op. cit., p. 406.

arrangement was to be permanent. The Goths were thus tied to the soil and distributed in the midst of the Roman population. Their king did not reign over the Romans. He was the general of his people, and their king, *rex Gothorum;* he was not *rex Aquitaniae.* The Goths were encamped in the midst of the Romans and held together by their king. Above him was the Emperor, but for the Roman population this German king was merely a general of mercenaries in the service of the Empire; and the stabilization of the Goths was regarded by the population as evidence of the power of Rome.

In 417 Rutilius Namatianus was still boasting of the eternal nature of Rome.[1]

The acceptance of the Visigoths as "allies of Rome" and their legal installation in Aquitaine did not result in their pacification. Twenty years later, when Stilicho had to recall the Legions from Gaul in order to defend Italy, while Genseric succeeded in conquering Africa, the Visigoths fell upon Narbonne (437), defeated the Romans at Toulouse (439), and on this occasion obtained a treaty which probably recognized them, not as allies, but as an independent people.[2]

The cause of this collapse of the Imperial power in Gaul was the fact that the Vandals, under Genseric, had crossed over into Africa.

Succeeding where the Goths had failed, Genseric, in 427, with the aid of the Carthaginian ships, crossed the Straits of Gibraltar and landed 50,000 men upon the African coast. For the Empire this was the decisive blow. The very soul of the Republic—says Salvian—was destroyed. When in 439 Genseric captured Carthage —that is, the great naval base of the West—and then, shortly afterwards, took possession of Sardinia, Corsica and the Balearics, the position of the Empire in the West was completely shaken. It had lost the Mediterranean, which had hitherto been its great weapon of defence.

[1] F. LOT, PFISTER and GANSHOF, *Histoire du Moyen Age,* vol. I, p. 51, state that in 423, when Honorius died, the Empire re-established its authority in Africa, Italy, Gaul and Spain.

[2] E. STEIN, *op. cit.,* p. 482.

The provisioning of Rome was imperilled, and also the revictualling of the army, and this was afterwards the point of departure of Odoacer's rebellion. The Barbarians had control of the sea. In 441 the Emperor sent against them an expedition which on this occasion was unsuccessful, for the opposing forces were equally matched; the Vandals, no doubt, opposing the fleet of Byzantium with that of Carthage. Valentinian was obliged to recognize their establishment in the richest portions of Africa— in Carthage, Byzacium and Numidia (442).[1]

But this was only a truce.

Genseric has been regarded as a man of genius. The great part which he played in history was doubtless explained by the position which he occupied. He succeeded where Alaric and Wallia had failed. The most prosperous province of the Empire was in his hands. He was living in the midst of abundance. From the great seaport which was now in his power he could undertake profitable ventures of piracy. He could threaten the East no less than the West, and he felt that he was strong enough to defy the Empire, whose titles he regarded with indifference.

If we seek for the explanation of the Empire's inactivity where he was concerned for the years following the truce of 442, we shall find it in the Huns.

In 447, advancing from the plains of the Theiss, Attila ravaged Moesia and Thrace as far as Thermopylae. Then, turning westward, he marched upon Gaul, crossing the Rhine in the spring of 451 and laying waste the countryside as far as the Loire.

Aetius, supported by the Germans, Franks, Burgundi and Visigoths,[2] who behaved as loyal allies, checked him in the neighbourhood of Troyes. The military art of the Romans and the valour of the Germans collaborated. Theodoric I, king of the Visigoths, in fulfilling Ataulf's ambition to become the restorer of the Empire, was slain. The death of Attila in 453 spelt the ruin of his ephemeral achievements, and saved the West from the Mongol peril. The

[1] F. LOT, PFISTER and GANSHOF, *Histoire du Moyen Age*, vol. I, p. 63.
[2] L. HALPHEN, *op. cit.*, p. 32.

Empire then turned upon Genseric. Realizing his danger, he was first in the field.

In 455, taking advantage of the assassination of Valentinian, he refused to recognize Maximus. On June 2nd, 455, he entered Rome and sacked the city.[1]

On the same pretext, Theodoric II, king of the Visigoths (453–466), broke with the Empire, favouring the election of the Gaulish Emperor Avitus; and being sent by him to fight the Suevi in Spain he immediately marched in the direction of the Mediterranean. Avitus, defeated and captured by Ricimer, became a bishop,[2] but the Visigoths continued their campaign. Meanwhile the Burgundi, who, defeated by Aetius, were established as allies in Savoy in 443,[3] seized the city of Lyons (457).

Majorian, who had just ascended the throne, confronted this new peril. He recaptured Lyons in 458, and then hurriedly turned upon Genseric. In 460 he crossed the Pyrenees in order to reach Africa by way of Gibraltar, but was assassinated in Spain (461).

Lyons immediately fell into the hands of the Burgundi, who filled the whole valley of the Rhone, as far as the frontiers of Provence.

Theodoric II continued his conquests. He failed to take Arles, whose resistance saved Provence, but he captured Narbonne (462). After him, Euric (466–484) attacked the Suevi of Spain, drove them back into Galicia, and conquered the Peninsula. A feigned truce and the use of fire-ships resulted in his defeat off Cape Bon. With this the game was lost.

In order to resist its enemies the Empire had at any cost to recover the control of the sea. The Emperor Leo, in 468, made

---

[1] E. GAUTIER, Genséric, pp. 233–235.

[2] A. COVILLE, Recherches sur l'histoire de Lyon du Vᵉ siècle au IXᵉ siècle (450–800), Paris, 1928, p. 121.

[3] They were established in Savoy in accordance with the principle of the tertia. As BRUNNER has observed, op. cit., vol. I, 2nd ed., pp. 65–66, they were a vanquished people. This kind of settlement, which was practised in the case of the Visigoths and Ostrogoths, was therefore of Roman origin.

preparations for a great expedition against Africa. He is said to have spent 9,000,000 *solidi* and equipped 1,100 vessels.

At Ravenna the Emperor Anthemius was rendered powerless by Ricimer, the *magister militiae*. All that he could do was to delay by negotiations (for he no longer had a fleet) the occupation of Provence, which was threatened by Euric. The latter was already the master of Spain and Gaul, which he had conquered as far as the Loire (in 469).

The fall of Romulus Augustulus delivered Provence into the hands of the Visigoths (476); and from this moment the whole of the Western Mediterranean was lost.

When everything is taken into account, we may ask ourselves how the Empire could have held out so long, and we cannot but admire the obstinacy with which it resisted its destiny. A Majorian who recaptured Lyons from the Burgundi and marched through Spain upon Genseric is still worthy of admiration. For its defence, the Empire could count only upon allies, who continually betrayed it, like the Visigoths and the Burgundi, and mercenary troops whose loyalty could not resist misfortune, and which found it difficult to revictual themselves, since Africa and the islands were in the possession of the Vandals.

The East itself was threatened along the Danube, and was powerless. Its only effort was made against Genseric. Assuredly, if the Barbarians had wished to destroy the Empire they had only to agree among themselves, and they must have succeeded.[1] But they did not wish to destroy it.

After Majorian (d. 461) there were none but contemptible Emperors in Ravenna, living at the mercy of the Barbarian commanders and their troops of Suevi: Ricimer (472), and the Burgundian Gundobald, who, having returned to Gaul in order to become king over his people, was replaced by Orestes, of Hunnish origin, who deposed Julius Nepos, and gave the throne to his own son Romulus Augustulus.

---

[1] L. HALPHEN, *op. cit.*, p. 35, speaks inaccurately of the "methodical" efforts of the Barbarians.

But Orestes, who refused to give land to the soldiers,[1] was massacred, and their general Odoacer[2] was proclaimed king by the troops. He was opposed only by Romulus Augustulus, the son of Orestes, whom he sent to the villa of Lucullus on Cape Miseno (476).

Zeno, Emperor of the East, went so far as to recognize Odoacer as a patrician of the Empire. As a matter of fact, nothing was changed; Odoacer was an Imperial functionary.

In 488, in order to get the Ostrogoths out of Pannonia, where they threatened the Empire,[3] Zeno sent them to conquer Italy, employing Germans against Germans, after granting their king Theodoric the title of patrician. In 489 the battle of Verona was fought, in 490 the battle of the Adda, and finally, in 493, Odoacer was captured and assassinated in Ravenna. Theodoric, being duly authorized by Zeno, took over the government of Italy, while remaining king of his people, who were settled in accordance with the principle of the *tercia*. After this, there was not again an Emperor in the West (except for a moment, in the 6th century) until the reign of Charlemagne. As a matter of fact, the whole of the West was a mosaic of Barbarian kingdoms: Ostrogoths in Italy, Vandals in Africa, Suevi in Galicia, Visigoths in Spain and to the south of the Loire, and Burgundi in the valley of the Rhone. That portion of Northern Gaul which had remained Roman under Syagrius was conquered by Clovis in 486. He overwhelmed the Alamans in the valley of the Rhine and drove the Visigoths into Spain. Lastly, the Anglo-Saxons had established themselves in Britain. Thus, at the beginning of the 6th century there was not an inch of soil in the West still subject to the Emperor. At first

---

[1] L. SCHMIDT, *op. cit.*, p. 317. The Imperial granaries could not revictual them. Once more we see the importance of the Mediterranean. They wanted to settle down and still remain Roman soldiers.

[2] On August 23rd, 476, Odoacer commanded, not a people, but troops of many nationalities. He was a king, but not a national king. He seized power by means of a military pronunciamento. Odoacer sent the Imperial insignia back to Constantinople; he did not take them for himself.

[3] L. HALPHEN, *op. cit.*, p. 45. Although they were settled there as allies after the death of Attila, they threatened Constantinople in 487 (*ibid.*, p. 46).

sight the catastrophe seems enormous; so enormous that the fall of Romulus has been regarded as beginning a second act of the world-drama. But if we examine it more closely it seems less important.

For the Emperor still had a legal existence. He had abdicated nothing of his sovereignty. The old fiction of the allies was maintained. And the new upstarts themselves acknowledged his primacy. The Anglo-Saxons alone ignored him. For the others he was still a pre-eminent sovereign. Theodoric governed in his name. The Burgundian king Sigismond wrote to him in 516–518: *Vester quidem est populus meus.*[1] Clovis prided himself upon receiving the title of consul.[2] No one ventured to assume the title of Emperor;[3] there was no Emperor in the West before Charlemagne. Constantinople remained the capital of this complex, and to Constantinople the Visigoth, Ostrogoth and Vandal kings appealed, as the arbiter of their disputes. The Empire subsisted, in law, as a sort of mystical presence; in fact—and this is much more important—it was "Romania" that survived.

3. *The Germans in "Romania"*

In reality, "Romania" had lost very little: a strip of frontier in the north, and Great Britain, where the Anglo-Saxons had taken the place of the more or less Romanized Britains, many of whom migrated to Brittany. The portion lost in the North[4] may be estimated by comparing the old Rhine–Danube *limes* with the present linguistic frontier between the Germanic and Latin languages. There Germania had gained upon the Empire.

---

[1] *Lettres de Saint-Avit*, ed. PEIPER, M.G.H.SS.ANTIQ., vol. VI[2], p. 100.

[2] GREGORY OF TOURS, *Hist. Franc.*, II, 38.

[3] Even Odoacer did not dare to do so, and this proves that SCHMIDT is mistaken in believing that Alaric and Wallia wished to replace the Roman by a Germanic Empire. All those Germans who were strong enough—Ricimer, etc.—appointed Roman puppets as Emperors. Odoacer was the first to abandon this practice and acknowledge the Emperor in Constantinople.

[4] F. LOT, *Les Invasions*, p. 128, estimates that it was one-seventh of Gaul. It should be noted that it did not comprise any region of essential importance.

Cologne, Mayence, Trèves, Ratisbon and Vienna are today German cities, and the *extremi hominum* are found upon Flemish soil.[1] Of course, the Romanized population did not suddenly disappear. While it seems to have been completely effaced in Tongres, Tournai and Arras, there were still Christians—that is, Romans—in Cologne and Trèves. But those who continued there gradually became Germanized. The *Romani* to whom the Salic Law refers attest the presence of these survivors, and the *Vita Sancti Severini* affords us a glimpse of the intermediary state in Noricum.[2] We know, also, that there were Romans who held their own for a long while in the mountains of the Tyrol and Bavaria.[3] Here, then, colonization took place; the substitution of one population for another; Germanization. The establishment *en masse* of the Western Germans on their own frontiers offers a strange contrast with the formidable migrations which led the Goths from the Dnieper into Italy and Spain, the Burgundi from the Elbe to the Rhine, and the Vandals from the Theiss to Africa. The Germans confined themselves to crossing the river upon which Caesar had established them. Are we to seek the explanation in race? I do not think so. The Franks, in the 3rd century, pushed forward to the Pyrenees, and the Saxons invaded England.

I am more inclined to believe that the explanation is to be sought in the geographical situation. By installing themselves on the frontiers of the Empire the Germans did not directly menace its vital points—Constantinople, Ravenna and Africa. It was therefore possible to allow them to settle down and attach themselves to the soil, a privilege which the Emperors had always refused the Germans of the East until the Visigoths were settled in Aquitaine. In order to make them keep to the frontiers, however, Julian undertook certain expeditions against the Franks and the Alamans; the Roman population retreated before them; they were not installed,

[1] A. DEMANGEON and L. FEBVRE, *Le Rhin. Problèmes d'histoire et d'économie*, Paris, 1935, pp. 50 *et seq.*

[2] Ed. H. SAUPPE, M.G.HSS.ANTIQ., vol. I, 1877.

[3] For the Roman vestiges in Alsace, Switzerland and Bavaria see LOT, *Les Invasions*, pp. 217 and 220.

as mercenary troops, in accordance with the system of the *tercia*, but they slowly colonized the occupied country, attaching themselves to the soil like a people taking root. This explains why, in 406, when the Legions had been withdrawn, the Germans were held up by the small military posts and *castella* of the Roman frontier along the line Bavai–Courtrai–Boulogne and Bavai–Tongres.[1] They advanced very slowly towards the South, capturing Tournai in 446. They were not a conquering army, but a people on the move, who settled down on such fertile soil as was available. And this means that they did not mingle with the Gallo-Roman population, which gradually made way for them; and it explains why they preserved their manners, their epic traditions, and what one may call the Germanic spirit. They imported their religion and their language and introduced new place-names. Germanic names ending in *ze(e)le*, and *inghem*, derive from the family names of the first colonists.

To the south of the territory which they completely submerged they advanced by a process of gradual infiltration, thus creating a zone of mixed population, corresponding more or less to Walloon Belgium, the north of France, and Lorraine. Here many of the place-names attest the presence of a Germanic population which afterwards became Romanized.[2] This infiltration reached as far as the Seine.[3]

But on the whole, Germanization *en masse* had occurred only where the German language was retained. "Romania" had disappeared only in the latest conquests of Rome, along the outer

[1] G. DES MAREZ, *Le problème de la colonisation franque et du régime agraire dans la Basse-Belgique*, Brussels, 1926, p. 25.

[2] Names in *baix*, *stain* (*stein*), etc. Cf. F. LOT, *De L'origine et de la signification historique et linguistique des noms de lieux enville et encourt*, ROMANIA, vol. LIX (1933), pp. 199 *et seq*. See also M. BLOCH's observations in ANNALES D'HISTOIRE ÉCONOMIQUE ET SOCIALE, 1934, pp. 254-250, and J. VANNÉRUS, in the REVUE BELGE DE PHILOLOGIE ET D'HISTOIRE, vol. XIV, 1935, pp. 541 *et seq*. G. KURTH, in his *Etudes franques*, vol. I, p. 262, finds hardly any Frankish names in Touraine.

[3] GAMILLSCHEG, *Romania Germanica*, vol. I, 1934, p. 46: *Das Land zwischen Seine und Loire ist fränkischer Kulturgebiet, aber nicht mehr Siedlungsgebiet.*

rampart which protected the Mediterranean: the two Germanies, part of the Belgiums, Rhaetia, Noricum and Pannonia.

Apart from this, "Romania" had remained intact, and could hardly have done otherwise. The Roman Empire continued to be Roman, just as the United States of North America, despite immigration, have remained Anglo-Saxon.

As a matter of fact, the newcomers were in a very small minority. Without figures, we cannot speak with scientific accuracy, but we have no documents which would furnish such information. What was the population of the Empire?[1] 70 millions? I do not think we can accept the estimate of C. Jullian, who gives Gaul a population of 20 to 40 millions.[2] It is impossible to speak precisely. The only thing that is obvious is, that the Germans disappeared in the mass of the population.

Dahn[3] estimates that the Visigoths admitted to the Empire by Valens may have numbered a million; L. Schmidt, following Utropius, and the figures relating to the battle of Andrinople, speaks of 8,000 warriors and 40,000 souls in all.[4] It is true that these must have been augmented subsequently by Germans, slaves, mercenaries, etc. Schmidt assumes that when Wallia entered Spain (416) the Visigoths numbered 100,000.

Gautier[5] estimates that the tribes of the Vandals and Alains, men, women, children and slaves, when they crossed the Straits of Gibraltar, must have numbered 80,000. This figure is given by Victor de Vita: *Transiens quantitas universa.*[6] Gautier[7] believes that this may be accepted as accurate, since it was easy to calculate the capacity of the fleet.[8] He also estimates,[9] plausibly enough, that

---

[1] E. STEIN, *op. cit.*, p. 3, gives 50 millions at the end of the 3rd century.

[2] C. JULLIAN, *Histoire de la Gaule*, vol. 5, p. 27, estimates the population of Gaul in the 2nd century as 40 millions; he considers that in the 4th century this figure was halved (*ibid.*, vol. VII, p. 29).

[3] DAHN, *Die Könige der Germanen*, vol. VI, p. 50.

[4] L. SCHMIDT, *op. cit.*, p. 403.   [5] E. GAUTIER, *Genséric*, p. 97.

[6] *Historia persecutionis Africanae provinciae*, I, I, ed. HALM, M.G.H.SS.ANTIQ., vol. III, p. 2.   [7] *Ibid.*, p. 138.

[8] E. STEIN, *Gesch. des Spät. Röm. Reiches*, vol. I, 1928, p. 477, also accepts this figure.   [9] E. GAUTIER, *Genséric*, p. 141.

Roman Africa may have had a population equal to that of today —namely, 7 to 8 millions—which means that the Roman population would have been a hundred times more numerous than the horde of Vandal invaders.

We can hardly assume that the Visigoths were much more numerous in their kingdom, which extended from the Loire to Gibraltar, so that Schmidt's figure of 100,000 may be accepted as probable.

The Burgundi[1] do not seem to have numbered more than 25,000 souls, of whom 5,000 would be warriors.

In the 5th century, according to Doren,[2] the total population of Italy may be estimated at 5 or 6 millions. But we know nothing definite. As for the numbers of the Ostrogoths, Schmidt[3] estimates it at 100,000, of whom 20,000 were warriors.[4]

All this is conjecture. Our estimate would doubtless be in excess of the truth if, for the Western provinces beyond the *limes*, we reckoned the Germanic element as constituting 5 per cent of the population.

As a matter of fact, a minority can transform a people when it wishes to dominate it effectively, when it has only contempt for it, regarding it as fit only for exploitation; as was the case with the Normans in England, the Musulmans wherever they appeared, and even the Romans in the conquered provinces. But the Germans

[1] L. SCHMIDT, *op. cit.*, p. 168. In 406 they were established in Germania. Cf. in this connection the recent theory expounded by M. H. GRÉGOIRE, *La Patrie des Nibelungen*, BYZANTION, vol. IX, 1934, pp. 1–40, and the objections formulated by M. E. GANSHOF in the REVUE BELGE DE PHILOLOGIE ET D'HISTOIRE, vol. XIV, 1935, pp. 195–210. Their king, Gundachar, having attempted to enter Belgium, was crushed in 435–436 by Aetius, who in 443 removed the rest of the Burgundi to *Sapaudia*. Cf. LOT, PFISTER and GANSHOF, *Histoire du Moyen Age*, vol. I, pp. 58–59. COLVILLE, *op. cit.*, pp. 153 *et seq.* arrives by arbitrary calculations at the figure of 263,700.

[2] DOREN, *Italienische Wirtschaftsgeschichte* (Collection BRODNITZ), vol. I, 1934, p. 29.

[3] L. SCHMIDT, *op. cit.*, p. 293.

[4] According to L. HARTMANN, *Das Italienische Königreich*, vol. I, p. 72 (in *Geschichte Italiens im Mittelalter*, vol. I), who follows DAHN, Theodoric must have been accompanied by hundreds of thousands of Ostrogoths.

wished neither to destroy nor to exploit the Empire. Far from despising it, they admired it. They did not confront it with any superior moral strength. Their heroic period ended with their settlement. The great poetic memories that remained,[1] like the legends of the Nibelungen, were developed at a much later date, and in Germany. Consequently, in every case the triumphant invaders accorded the provincials a juridical status equal to their own. The truth is that in every respect they had much to learn from the Empire. How could they resist its influence?

It was not even as though they were gathered into compact groups. With the exception of the Vandals, they were dispersed amidst the Roman population in accordance with the rules of "hospitality." The distribution of the domains made it necessary to comply with the agricultural usages of the Romans.

But what of marriage, or their relations with the Roman women? It is true that until the reign of Reccared, in the 6th century, there was no *connubium*. But this was a juridical, not a social obstacle. The number of unions between Germans and Roman women must have been fairly constant, and the child, we know, speaks the language of his mother.[2] Evidently these Germans must have become Romanized with astonishing rapidity. Some have supposed that the Visigoths preserved their own language, but they have supposed this because they wished to believe it.[3] Nothing can be cited in confirmation of this belief. As for the Ostrogoths, we know from Procopius that there were still some who spoke Gothic in Totila's army, but these must have been a few isolated individuals from the North.

The Gothic language would have been retained only if the Goths had brought with them a culture comparable to that of the Anglo-Saxons. But they had no such culture. Ulfila had no suc-

---

[1] DAWSON, *The Making of Europe*, 1932, p. 98.

[2] *Re* the disappearance of the Gothic language among the Visigoths, see Gamillscheg, *Romania Germanica*, 1934, vol. I, p. 394, and L. SCHMIDT, *op. cit.*, p. 527.

[3] MARTROYE, Genséric. *La conquête vandale en Afrique et la destruction de l'Empire d'Occident*, Paris, 1907, p. 308.

cessor. We have not a single text or charter in the Germanic language. The liturgy in the Churches was sung or recited in the Germanic tongue, yet no trace of it remains. The Franks of the pre-Merovingian epoch were perhaps alone in drafting the Salic Law in the vulgar tongue, and the Malberg Glosses would be vestiges of this language. But Euric, the earliest Germanic legislator any of whose texts have come down to us, wrote in Latin, and all the other German kings did the same.

As for an original decorative art, we find no trace of such a thing among the Visigoths after their acceptance of Catholicism in 589, and Zeiss[1] supposes that such art existed only among the people.

For a time, no doubt, <u>Arianism</u> may have prevented any very intimate contact between the Romans and the Germans. But we must not exaggerate the importance of this factor. The only kings who really favoured Arianism were the kings of the Vandals, and they did so for military reasons. Gondobald is suspected of having been a Catholic. Sigismond was a Catholic from the year 516. However, there were still Arians in 524. And then came the Frankish conquest, which was accompanied by the triumph of orthodox Catholicism. After all, Arianism was never very influential, even among the Burgundi.[2] Soon it had everywhere disappeared. The Vandals abandoned it when conquered by Justinian in 533; among the Visigoths it was abolished by Reccared (586–601).[3] Moreover, this Arianism was superficial, for its suppression was nowhere followed by any disturbance. According to Dahn,[4] the Gothic language may have disappeared at the time of Reccared's acceptance of Catholicism, or if it survived it did so only among the poorer classes.

It is therefore difficult to see how the Germanic element could have maintained itself. The indispensable condition of its survival would have been the constant arrival of fresh recruits from Ger-

---

[1] H. ZEISS, *Die Grabfunde aus dem Spanischen Westgotenreich,* Berlin, 1934, pp. 126 and 138.   [2] COLVILLE, *op. cit.,* pp. 167 *et seq.*
[3] Reccared was converted in 589.   [4] *Op. cit.,* vol. V, p. 170.

mania. But neither the Vandals nor the Visigoths—who had no longer any contact with Germania—received such recruits. The Ostrogoths may possibly have remained more or less in touch with the Germans by way of the Alpine passes. As for the Franks of Gaul, once the country was conquered no further Barbarian contingents made their appearance. To read Gregory of Tours is to be convinced of this.

There is another irrefutable argument. If the Gothic language had been preserved it would have left some traces in the Latin tongues. Now, apart from certain borrowed words no such traces are found. Neither the phonetics nor the syntax of the Latin languages betrays the faintest Germanic influence.[1]

The same may be said of the physical type. Where do we find the Vandal type in Africa,[2] the Visigoth type in Italy? There are fair-haired people in Africa, but Gautier[3] calls our attention to the fact that there were such people in Africa before the arrival of the Barbarians. However, it may be said that the Germanic law survived—that there was Roman law for the Romans, and Germanic law for the Germans; and this is quite true. But even in the legislative measures of Euric this Germanic law was already interpenetrated with Romanism. And after Euric the Roman influence became more and more marked.

Among the Ostrogoths there was no special code in force; they were subject to the Roman law of the country. But as soldiers they were amenable only to the military tribunals, which were purely Gothic.[4] This is the essential thing to remember. The Germans were soldiers and Arians, and it was perhaps in order to keep them soldiers that the kings protected Arianism.

[1] We find borrowed words only in the French language (cf. LOT, *Invasions*, pp. 225 *et seq.*, and GAMILLSCHEG, *op. cit.*, vol. I, pp. 293-295): that is to say, where from the 4th century the population was in contact with the Germans. There was no such borrowing of words in Aquitaine, Spain (Visigoths), Africa (Vandals), or Italy (Ostrogoths). The Germanic additions to the French language are said to number some 300 words.

[2] The population of Spain has nowhere preserved the Germanic type. E. PITTARD, *Les ras et l'histoire*, 1924, p. 135.

[3] GAUTIER, *op. cit.*, p. 316.   [4] HARTMANN, *op. cit.*, vol. I, p. 93.

Among the Burgundi and the Vandals the influence of Roman over Germanic law was as manifest as among the Visigoths.[1] For that matter, how could we expect that the pure Germanic law would be preserved where the consanguinous family, the *Sippe*, the essential cell of the juridical system, had disappeared?

As a matter of fact, there must have been laws relating to personal property, just as there were laws relating to the *connubium*. Germanic law survived only in countries colonized by the Anglo-Saxons, the Salic and Ripuarian Franks, the Alamans and the Bavarians.[2]

That the Salic Law was the law of Gaul after the reign of Clovis is quite a mistaken belief. Outside Belgium there were hardly any Salians, apart from the magnates about the king. We do not find a single allusion to this law and its procedure in Gregory of Tours. We must conclude that its sphere of application was confined to the extreme north.

We find no mention of *rachimburgii* to the south of the Seine. Do we find any *sculteti* or *grafiones*? The Malberg Gloss proves, moreover, that we have to do with a code established for a procedure in which the Germanic language was employed. How many of the Counts, nearly all of whom were Roman, could have understood it? All that it tells us concerning agrarian usages and the arrangement of the houses holds good only for the North, colonized by the Germans. One would have to be blinded by prejudice to imagine that a law as rudimentary as the Salic Law could have been applied to the south of the Loire.

[1] H. BRUNNER, *Deutsche Rechtsgeschichte*, vol. I, 2nd ed., 1906, p. 504. Note that although barely fifty years had passed between the establishment of the Burgundi in Gaul and the drafting of the *Lex Gundobada*, the latter betrays "marked influences of Roman culture," and lacks the "fresh Germanic originality" which was afterwards to be seen in the Lombard laws.

[2] What F. LOT has said, in F. LOT, PFISTER and GANSHOF, *Histoire du Moyen Age*, vol. I, p. 390, concerning the interpenetration of the population in the Merovingian epoch seems to be entirely mistaken. Moreover, he contradicts himself when, in *Les Invasions*, p. 274, he says: "Although ethnically speaking (contemporary) France contains some Germanic elements, they entered it before the conquest of Gaul by Clovis."

41

Shall we say that the Germans brought with them the morality of a young people—that is, a people in whom personal ties of loyalty came before subjection to the State? It is a convenient theory. It is at the same time a romantic theory, and a dogma among certain Germanic historians. They are fond of citing Salvian and his comparison of the moral decadence of the Romans with the virtues of the Barbarians. But these virtues did not survive the establishment of the Germans in the midst of the Romanized population. *Mundus senescit*, we read, at the beginning of the 7th century, in the chronicle of the pseudo-Fredegarius.[1] And we have only to run through Gregory of Tours to find, on every page, the traces of the grossest moral decadence: drunkenness, debauchery, cupidity, adultery, murder, abominable acts of cruelty, and a perfidy which prevailed from top to bottom of the social order. The court of the Germanic kings witnessed as many crimes as that of Ravenna. Hartmann[2] makes the observation that "*Germanische Treue*" is a convenient fable. Theodoric had Odoacer assassinated after swearing to him that his life should be spared. Gontran begged the people not to assassinate him. All the Visigoth kings, with rare exceptions, died by the assassins' knife.

Among the Burgundi, in 500, Godegesil betrayed his brother Gondebaud that Clovis might benefit.[3] Clodomir, the son of Clovis, had his prisoner Sigismond, king of the Burgundi, thrown into a well.[4] The Visigothic king Theodoric I betrayed the Romans. And consider how Genseric treated the daughter of the Visigothic king, his own daughter-in-law.

The court of the Merovingians was a brothel; Fredegond was a frightful termagant. Theodahat had his wife assassinated. Men were always lying in wait for their enemies, and an almost incredible amorality was universal. The story of Gondebaud is characteristic. Drunkenness seems to have been the usual condition of all. Women got their lovers to murder their husbands. Every-

---

[1] Ed. B. KRUSCH, M.G.H.SS.RER.MEROV., vol. II, p. 123.
[2] *Das Italienische Königreich*, vol. I, of the *Geschichte Italiens*, p. 76.
[3] L. SCHMIDT, *op. cit.*, p. 151.   [4] *Ibid.*, p. 163.

body could be purchased for gold; and all this without distinction of race, for the Romans were as bad as the Germans. The clergy themselves—even the monks[1]—were corrupt, though morality should have taken refuge in their ranks. But among the people piety did not rise above the level of a crude thaumaturgy. But there was a partial disappearance of the urban vices, of the mimes and the courtesans; though not everywhere. They were still to be found among the Visigoths, and above all, in Africa, among the Vandals, although the latter were the most Germanic of the Southern Barbarians. They were effeminate, living in luxurious villas and spending much time at the baths. The poems written under Huneric and Thrasamund are full of priapic allusions.

We may conclude that after their establishment within the Empire all the heroic and original characteristics of the Barbarians disappeared, yielding to the influences of their Roman environment. The soil of "Romania" had sapped the Barbarians' vitality. And how could it have been otherwise, when the example was set them by their superiors? At first, of course, the kings were but imperfectly Romanized. Euric and Genseric knew but little Latin. But what shall we say of the greatest of all of them, Theodoric? Beyond the Alps he was known as Dietrich of Berne, but in him it was the Byzantine influence that was predominant.

At the age of seven his father gave him as hostage to the Emperor,[2] and he was educated in Constantinople until he was eighteen years of age. Zeno made him *magister militum* and patrician, and in 474 even went so far as to adopt him. He married an imperial princess.[3] In 484 the Emperor made him consul. Then, after a campaign in Asia Minor, a statue was raised to him in Constantinople. His sister was lady-in-waiting to the Empress.

In 536 Evermud, his son-in-law, promptly surrendered to Belisarius, preferring to live as a patrician in Constantinople rather

[1] GREGORY OF TOURS, *Hist. Franc.*, X, 15.

[2] HARTMANN, *op. cit.*, vol. I, p. 64.

[3] See his letter to the king of the Thuringians, to whom he sent his niece. CASSIODORUS, *Variae*, IV, I, 2nd ed. TH. MOMMSEN, M.G.H.SS.ANTIQ., vol. XII, p. 114. Cf. SCHMIDT, *op. cit.*, p. 340.

than defend the cause of his fellow Barbarians.[1] His daughter Amalasontha was completely Romanized.[2] Theodahat, his son-in-law, boasted that he was a follower of Plato.[3]

And even among the Burgundi, what a fine type of national king was Gondebaud (480–516), who in 472, after the death of Ricimer, succeeded to him as patrician of the Emperor Olybrius, and on the death of the latter had Glycerius made Emperor,[4] and then, in 480, himself succeeded to his brother Chilperic as king of the Burgundi!

According to Schmidt,[5] he was highly cultivated, eloquent, and learned, was interested in theological questions, and was constantly in touch with Saint Avitus.

It was the same with the Vandal kings. And among the Visigoths, the same development may be remarked. Sidonius praises the culture of Theodoric II. Among his courtiers he mentions the minister Leo, historian, jurist and poet, and Lampridius, professor of rhetoric and a poet.[6] It was Theodoric II who in 455 made Avitus Emperor. These kings were entirely divorced from the old traditions of their peoples; it was left to Charlemagne to revive them.

And among the Franks there was the royal poet Chilperic.[7]

As time went on the process of Romanization became accentuated. Gautier[8] remarks that after Genseric the Vandal kings re-entered the orbit of the Empire. Among the Visigoths, Romanization made constant progress. By the end of the 6th century Arianism had everywhere disappeared.

Once again, it was only in the North that Germanism held its own, together with paganism, which was not extirpated there until the 7th century. When the Austrasian armies entered Italy in aid of the Ostrogoths they disgusted the latter,[9] who would pro-

[1] HARTMANN, op. cit., vol. I, p. 261.   [2] Ibid., p. 233.
[3] PROCOPIUS, ed. DEWING (The Loeb Classical Library), vol. III, pp. 22–24.
[4] COVILLE, op. cit., pp. 175 et seq.
[5] SCHMIDT, op. cit., pp. 146 and 149.   [6] Ibid., pp. 527–528.
[7] GREGORY OF TOURS, Hist. Franc., V, 44, and VI, 46.
[8] GAUTIER, op. cit., p. 270.   [9] HARTMANN, op. cit., vol. I, p. 284.

bably have preferred to own allegiance to Byzantium rather than to the Franks.

In short, "Romania," though somewhat diminished in the North, still survived as a whole.[1] It had, of course, altered greatly for the worse. In every domain of life, in the arts, literature and science, the regression is manifest. *Pereunte . . . liberalium cultura litterarum,* as Gregory of Tours very truly says.[2] "Romania" survived by virtue of its inertia. There was nothing to take its place, and no one protested against it. Neither the Church nor the laity conceived that there could be any other form of civilization. In the midst of the prevailing decadence only one moral force held its own: the Church, and for the Church the Empire still existed. Gregory the Great wrote to the Emperor that he reigned over men, the Barbarians over slaves.[3] The Church might quarrel with the Emperors of Byzantium, but it remained loyal to them. Had not the Fathers told it that the Roman Empire existed in accordance with the will of God, and that it was indispensable to Christianity? Had it not modelled its organization upon that of the Empire? Did it not speak the language of the Empire? Had it not preserved the law and the culture of the Empire? And were not all its dignitaries recruited from the ancient senatorial families?

4. *The Germanic States in the West*

It is so obvious that the point need not be emphasized, that the tribal institutions of the Germans could not be preserved in the new kingdoms, founded on the soil of the Empire,[4] in the midst of the Roman population. They were able to survive only in small

---

[1] Nothing was borrowed from the Germans with the exception of proper names, and these are no proof of nationality; they were bestowed out of flattery.

[2] *Hist. Franc. Praefatio,* ed. ARNDT, M.G.H.SS.RER.MEROV., vol. I, p. 7.

[3] GREGORY THE GREAT, *Regist.,* XIII, 34, ed. HARTMANN, M.G.H.EPIST., vol. II, p. 397.

[4] There can be no question of speaking, as certain writers have done, of the social policy of these kings, and of their "conservative attitude" in respect of the Imperial institutions.

kingdoms, like those of the Anglo-Saxons, which were peopled by Germans.

No doubt the Germanic kings installed in the Empire were national kings to their peoples—*reges gentium*, in the words of Gregory the Great.[1] They called themselves *reges Gothorum, Vandalorum, Burgondionum, Francorum*. But for the Romans they were Roman generals to whom the Emperor had abandoned the government of the civil population. It was as Roman generals that they approached the Romans,[2] and they were proud to bear the title on such occasions: we have only to recall the cavalcade of Clovis when he was created honorary consul. Under Theodoric an even simpler state of affairs prevailed. He was really a Roman viceroy. He promulgated not laws but edicts only.

The Goths constituted the army merely.[3] All the civil magistrates were Roman, and as far as possible the entire Roman administration was preserved. The Senate still existed. But all the power was concentred in the king and his court—that is, in the consecrated palace. Theodoric assumed merely the simple title of *rex*, as though he wished his Barbarian origin to be forgotten. Like the Empress, he lived in Ravenna. The division of the provinces was retained, with their *duces, rectores, praesides*, and the municipal constitution with its *curiales* and *defensores*, and the fiscal organization. Theodoric struck coins, but in the name of the Emperor. He adopted the name of Flavius,[4] a sign that he had adopted the Roman nationality. Inscriptions call him *semper Augustus, propagator Romani nominis*. The king's guard was organized on the Byzantine model, and so was all the ceremonial of the court.

---

[1] JAFFÉ-WATTENBACH, *Regesta pontificum Romanorum*, vol. I, 2nd ed., p. 212, No. 1899.

[2] Authors have sought in vain to insist on their Germanic character. See the amusing story of the ox-wagon. H. PIRENNE, *Le char à bœufs des derniers Mérovingiens. Note sur un passage d'Eginhard*, MÉLANGES PAUL THOMAS, 1930, pp. 555–560.

[3] Cassiodorus calls them officially: *barbari* or *milites*. Cf. L. SCHMIDT, *Zur Geschichte Rätiens unter der Herrschaft der Ostgoten*, ZEITSCHRIFT FUR SCHWEIZERISCHE GESCHICHTE, vol. XIV, 1934, p. 451.

[4] His title was *Flavius Theodoricus rex*.

The organization of the judiciary was entirely Roman, even for
the Goths; and the Edict of Theodoric was thoroughly Roman.
There was no special law for the Goths. As a matter of fact,
Theodoric opposed the private wars of the Goths, and their Germanic barbarism. The king did not protect the national law of
his people.[1] The Goths constituted the garrisons of the cities, living
on the revenues of their lands,[2] and in receipt of a salary. They
could not undertake civil employments. They could not exert the
slightest influence upon the Government, apart from those who,
with the Romans, constituted the king's entourage. In this kingdom,
ruled by their king, they were in reality foreigners, but well-paid
foreigners: a military caste, whose profession furnished them with
a comfortable livelihood. It was this fact, and not their alleged
national character, that bound them together, and explained the
vigour of their resistance under Justinian. L. Schmidt[3] admits that
from the time of its establishment in Italy the Gothic conception
of royalty was lost.[4] Theodoric was merely a functionary of Zeno's.
Almost as soon as he had arrived in Italy the Church and the
population acknowledged him as the representative of legal order.
The personal power of the king was exercised by *sajones*, who, for
all their Gothic name, were merely an imitation of the Roman
agentes in rebus.[5] In short, the Goths were the military basis of the
royal power, which in other respects was Roman.

We do not, of course, find that the Roman influence was so
profound among the other Barbarians. Among the Vandals, despite
their rupture with the Empire, there were no Germanic features
in the organization of the State. Yet in this case, despite the fiction
of the treaties, there was really a complete break with the Empire,

---

[1] SCHMIDT, *op. cit.*, p. 387.

[2] The Goths had to pay the land tax. But the king saw to it that they were
able to obtain corn at a low price.

[3] SCHMIDT, *op. cit.*, p. 292, "*das gotische Volkskönigtum Theoderichs war
erloschen.*"

[4] Nevertheless, the Ostrogoths were more Germanic than the Visigoths
when they settled in Italy.

[5] HARTMANN, *op. cit.*, vol. I, p. 100.

and it would be absurd to regard Genseric merely as a functionary. His position may be contrasted with that of Theodoric. Instead of considering and flattering the Roman population as Theodoric had done, he treated it with severity and persecuted its religion. There was no question of the *tercia* here. The Vandals were established *en masse* in Zeugitania (Northern Tunisia), dispossessing or expropriating the Roman landowners. They lived on the revenue of their "colonies," and were exempted from taxation. Their organization in "thousands"[1] which Procopius calls *chiliarchs*, was entirely military.

Vandal in Africa

But all Germanic law, or rather, all Germanic institutions had disappeared when, in 442, Genseric, having crushed an insurrection of the nobles, who were endeavouring for their own advantage to preserve the relics of the tribal organization, established an absolute monarchy.[2] His was a Roman government. He struck coins which bore the effigy of Honorius. The inscriptions were Roman. Genseric's establishment in Carthage was like Theodoric's in Ravenna: there was a *palatium*. It did not meddle with the economic life of the country, or deal with the realities of daily existence. It seems that the Vandal kings even continued to send presentations of oil to Rome and Constantinople.[3] When Genseric established the order of succession to the throne he did so in a codicil drawn up in accordance with the prescriptions of Roman legislation.[4]

The Romanized Berbers continued, under the Vandals, to live as they had lived in the preceding epoch.[5] The chancellery was Roman;[6] there was a *referendarius* at its head—Petrus, some of whose verses have been preserved. Under Genseric the *termi* of

---

[1] GAUTIER, *op. cit.*, p. 207. [2] SCHMIDT, *op. cit.*, p. 113.

[3] ALBERTINI, *Ostrakon byzantin de Négrine (Numidie)*, in CINQUANTENAIRE DE LA FACULTÉ DES LETTRES D'ALGER, 1932, pp. 53–62.

[4] MARTROYE, *Le testament de Genséric*, in BULLETIN DE LA SOCIÉTÉ DES ANTIQUAIRES DE FRANCE, 1911, p. 235.

[5] ALBERTINI, *Actes de vente du Ve siècle, trouvés dans la région de Tebessa (Algérie)*, JOURNAL DES SAVANTS, 1930, p. 30.

[6] R. HEUBERGER, *Ueber die Vandalische Reichskanzlei und die Urkunden der Könige der Vandalen*, MITTEILUNGEN DES OESTER. INSTITUT FUR GESCHICHTSFORSCHUNG, XI ERGANZUNGSBAND, O. REDLICH ... ZUGEEIGNET, 1929, pp.76–113.

Tunis were constructed. Literature was still practised.[1] Victor Tonnennensis still believed in the immortality of the Empire.[2] The kings followed the paths laid down by Rome, as the Restoration followed those laid down by Buonaparte. For example, in 484 the edict of Genseric against the Catholics was modelled upon that which Honorius published against the Donatists in 412.[3] And we can see from this edict that the classes of the population had remained exactly the same. In short, among the Vandals there were even fewer traces of Germanism than among the Ostrogoths. It is true that Africa, at the time of their establishment there, was the most flourishing of the Western provinces, and from the first they were subject to its influences.

Spain and Gaul had not suffered so greatly from the invasions, and, moreover, were not so completely Romanized as Italy and Africa. Yet there too the Germanic character of the invaders was modified in an equal degree by Roman manners and Roman institutions. Among the Visigoths, before the conquest of Clovis, the kings lived in the Roman fashion in their capital of Toulouse, and later, in Toledo. The Visigoths established in accordance with the rules of "hospitality" were not regarded as juridically superior to the Romans. The king addressed his subjects as a whole, as *populus noster*. But each people retained its own laws, and there was no *connubium* between Romans and Germans. Perhaps the religious difference, the Visigoths being Arians, was one of the reasons for this absence of lawful union between the old Roman citizens and the invaders. The prohibition of the *connubium* disappeared under Leovigild (d. 586) and Arianism under Reccared. A community of law between Romans and Goths was established under Reccesvinth.

The *sortes* of the Goths were exempt from taxation. The provinces were retained with their *rectores*, or *judices provinciarum*,

---

[1] See later, pp. 101 *et seq.*

[2] *Chronicon*, ed. MOMMSEN, M.G.H.SS.ANTIQ., vol. XI, pp. 184–206.

[3] CH. SAUMAGNE, *Ouvriers agricoles ou rôdeurs de celliers? Les Circoncellions d'Afrique*, ANNALES D'HISTOIRE ECONOMIQUE ET SOCIALE, vol. VI, 1934, p. 353.

consulares, praesides; they were divided into *civitates*. And according to Schmidt, there was nothing Germanic about their agricultural organization.

The king was absolute: *dominus noster gloriosissimus rex*. He was hereditary, and the people did not participate in the power of government. Schmidt, unable to discover any evidence of true national assemblies, calls our attention to the traces of military assemblies, but as a matter of fact we find many such instances during the later Empire.

The king appointed all his agents. There were both Germanic and Roman dignitaries at his court, but the latter were by far the more numerous. The prime minister of Euric and Alaric II, Leo of Narbonne, combined the functions of *quaestor sacri palatii* and *magister officiorum* of the Imperial court. The king had no body-guard of warriors, but *domestici* of the Roman type. The dukes of the provinces and the *comites* of the cities were mainly Romans.

In the cities the curia was retained, with a *defensor* ratified by the king. The Visigoths were divided into thousands, five-hundreds, hundreds, and tens, with military leaders as to whose attributions we have little information. It does not appear that the Romans of the kingdom of Toulouse, while this endured, were subject to military service, so that the situation there was the same as among the Ostrogoths. For a time the Visigoths appear to have had, in the *millenarius*, a separate magistrate, like the Ostrogoths. But under Euric they were already amenable to the jurisdiction of the *comes*, who presided in the Roman fashion with the assistance of *assessores*, who were legists. There was not the faintest trace of Germanism in the organization of the tribunal.[1]

The Code of Euric, promulgated in 475 to regulate the relations between the Goths and the Romans, was drawn up by Roman jurists; this document is completely Romanized. As for the Breviary

[1] M. M. BLOCH has shown in the REVUE HISTORIQUE for March–April 1930 how absurd is the belief in certain alleged survivals of Germanism.

Concerning the extraordinarily rapid Romanization of the Visigoths, see GAMILLSCHEG, *Romania Germanica*, vol. I, pp. 394 *et seq.*

of Alaric (507), which affected the Romans, it is an example of almost purely Roman law. The Roman taxes were still collected, and the monetary system was also Roman.

The king's functionaries were salaried. As for the Church, it was subject to the king, who ratified the election of the bishops. With few exceptions, there was no real persecution of the Catholics. As time went on, the Romanization became more marked. Leovigild (568–586) suppressed the vestiges of special jurisdiction for the Goths, authorized marriage between the two races, and introduced the Roman laws of the family among the Visigoths.

At first the royal insignia were Germanic, but these were later replaced by Roman insignia.[1] The king's authority was a public function, and not a mere personal tyranny. The old military character of the Barbarians was disappearing. The Visigoths had so diminished in number that in 681 Ervigus compelled landowners to enrol in the army one-tenth of their armed slaves.

Under Reccared (586–608) the amalgamation of the two judicial systems was complete. This is proved by the *Liber judiciorum* promulgated by Reccesvinth in 634. It is Roman and ecclesiastical in spirit, for after the conversion of Reccared the Church played an enormously important part. The eighteen Councils which assembled between 598 and 701 were convoked by the king. To these Councils he summoned lay members of his court, who sat side by side with the bishops. The Councils were consulted on civil as well as ecclesiastical affairs.[2]

The Church, whose dignitaries the king continued to appoint, was thoroughly royalist, even in respect of the Arian kings.

When Athanagild revolted against Leovigild the Church remained loyal to the latter. It claimed the right to elect the kings

---

[1] LOT, *La fin du monde antique et le debut du Moyen Age*, in the collection L'EVOLUTION DE L'HUMANITÉ, Paris, 1927, p. 329: Reccesvinth, about 630, adopted Byzantine dress.

[2] LOT, *op. cit.*, p. 329.

in conjunction with the magnates (633), and introduced the rite of consecration.[1]

This, however, did not in any way modify the absolutism of the monarchy, which was supported by the Church: *Nefas est in dubium deducere ejus potestatem cui omnium gubernatio superno constat delegata judicio.*[2]

Chindasvinth, elected in May 642, had 700 aristocrats, who attempted to oppose his omnipotence, put to death or reduced to slavery.[3]

The king depended on the support of the Church only in order to hold his own against the aristocracy.[4] But the Church, whose bishops he appointed, was servile in its obedience. There was no theocracy. The monarchy was evolving in the direction of the Byzantine system. The election of the kings, which Lot[5] seems to take seriously, is believed by Ziegler to have been a mere phantasmagoria. In reality there was here, as in Byzantium, a mixture of inheritance and intrigue and sudden acts of violence. Leovigild married a Byzantine princess, which did not prevent his repelling the Byzantines. And these Visigoth kings had *spatharii* just like the Emperors.[6]

The Burgundian kings, whose ephemeral kingdom was annexed by the Frankish kings in 534,[7] were on the best of terms with the Empire, once they had succeeded in obtaining possession of Lyons. The Burgundi were established, like the Ostrogoths and Visigoths, in accordance with the rules of *hospitalitas.*[8]

Sidonius describes them, at the time of their settlement, as naïve

---

[1] There is evidence that Wamba was anointed in 672, but the rite is doubtless still more ancient, and may even date back to Reccared (586–608). M. BLOCH, *Les Rois thaumaturges*, 1924, p. 461.

[2] Text of the 30th canon of the 6th Council of Toledo, cited by ZIEGLER, *Church and State in Visigothic Spain*, 1930, p. 101.

[3] F. LOT, *op. cit.*, p. 329.   [4] ZIEGLER, *op. cit.*, p. 126.

[5] *Op. cit.*, p. 329.

[6] P. GUILHIERMOZ, *Essai sur l'origine de la noblesse en France au Moyen Age*, 1902, p. 13, n. 55.

[7] See the very detailed accounts in COVILLE, *op. cit.*, pp. 77–238.

[8] In 443, in Sapaudia, COVILLE, *op. cit.*, p. 109.

and brutal barbarians. But their kings were completely Romanized. Gondebaud was *magister militum praesentialis*. Their courts were full of poets and rhetoricians. King Sigismond boasted that he was a soldier of the Empire, and declared that his country was part of the Empire.[1] These kings had a *quaestor Palatii* and *domestici*. Sigismond was a tool of Byzantium, who received the title of patrician from the Emperor Anastasia. The Burgundi fought against the Visigoths as soldiers of the Emperor.

Thus, they regarded themselves as belonging to the Empire. They reckoned their dates from the accession of the consul—that is to say, of the Emperor; the king was *magister militum* in the Emperor's name.

In other respects the royal power was absolute and unique. It was not divided; when the king had several sons he made them viceroys.[2] The court was peopled mainly by Romans. There was no trace of warrior bands; there were *pagi* or *civitates*, with a *comes* over them. He had beside him, in order to administer justice, a *judex deputatus*, who was likewise appointed by the king, and who dispensed justice in accordance with the Roman usages.

The primitive *Sippe* had disappeared, although the memory of it survived in the name of the *Faramanni* (free men). The Roman municipal organization was in force at Vienne and Lyons. The organization of the taxes and of the currency was also entirely Roman.

The Burgundian king, like the Visigoth king, paid salaries to his agents. In this thoroughly Romanized kingdom the Burgundi and the Romans had the same juridical status: "*una conditione teneantur.*"[3] Here, although this was not the rule in the other so-called federate Germanic States, the Romans served in the army and enjoyed the *connubium* with the Burgundi.

Thus, the Ostrogoths, Visigoths, Vandals and Burgundi were

---

[1] HARTMANN, *op. cit.*, vol. I, pp. 218–219.

[2] L. SCHMIDT, *op. cit.*, pp. 169 and 178.

[3] *Lex Gundobada*, X, ed. R. DE SALIS, M.G.H.LEGES, vol. II, p. 50.

governed in the Roman manner. There was hardly a trace, or none at all, of "Germanic principles." Under the new kings the old system of government survived, though doubtless in an imperfect form. There was only one novelty: service in the army was gratuitous, thanks to the distribution of land. The State was relieved of the terrible war budget which had formerly crushed the people.

The administration, which had become somewhat rudimentary, was also less costly. The Church saw to everything else. But once more, everything that survived and functioned was Roman. Of the Germanic institutions, of the assemblies of free men, nothing was left. At the most we find, here and there, in the laws of the period, Germanic infiltrations, like that of the *Wehrgeld*. But this was a mere trickle in the flood of juridical Romanization: civil processes, contracts, testaments, etc. The West reminds us of those Italian palaces which have been turned into lodging-houses, and which, in all their degradation, have still preserved their ancient architecture. Here was decadence indeed, but it was a Roman decadence, in which there appeared no germ of a new civilization. Its only German characteristic, its Arianism, was itself an old heresy, without anything original about it, and this had little vogue save at first among the Vandals.

It has been supposed that matters were otherwise among the Franks,[1] to whom some have attributed an extraordinary importance, even at the outset of the invasions, because they did actually refashion Europe during the Carolingian epoch. But did they do anything of the kind as early as the 6th century? I think we can reply, very definitely, that they did not.

No doubt the Frankish State was the only one to retain, in its Northern regions, a purely Germanic population. But it played no important part during the Merovingian epoch. Almost as soon as the conquest of the country was begun the kings established themselves in the South in Roman territory, in Paris, Soissons,

[1] H. BRUNNER, in particular, upholds this point of view in his *Deutsche Rechtsgeschichte*; and also G. WAITZ in his *Deutsche Verfassungsgeschichte*.

Metz, Reims, Orleans, and their suburbs.[1] And if they did not go farther South, this was doubtless in order that they might the better resist Germania, towards which they adopted the defensive attitude of the Roman Emperors.[2]

In 531 Thierry, with the aid of the Saxons, overthrew the Thuringians.[3] In 555 Clotair led an expedition into Saxony and Thuringia and subdued Bavaria.[4] In 556[5] and 605[6] further wars were undertaken against the Saxons. In 630–631 Dagobert undertook an expedition against Samo.[7] In 640 Thuringia rebelled and became independent once more.[8] In 689 Pippin fought against the Frisians.[9]

These Germanic countries exercised no sort of influence during the Merovingian period. The Frankish State, until its submission to the Carolingians, was essentially Neustrian and Roman, from the basin of the Seine to the Pyrenees and the sea. However, the Franks who had established themselves there were very few in numbers.

We have no information as regards the Merovingian institutions until after the conquest of the Visigothic and Burgundian territories. We may be assured that the state of affairs existing in these territories, and also in the region governed by Syagrius, must have

[1] When a king of Austrasia became monarch of the whole kingdom he hastened to establish himself in Paris. F. LOT, *Les Invasions*, p. 208. The archaeological observations of ABERG, *Die Franken und Westgothen in der Völkerwanderungszeit*, Upsala, 1922, and GAMILLSCHEG's philological comments in *Romania Germanica*, vol. I, p. 294, show that from the middle of the 6th century the Franks of Gaul no longer exercised any influence over the regions of Germania.

[2] R. BRUNNER, *Die Provence in Merowingischer Zeit*, 1933, p. 2, n. 5. According to this author, Clovis differed from the other, and purely Mediterranean, German kings because he was aiming at both the Mediterranean and Germania. He does not see that his attitude, and even more so that of his successors, was purely defensive.

[3] G. RICHTER, *Annalen des fränkischen Reichs im Zeitalter der Merowinger* (1873), p. 48, and F. LOT, PFISTER and GANSHOF, *Histoire du Moyen Age*, vol. I, p. 205.

[4] RICHTER, *op. cit.*, p. 61.
[5] *Ibid.*, p. 63.
[6] *Ibid.*, p. 102.
[7] *Ibid.*, p. 160.
[8] *Ibid.*, p. 165.
[9] *Ibid.*, p. 177.

influenced the Frankish institutions.[1] But in one important respect the Franks differed from the Visigoths and the Burgundi; they knew nothing of the system of *hospitalitas* or the prohibition of the *connubium* with the Romans. Moreover, the Franks were Catholics. Their fusion with the Gallo-Roman population therefore took place with the greatest ease.

Nevertheless it is true that their Romanization was less effective, because their kings lived in Paris, in an environment which was less Romanized than were the cities of Ravenna, Toulouse, Lyons, or Carthage. Moreover, Northern Gaul had recently passed through a period of wars and successive invasions which had devastated the country. However, they preserved as much of the old Roman institutions as they were able, and they were not lacking in good-will. Their state was more barbarous, but it was not more Germanic.[2] Here again the organization of the taxes[3] and of the currency was retained. Here too there were Counts in each city, the provinces having disappeared.

The *grafio*, the *thunginus*, the *rachimburgi* were found only in the North.[4] The *leudesamio*, which Waitz believes to be Germanic, was according to Brunner[5] of Roman origin; as was the practice of the *commendatio*.[6]

Nearly all if not all the king's agents were recruited among the

---

[1] The agents of the Merovingian king were known as *judices*, as were those of the Emperor.

[2] This was fully realized by H. VON SYBEL, *Entstehung des Deutschen Königthums*, 2nd ed., 1881. See the arguments brought against him by G. WAITZ, *Deutsche Verfassungsgeschichte*, vol. II, part I, 3rd ed., 1882, pp. 81 *et seq.*

[3] WAITZ, *op. cit.*, vol. II, part 2, 3rd ed., p. 273, alleges that the Germans refused to pay the personal tax because it was regarded as incompatible with *ingenuitas*. But there was nothing Germanic in this. He cites, in Note 3, the text of a Council which constitutes manifest proof of his contention.

[4] WAITZ, *op. cit.*, vol. II, part 2, 3rd ed., pp. 122 *et seq.*, endeavours to prove that the Merovingian functionaries were not Roman. There was no longer any division between the military and the civil officers; they came at the king's summons, and received no salary! He admits, however, that the Germans knew nothing of administration (p. 124), and he overlooks the Roman officials and the servile functionaries.

[5] BRUNNER, *op. cit.*, vol. II, 2nd ed., pp. 77–80.   [6] *Ibid.*, pp. 364–365.

Gallo-Romans. Even the best of the generals of that period, Mummolus, appears to have been a Gallo-Roman.[1] And even in the governmental offices by which he was surrounded the king had Gallo-Roman *referendarii*.[2]

Not a trace was left of public assemblies.[3] It is true that the king himself seems to have been more Germanic than the kings of the other Barbarian peoples. Yet what was there specifically German about him? His long hair?[4] In this connection the prejudice is so obstinate that some have even invoked, as evidence of his Germanic character, Eginhard's caricature of the last Merovingian kings. Of all the Merovingians, only Thierry, the eldest son of Clovis (d. 534), is celebrated in Germanic poetry, doubtless on account of his terrible Thuringian expedition. He is the Hugdietrich of the *épopée*.[5]

The others were not remembered by their peoples as national heroes. The power of the monarch was much like that of the Emperor. The Frankish king, like the other Germanic kings, was the centre of all authority.[6] He was an absolute despot. He wrote in his *praeceptiones*: *Si quis praecepta nostra contempserit oculorum evulsione multetur*,[7] in which we have an expression of the essentially Roman notion of the *crimen laesae majestatis*.[8]

Although it is quite true that the king regarded himself as the owner of his kingdom, the character of the monarchy was not as private as has been argued by some. The king distinguished between

---

[1] F. LOT, PFISTER and GANSHOF, *Histoire du Moyen Age*, vol. I, p. 271.

[2] H. BRESSLAU, *Handbuch der Urkundenlehre*, vol. I, 2nd ed., 1912, pp. 360–362.

[3] WAITZ, *op. cit.*, vol. II, part 2, 3rd ed., p. 241.

[4] What WAITZ, *op. cit.*, vol. II, part I, 3rd ed., pp. 205 *et seq.*, says of the Germanic character of the king is quite without pertinence.

[5] LOT, PFISTER and GANSHOF, *op. cit.*, p. 200, n. 98.

[6] Although the word "ban" denotes power, it is not Germanic. The old military term was retained; that is all.

[7] GREGORY OF TOURS, *Hist. Franc.*, VI, 46; WAITZ, *op. cit.*, vol. II, part I, 3rd ed., p. 212, cites GREGORY OF TOURS, *Hist. Franc.*, IX, 8: "*agendo contra voluntate vestram atque utilitatem publicam.*"

[8] GREGORY OF TOURS, *Hist. Franc.*, V, 25; VI, 25; VI, 37; IX, 13; IX, 14; X, 19.

his private fortune and the public fisc.[1] Of course, the notion of the royal power was more primitive than among the Visigoths. At the death of the king his States were divided between his sons, but this was a result of the conquest, and was not especially Germanic.[2] It is also true that the Frankish kings had no Roman titles, except, sporadically, under Clovis. But they endeavoured to maintain contact with the Emperors of Byzantium.[3]

Thus even among the Franks the traditional Romanism was preserved.

If we consider these Barbarian kingdoms as a whole we shall find that they had three features in common. They were absolutist, they were secular, and the instruments of Government were the fisc and the treasury.

And these three features were Roman, or, if you will, Byzantine. The absolutism was no doubt spontaneous. The king was already extremely powerful as a military leader when the kingdom was established. Afterwards, on account of the provincials, his power was bound to assume the form of absolutism.[4] It could not have done otherwise, unless indeed the king had been in the position of the Anglo-Saxon sovereigns. Nothing could be less Germanic than the royalty of these military leaders. It was simply personal power; exactly what we find in the Empire.

In all these kingdoms the absolutism of the king is explained by his financial power. Everywhere, as the successor of the Emperor, he disposed of the fisc and the taxes. Now the wealth of the fisc was enormous. It included the Imperial domain, the forests, the waste lands, the mines, the ports, and the highways, and there

---

[1] Cf. the situation among the Anglo-Saxons. See w. STUBBS, *Histoire constitutionnelle de l'Angleterre*, edited and translated into the French by G. LEFEBVRE and CH. PETIT-DUTAILLIS, vol. I, 1907, p. 183.

[2] Such division was made only among the Franks, perhaps because at the moment of Clovis's succession there was no longer an Emperor in the West, and in any case the Franks were not then thinking of the Emperor.

[3] Theodebert is said to have thought of attacking Byzantium. LOT, PFISTER and GANSHOF, *Histoire du Moyen Age*, vol. I, p. 208.

[4] There were no hereditary functions. The king, like the Emperor, chose his functionaries at will.

were also the taxes and the mint. Thus the king was a landed proprietor of enormous wealth, and he also possessed a formidable treasury of minted gold. No prince in the West, before the 13th century, can have been so rich in money as these kings. The description of their treasuries calls up the image of a river of gold. Above all, this wealth enabled the king to pay his functionaries.[1] The Merovingian kings granted large assignations from their treasuries: before 695 the Abbot of St. Denis drew an annuity of 200 gold *solidi* from the treasury and another of 100 *solidi* from the magazines of the fisc (*cellarium fisci*);[2] they lent money to the cities,[3] paid missionaries, and bought or corrupted men at will. The retention of the Roman impost and the market-toll (*tonlieu*) were the essential sources of their power. To regard them, as they have often been regarded, merely as great landed proprietors is a manifest error, of which the only explanation is that they have been compared with the kings who came after them.[4] But the fact is that owing to their wealth in money they were far more akin to the Byzantine kings than to Charlemagne.

And they did everything they could to increase the treasure upon which their power was based. Hence the innumerable confiscations. Chilperic made in all parts of his kingdom *descriptiones novas et graves*.[5] There was a whole complicated financial administration, with its registers, its revisors, etc. It was to seize one another's treasuries that the kings fought and slew one another.[6]

Moreover, they drew enormous subsidies from Byzantium. The Emperor Maurice sent 50,000 gold *solidi* to Childebert as payment

[1] DAHN, *op. cit.*, vol. VI, p. 290.

[2] H. PIRENNE, *Le cellarium fisci*, ACADÉMIE ROYALE DE BELGIQUE, BULLETIN DE LA CLASSE DES LETTRES ET DES SCIENCES MORALES ET POLITIQUES, 5th series, vol. XVI, 1930, nos. 5–7, p. 202.

[3] GREGORY OF TOURS, *Hist. Franc.*, III, 34.

[4] H. PIRENNE, *Liberté et propriété en Flandre du VIIe au XIe siècle*, ACADÉMIE ROYALE DE BELGIQUE, BULLETIN DE LA CLASSE DES LETTRES, 1911, pp. 522–523.

[5] GREGORY OF TOURS, *Hist. Franc.*, V, 28.

[6] FUSTEL DE COULANGES, *Les transformations de la royauté pendant l'époque carolingienne*, p. 19.

for his alliance against the Lombards.[1] The dowry given to Riguntis in 584,[2] the 6,000 *solidi* of alms given by Childebert to the Abbé of Saint-Germain for the poor,[3] and the munificence of Dagobert I, who covered the apse of Saint-Denis with silver,[4] give us some idea of the wealth of the Frankish kings. Like the Byzantines, they employed their treasure largely for political purposes; for example, Brunhild in 596 was able, by means of a money payment, to prevent the Avars from attacking Thuringia.[5]

It therefore cannot be said that the kings accumulated wealth only for themselves.

But the Ostrogothic sovereigns were even richer. It is enough to recall the sumptuous buildings erected by Theodoric. And the same may be said of the Visigoths: in 631 the pretender Sisenand offered 200,000 gold *solidi* to Dagobert in order to obtain his support against Svinthila;[6] and Leovigild promised 30,000 to the Emperor's lieutenant if he would take his part against his son.[7]

The importance of the revenue from the *tonlieux* among the Visigoths may be deduced from the fact that breaches of trust on the part of the farmers were punished by death, as under Roman law.[8] The registers of the taxes were always kept by them,[9] and the kings paid their officials.[10] The description given by Venantius Fortunatus of the treasure brought by Galswinth gives us some idea of their wealth.[11]

Gold, in short, continually played its part in their policy as it did in that of Byzantium; the kings bought one another and sold themselves.

---

[1] GREGORY OF TOURS, *Hist. Franc.*, VI, 42.

[2] *Ibid.*, VI, 45; VII, 9; VII, 15.

[3] S. DILL, *Roman Society in Gaul in the Merovingian Age*, 1926, p. 280.

[4] *Gesta Dagoberti regis*, c. 17, M.G.H. SS.RER.MEROV., vol. II, p. 406.

[5] RICHTER, *op. cit.*, vol. I, p. 98. [6] *Ibid.*, vol. I, p. 161.

[7] GREGORY OF TOURS, *Hist. Franc.*, V, 38.

[8] DAHN, *Könige der Germanen*, vol. VI, p. 290.

[9] *Ibid.*, p. 260. [10] *Ibid.*, p. 275.

[11] *Carmina*, VI, 5, ed. KRUSCH, M.G.H. SS. ANTIQ., vol. IV, pp. 136 *et seq.*

But there was yet another direction in which the Barbarian States continued the tradition of antiquity: namely, they were secular States. The entire administration, in all its phases, was secular. Although the kings were generally on good terms with the bishops, not one of the latter filled a governmental office: and here was one great difference between this period and the Middle Ages. On the other hand, many of the bishops had been royal *referendarii*.[1] Here we have a striking contrast with the policy of Charlemagne, which was based upon the *missi*, half of whom were necessarily bishops, or that of Otto, who entrusted the reins of government to the Imperial bishops. The fact is that on the morrow of the invasion the laity, as we shall presently see, was still educated.[2]

The profane Merovingian State was therefore very definitely unlike the religious Carolingian State. And the same may be said of all the other States: Ostrogothic, Visigothic, Vandal, Burgundian. In this respect, then—and this is the essential point—the ancient order of things continued. The king himself was a pure layman, and his power did not depend upon any religious ceremony.

The Church was subject to the king. Though in theory the bishops were appointed by the clergy, in practise they were very often appointed directly by the king. And here, again, we have the ancient tradition of the State Church. As in the East, the Frankish bishops worked hand in hand with the kings.[3] The kings convoked the Councils. And although the Merovingians abstained from directing the Councils, in the Visigothic kingdoms, from the

---

[1] Didier de Cahors was the king's treasurer and prefect of Marseilles; Saint Ouen was referendar in Neustria.

[2] H. BRESSLAU, *op. cit.*, vol. I, 2nd ed., pp. 364–367, cites some instances of referendars who became bishops. See also H. SPROEMBERG, *Marculf und die frankische Reichskanzlei*, NEUES ARCHIV, vol. XLVII, 1927, pp. 124–125.

LOENING, *Geschichte des Deutschen Kirchenrechts*, vol. II, 1878, p. 262, perfectly understands that the State was secular, although he is mistaken in the explanation of the fact. See also DAWSON, *op. cit.*, pp. 221–222.

[3] L. DUCHESNE, *L'eglise au VIᵉ siècle*, 1925, p. 528.

reign of Reccesvinth, the Councils were associated with the government. Nevertheless, the Church remained servile, completely subject to the king.[1]

But the kings had the greatest respect for the Church over which they ruled. The royal ideal, according to Gregory of Tours, was to protect the churches and the poor.[2] They were lavish of their favours, endowed the Church with their wealth, and surrounded it with every mark of respect, although, with the exception of a few women, they or their relatives did not enter the cloister. Their personal piety does not seem to have been remarkable, but they regarded the bishops as the heads of the Church—that is, of a very great and divine power. Moreover, these bishops enjoyed an enormous prestige among the people. They could serve—as they did, for example, among the Visigoths—as a useful counterweight against the lay aristocracy.

5. Justinian (527–565)

There could be no greater mistake than to suppose that the idea of the Empire disappeared after the dismemberment of the Western Provinces by the Barbarians. There is no justification for doubting that the βασιλεὺς who reigned in Constantinople still extended his theoretical authority over the whole Empire. He no longer governed, but he still reigned. And it was toward him that all men's eyes were turned.

The Church above all, for which the Empire was a creation of Providence, could not dispense with him. The head of the Church

[1] See the curious anecdote related by GREGORY OF TOURS, Liber vitae patrum, VI, 3, M.G.H. SS. RER. MEROV., vol. I, pp. 681–682. An electoral intrigue was foiled by the king, who none the less appointed the desired candidate, in consideration of handsome presents, and gave a banquet in the episcopal city. In short, everything depended on the king. See ibid., pp. 727 et seq., for the life of Saint Nicetus, Bishop of Trèves, appointed by one king, exiled by another, and restored by a third.

[2] GREGORY OF TOURS, Hist. Franc., III, 25.

in Rome, and the city of Rome, acknowledged him as the legitimate sovereign of the *ecclesia*.[1]

With the exception of the king of the Vandals, the Barbarian kings regarded him as their master, striking his effigy on their coins, and they solicited and obtained titles and favours from him. Justinian adopted Theodebert,[2] as Maurice afterwards adopted Childebert.

It was to Constantinople that the kings submitted their disputes, and it was there that they endeavoured to concoct their intrigues. The Emperor himself had made no concessions; it was therefore quite natural that when the occasion offered itself he should seek to recover his property. And in the case of Justinian, his desire to recover what was his was reinforced by his anxiety to re-establish the orthodox religion. Even though she had lost nearly the whole of the Mediterranean coast, Byzantium was still capable of attempting the great enterprise of reconstituting the Empire.

Byzantium had a navy which gave her the control of the sea. She was supported by the Church, with which Theodoric had just quarrelled. In Italy she could count on the support of the great Roman families, and in Africa she could rely on the friends of the refugees of the Vandal aristocracy, who had sought in the Imperial Court a refuge against the persecutions of the monarchy. Perhaps, too, she counted on the revolt of the provincial population. In order to ensure the maximum chance of success, Justinian, before entering upon his campaigns, concluded peace with the Persian Empire (532), and, by means of subsidies, immobilized the Barbarians of all sorts who were prowling about the frontiers.

Byzantium had not to deal with a single front only. There was no Germanic policy. Theodoric, indeed, had endeavoured to group

---

[1] See the work of Gregory the Great; though this, it is true, is later in date than Justinian. It is enough to read the writings of Marius of Avenches (d. 594), Victor Tonnennensis (d. 569), and John of Biclaro to realize that for them the Empire still existed. Cf. EBERT, *Histoire de la littérature du Moyen Age en Occident*, trans. AYMERIC and CONDAMIN, vol. I, 1883, p. 618.

[2] Theodebert wrote to Justinian as humbly as possible. A. VASILIEV, *Histoire de l'Empire byzantin*, French trans., Paris, 1932, vol. I, p. 203, n. 2.

the other States under his hegemony. But his object had been simply to safeguard Italy. With this purpose in view he had supported the Visigoths against the Franks, and had saved them from being completely crushed after the battle of Vouillé; in 509 he made Clovis surrender Provence to him, and in 523 he intervened in order to prevent the Franks from destroying Burgundy.[1]

Far from conciliating the Frankish kings, his policy had made the Merovingians his implacable enemies.

If Byzantium did not intervene in order to prevent Theodoric from establishing himself so firmly in Italy, this was because she did not feel strong enough to do so. She had tolerated the occupation of Italy, and had maintained peaceful relations with Theodoric, but she had not accepted the accomplished fact.

In the Franks, Byzantium was soon to find natural allies against the Ostrogoths.

In 526 Theodoric died. Like a Roman Emperor,[2] and in absolute opposition to the Germanic custom, he had appointed his successor on his death-bed: his grandson Athalaric, aged ten, who was to reign under the regency of his mother Amalasontha.

The latter assumed power only with the consent of Justinian, and on this occasion she treated Justinian with such deference that he may perhaps have felt that it would be possible to secure the return of Italy to the Empire without drawing the sword.

It was therefore against the Vandals that Justinian directed his offensive. In 533, in a single campaign, Belisarius triumphed over the usurper Gelimer, who then occupied the throne, and took possession of the whole coast of Africa as far as Ceuta.

Justinian made haste to re-establish a *limes* there. For the rest, he immediately took over the government of the country, in which the entire Roman administrative system had been preserved.

The Vandals did not react against their defeat. They became submerged at once in the mass of the Roman population, and they never again caused any trouble.

---

[1] BUCHNER, *Die Provence in Merowingischer Zeit*, 1933, p. 3.

[2] HARTMANN, *op. cit.*, vol. I, p. 229; F. LOT, *La fin du monde antique*, p. 303.

Africa, the wealthiest of the provinces of the Empire, was once more attached to the latter. The Moors alone continued to resist, but they were finally subjected in 548.[1]

Shortly after Justinian had recovered possession of Africa (533), the young king of the Ostrogoths, Athalaric, died (534). In order to retain her power, his mother Amalasontha married her cousin Theodahat, but in the following year (535) her husband had her put to death.

Justinian immediately intervened. Belisarius took possession of Sicily (535), thus completing the conquest of Africa. Acclaimed by the population, he marched northwards, made himself the master of Naples, and entered Rome in 536.

The Romanized dynasty of the Ostrogoths offered no resistance. Theodahat prided himself on being a follower of Plato, and despised the profession of arms, and his brother Evermud immediately surrendered to Belisarius, preferring to live as a patrician in Rome rather than defend the cause of his Barbarian compatriots.[2]

Nevertheless, Belisarius was suddenly confronted with a desperate resistance.

Feeling that their possession of the lands which had been allotted to them was threatened, the Ostrogoths lifted one of their officers, Vitiges, upon their shields, and acclaimed him king. He immediately marched upon Rome, where Belisarius had shut himself up (537), but he could not force his way into the city, and being presently compelled to retreat he entrenched himself in Ravenna.

Fearing that he might be assailed in the North by the Franks he surrendered Provence to them, which Justinian hastened to acknowledge as their possession.[3]

Then, being unable to hold his own against the troops of Belisarius, Vitiges negotiated for peace.

On condition that he left them in possession of their lives and

---

[1] A. VASSILIEV, *op. cit.*, vol. I, p. 178.
[2] HARTMANN, *op. cit.*, vol. I, p. 261.
[3] F. KIENER, *Verfassungsgeschichte der Provence*, 1900, p. 22.

their land, the Goths offered Belisarius the royal crown. Belisarius accepted the offer, or feigned to accept it, and entered the city (540). A treaty was signed. The Gothic garrisons took the oath of fidelity to their new king; and Belisarius, having completed his mission, was recalled by the Emperor. To the amazement of the Goths, who could not understand how he could continue to serve another when he might have been an independent king, Belisarius obeyed. He took with him Vitiges, and a number of Goths who followed him, who afterwards took part with him in the wars against the Persians.

This conduct on the part of Belisarius, which brought into Italy a prefect of the Praetorium and the regular government of Rome, constituted an act of treason in the eyes of the Goths. Those of the North of Italy, whose territory had not yet been occupied by the Imperial forces, rebelled, and offered the crown to an officer, Uraias, who refused it, and then to Ildibald, the nephew of the Visigoth king Theudis;[1] and the latter undertook to reconquer Italy.

At this time the Italian population was crushed by the burden of taxation. Belisarius had taken with him the greater part of the troops; the forces·that remained in the country were distributed in garrisons, and were under no general command.

Starting from Pavia with a thousand men, Ildibald, thanks to the hostility of the population against the new Imperial government, won some important victories. He defeated the Roman army, commanded by the *magister militum per Illyricum*, but in the moment of his triumph he was assassinated.[2]

His successor Eraric, who was not a Goth, but a Rugian, immediately attempted to negotiate with Justinian, offering to betray his army and to take up his residence in Constantinople in return for the title of patrician. He was assassinated before he could put his plan into execution (541), and was followed by Totila, a cousin of Ildibald's. Prepared to acknowledge Justinian's authority before

---

[1] HARTMANN, *op. cit.*, vol. I, pp. 289–290.
[2] HARTMANN, *op. cit.*, vol. I, p. 301.

his accession to the throne, he behaved, once he was king, with remarkable energy.[1]

His army was enlarged by the addition of Imperial deserters, slaves, and Italian colonists, who were drawn to him by his hostility to the great landowners. With this army he captured Rome (December 17th, 546). He then attempted to negotiate with Justinian, who regarded him as a tyrant, and would not condescend to listen to him. He asked nothing better than to conclude peace, if Justinian would agree that he should pay tribute to the Emperor and furnish military service.[2] Under the circumstances it seems difficult to regard him as a national hero. But he was certainly one of the most intelligent and most civilized of the Germanic kings, and his victories were largely due to his humanity, which reconciled the unhappy and embittered Roman populations.

Being compelled to make war by the Emperor's refusal to negotiate with him, Totila reconquered Sicily, Sardinia and Corsica, and organized a fleet of captured Byzantine ships, which enabled him to make himself the master of the Adriatic; and having reconquered the whole of Italy he governed it as Theodoric had done.

But Justinian had not abandoned Italy. In 551 Narses landed on Italian soil with 20,000 men. He defeated Totila, who fell on the field of battle. His successor Teias, after a desperate struggle, was defeated and slain, in 553, at the foot of Vesuvius.

At the end of their powers, the Goths appealed to the Franks and the Alamans. But the Frankish and Alamanish bands which responded to their appeal, after pillaging Goths and Romans indiscriminately, were defeated by the Byzantines near Capua in 554. The rest of the Goths finally surrendered, and were sent to Asia to fight the Persians. Italy was reorganized as a Roman province. The exarch or patrician installed himself in Ravenna. But the country had been bled white.

[1] LOT, PFISTER and GANSHOF, *Histoire du Moyen Age*, vol. I, p. 157, say that he was chivalrous and thought only of saving his people. HARTMANN, *op. cit.*, vol. I, p. 302, seems to take a more probable view: in his opinion Totila identified himself with the people only in so far as it served his own interest to do so.　　　　[2] HARTMANN, *op. cit.*, vol. I, p. 328.

During this twenty years' struggle between the Byzantines and the Ostrogoths the Franks did their best to profit by the situation. In 532 they took possession of Burgundy; in 535, by threatening to march against Vitiges, they obtained the cession of Provence, which was immediately recognized by Justinian.

In spite of this, in 539 Theudebert descended upon Italy with a great army, and besieging Vitiges in Ravenna, seized the greater part of Venetia and Liguria. Compelled to withdraw by reason of the maladies that decimated his troops, Theudebert nevertheless retained a portion of Venetia, leaving a duke there, whom he afterwards persuaded Totila to recognize. It may be that he thought of utilizing Venetia as the basis of an attack upon Constantinople.[1]

It was from Venetia, in 552–553, that the Frankish and Alaman bands spread throughout Italy, only to be finally crushed by the Byzantines. At the same time the Franks lost Venetia.

There was never for a moment any thought of an alliance between the Franks and the Ostrogoths, who together might have opposed a united front to the Empire. As it was, the Empire met with no united resistance on the part of the Germanic peoples.

Africa and Italy once reconquered, Justinian turned to Spain. An intestine struggle was in progress there, which enabled him to intervene. When Athanagild appealed for his help against Agila he ordered Liber, who had just reconquered Sicily, to land in Spain. Agila, defeated at Seville, was slain by his own men, who in 554 acclaimed Athanagild, the loyal servant of the Emperor.

The Romans now held all the shores of the Tyrrhenian Sea, with the exception of Provence. The Visigothic monarchy, though it acknowledged the Imperial suzerainty,[2] was cut off from the sea.

The Mediterranean was once more a Roman lake.

The Empire had made a prodigious effort. In order to triumph it

---

[1] RICHTER, *op. cit.*, pp. 57–58.

[2] Leovigild, who succeeded to Athanagild (567), asked the Emperor Justin II to confirm his accession to the throne. F. LOT, *La Fin du Monde Antique*, p. 310.

had had to fight upon two fronts: for while it was battling in Italy, the Persians,[1] incited by the Ostrogoths, had declared war upon the Empire; and in the Balkans the Slavs had to be driven back from the frontiers which they were attacking.

In the midst of these incessant and victorious wars, on the other hand, the Empire was adapting itself to the deep-seated process of evolution which was transforming society and manners. The Code which bears the name of Justinian is one of the great juridical achievements of all ages.

The Roman civilization was once more brilliant and flourishing, and in order to commemorate this wonderful renaissance of the Empire, Saint Sophia was built in the centre of the capital, like an immense triumphal monument to the glory of God and Byzantium.

When Justinian died the Empire was reconstituted, and surrounded with fortresses, but it was profoundly exhausted. Yet it was soon compelled to enter upon new and terrible conflicts.

The period that followed the reign of Justinian, from 565 to 610, is one of the most depressing of Byzantine history.[2] War was raging on all the frontiers; the Persians, the Slavs, and the Avars flung themselves upon the Empire, and in 568 the Lombards invaded Italy from the North.

Nevertheless, to contemporary eyes Byzantium did not appear decadent; no one foresaw the catastrophe. After all, the Empire had recovered its footing throughout the West, and had powerful resources at its disposal: its fleet, thanks to which it maintained contact with Ravenna, Spain and Africa, its treasury, and its diplomacy. And another thing was in its favour: its enemies were quite incapable of coming to an understanding among themselves.

Yet before long the Empire was yielding on every front. The most important event of this period was undoubtedly the Lombard invasion.

The Lombards invaded Italy, and although by 575 they had reached Spoleto and Benevento, they did not succeed in taking either Rome, or Ravenna, or Naples.

[1] VASILIEV, *op. cit.*, vol. I, p. 181. [2] *Ibid.*, vol. I, pp. 220–221.

On the other hand, the Visigoths reconquered Spain; in 614 the Empire retained only the Balearic Isles.[1]

Yet the Mediterranean was not lost; Africa, Sicily and Southern Italy were still Roman.

The Lombards who entered Italy were almost as Germanic as the Anglo-Saxons who invaded Britain. Here, for the first time, Italy was invaded by strangers who had no points of resemblance to the Roman armies or their allies. They overran the population, took its land, and reduced it to the condition of a vanquished enemy. Their occupation was in striking contrast with that of Theodoric's Goths. Their dukes and kings, elected by the army, were purely Germanic. The Lombard people were still living under the régime of the *Farae*—that is, of the *Sippen*. Their laws and customs had not been modified in any way by the influence of Rome.

Everything was in their favour, for Byzantium was paralysed by the war against the Persians and the Slav invasions. But they consisted merely of bands of pillagers. Incapable of seizing the Roman strongholds, by their depredations and the stupidity of their policy they incurred the hostility both of the Church and the Franks.

Their appearance in Italy forced the Papacy to fall back on Byzantium, for it saw no hope of support except from the Emperor. From this moment the Pope, in his ruined city, became the true governor of Rome, but he held it for the Empire. He applauded the election of the abominable Phocas. Gregory the Great was prodigal of promises of devotion to the Emperor. This rapprochement between the Pope and the Emperor was all the more readily effected inasmuch as since the Acacian schism (489–519) there had been, thanks to Justinian, no further religious conflicts. Nor were there any more until the crisis of Monophysism (640–681). The election of the Pope was ratified by the Exarch, a clear indication of his subordination to the Empire. He was still living within the Empire, and he still regarded himself as its subject. The Lombard

[1] VASILIEV, *op. cit.*, vol. I, p. 261.

invasion resulted also in closer relations between the Emperor and the Franks, who had been so hostile under Justinian. The unsuccessful expeditions of the Lombards into Gaul, between 569 and 571, led to an understanding between the Franks and Byzantium. In 576, when the Roman Senate appealed for help to the Emperor, the troops which he was able to send were quite insufficient, and he advised the Senate to appeal for assistance to the Franks and to corrupt the Lombard dukes with gold.

In 574 the Lombards made a fresh attack upon Gaul,[1] which ended in utter defeat, and this led them to sign a treaty of peace with Gontram of Burgundy and his ally Childebert II of Austrasia. This constituted a serious danger to the Empire.

The Imperial diplomacy—which was not sparing of gold—endeavoured to maintain, between the Franks and the Lombards, the antagonism which alone might preserve Italy for Byzantium. Supported by the Pope, the Emperor entered into negotiations with Chilperic of Neustria, who in 581 detached Childebert from Gontram. At the same time, the pretender Gondovald, who was living in Constantinople, was sent into Gaul, well provided with money, in order to dispute the throne with Gontram. On the other hand, Duke Grasulf of Friuli, who had been won over by means of gold, entered into negotiations with Childebert and his mother Brunehaut, to whom, in 583, the Emperor sent 50,000 gold *solidi*.[2]

He persuaded Childebert to undertake a campaign in Italy against the Lombards. Childebert returned from Italy after making peace with the Lombards in consideration of a money payment.

By this time many of the Lombard dukes had been purchased by Byzantium. Those who had remained independent, being doubtless aware that the alliance between the Empire and the Franks was dangerous to them, restored the monarchy in 584 in favour of Authari, who immediately resumed hostilities, and but for the intervention of the Imperial fleet would have made himself the master of Ravenna.

---

[1] HARTMANN, *Geschichte Italiens im Mittelalter*, vol. II, part I, 1900, pp. 58 *et seq.*
[2] GASQUET, *L'Empire byzantin et la monarchie franque*, p. 198.

But Authari threatened the Franks as well as the Emperor. Consequently, in 588–589 Childebert and his mother Brunehaut sent ambassadors to Constantinople in order to consult with the Emperor in respect of preparations for a war against the Lombards.[1]

And in the year 590 a great Frankish army, under the command of twenty-two dukes, descended into Lombardy.

On the other hand, the Exarch of Ravenna marched against Authari, who took refuge in Pavia. The Lombard kingdom, which was all but lost, was saved by the lack of understanding between its enemies. At this moment, the war against the Persians having come to an end, the Exarch resumed the offensive, seizing Altinum, Modena and Mantua.[2]

The Empire, having now the free disposal of its forces, and cherishing hopes of the complete reconquest of Italy,[3] broke with the Franks. This was a disastrous move.

The end of the active alliance between Byzantium and the Franks was the beginning of a period of great success for the Lombards. Moreover, the Empire was obliged once more to make war upon the Persians and to oppose the invasion of the Avars, leaving the Lombards to do as they willed.

The Franks, on the other hand, refrained from intervention in Italy. One expedition, which they organized in 662–663, was a failure; and this was to be the last before the reign of Charlemagne.

A series of truces prepared the way for the peace which was finally signed in 680 between the Emperor and the Lombards, dividing Italy between them.

Despite this partial check of the Empire in Italy, it still retained its formidable prestige. In 629 Heraclius triumphed over the

---

[1] Already, in 587, Duke Gontram had been sent as ambassador to the Emperor Maurice. See GASQUET, *L'Empire byzantin et la monarchie franque*, pp. 185 *et seq.*

[2] HARTMANN, *op. cit.*, vol. II, part I, p. 72.

[3] In Italy itself this reconquest seemed probable, for in 590 the Patriarch of Aquileia proposed to postpone until the reconquest the settlement of the dispute between himself and Rome in respect of the three Chapters. HARTMANN, *op. cit.*, vol. II, p. 89.

Persians, and Dagobert sent him an embassy to congratulate him on his victory.[1] Gregory the Great acted as intermediary between the Emperor and the Catholic Visigoths.[2] Ebroin (d. 680–683) allowed Anglo-Saxon pilgrims to pass through Gaul, once he was convinced that they were not a *legatio imperatorum contra regnum*.[3]

All those persons who were concerned with political or ecclesiastical intrigues[4] converged upon Constantinople, as a great international and intellectual centre.[5]

In short, despite its losses, the Empire was still the only world-power,[6] and Constantinople was the greatest of civilized cities. The foreign policy of the Empire embraced all the peoples of Europe, and completely dominated the policy of the Germanic State. Until the 8th century[7] the only positive element in history was the influence of the Empire. And it is an undeniable fact that this Empire had become Oriental.

The process of orientalization, which had manifested itself without interruption since the reign of Diocletian, was becoming more and more accentuated. It was evident also in the Church, where it gave rise to dangerous dissensions.

Yet we must not exaggerate. Apart from momentary ruptures, Rome remained the capital of the Church, and as soon as the Emperors ceased to support the Eastern heresy the Popes returned to their old loyalty.

From Constantinople, Byzantinism gradually made its way westward, for the West had nothing to oppose to it. Its fashions and its art were spread throughout the West by means of navigation. It obtained a foothold in Rome, where there was a host of Greek monks, and everywhere in Southern Italy. Its influence was per-

---

[1] VASILIEV, *op. cit.*, vol. I, p. 263.

[2] HARTMANN, *op. cit.*, vol. II, p. 176.

[3] *Ibid.*, vol. II, part 2, 1903, p. 198, n. 2.

[4] GREGORY OF TOURS, *Hist. Franc.*, VI, 24.

[5] It seems that intending physicians went to Constantinople to study medicine. GREGORY OF TOURS, *Hist. Franc.*, X, 15.

[6] HARTMANN, *op. cit.*, vol. II, part 1, p. 85.

[7] DAWSON, *op. cit.*, p. 221.

ceptible in Spain, and of course throughout Africa. In Gaul the *cellarium fisci* was reminiscent of the Byzantine commerciaries. Venice was gravitating into the orbit of Constantinople. The Greek Fathers are indispensable if we are to understand the religious thought of the West. Of course, in the 8th century, when the Emperor had become βασιλεὺς τῶν Ῥωμαίων, the rupture between the Greeks and the Latins was final. The beginning of the great crisis may be dated from Monophysism (640–681), and above all Iconoclasty (726–843); but how many tergiversations there were before the complete rupture!

The influence of the Syrians was greatly increasing in Rome, and they were becoming numerous in the city; there were even to be several Syrian Popes. Evidently the future was to see the Byzantinization of the West, more or less modified by Hibernianism and Anglo-Saxonism. The difference of languages was no obstacle; the superiority of the one culture over the other was too great. Once the Mediterranean became and remained the great means of communication between the East and the West the preponderance of the first over the second was inevitable. The sea, which the Byzantines continued to control, spread their influence in all directions. And the civilization of the period was found beside the sea, both in the West and in the East. From Germanism in itself nothing more was to be expected. The Lombards, in the 7th century, were undergoing a process of Romanization. A new centre of culture had indeed made its appearance among the Anglo-Saxons, but this culture had come to them direct from the Mediterranean.

THE ECONOMIC AND SOCIAL SITUATION
AFTER THE INVASIONS
AND THE MEDITERRANEAN NAVIGATION

1. *Personal Property and the Soil*

As regards the government of persons and territories, "Romania" was not greatly altered by the invasions. There was, of course, a certain amount of pillage and violence. The *Carmen de providentia divina*, which was written in Southern Gaul on the advent of Ataulf's Visigoths, compares their ravages with those of an ocean flood.[1] But calm returned after the tempest. Paulinus of Pella, who was ruined by the invasion, and who fled before it, relates that he was saved by a Goth, who bought a small estate which he owned in the neighbourhood of Marseilles.[2] One could hardly wish for a better illustration of the way in which pillage was followed by social equilibrium. Here was a deserted estate, yet the invaders did not seize it. As soon as the Germans were established in the country in accordance with the rules of *hospitalitas*, society became once more stabilized. But how was the process of settlement conducted? We may suppose that the Germans took advantage of their position, but their settlement did not involve any absolute upheaval. There was no redistribution of the soil, and no introduction of novel methods of agriculture. The Roman colonists remained tied to the soil to which the impost had attached them. Instead of paying a Roman, they paid a German master. The slaves were divided among the conquerors. As for the peasants, they cannot have noticed any very great change. There does not appear to have been, in any part of "Romania," such a substitution of one system of agriculture for another as occurred in England.

[1] MIGNE, *Patr. Lat.*, vol. 51, *circa* 617.
[2] *Eucharisticos*, ed. BRANDES, *Corp. Script. Eccles. Latin.*, vol. XVI, 1888, p. 311.

The Imperial domains were taken over by the royal fisc, without any further change.[1] The great Gallo-Roman or Hispano-Roman or Italo-Roman estates survived. There were still enormous *latifundia*; there is record of one which numbered 1,200 slaves. The great landowners retained their *villae*, their fortresses. As for the territorial possessions of the Church, already very extensive under the Roman régime, they were unaffected. It does not appear that Arianism brought about any change in the situation.

Even among the Vandals the newcomers merely replaced the old proprietors of the soil. The Vandals lived in the Roman *villae* as the Romans had done before them.

Albertini has shown that the territorial system, and the prestations of oil furnished to the treasury, remained unchanged in Africa during the conquest.[2]

If there were systematic changes, if communal usages unknown to the Romans were introduced, this was only in the colonial territories in the extreme north of the Empire.

Thus, everything remained on the same footing. The retention of the land taxes, for that matter, shows that there was no profound upheaval.

As for the organization of the great estates, this too was unchanged. They were entrusted to *conductores* who farmed them and collected the revenues from the colonists.

On the other hand, the entire system of Roman tenures survived, in the form of precarious tenures and benefices. The contemporary documents contain evidence of perpetual leases, and the whole system was identical, or nearly so, with the Roman system.

The great estates were still prosperous. Gregory of Tours[3] mentions one Chrodinus who established *villae*, planted vineyards, erected farm buildings, and organized estates, which he gave to the bishops.

Gregory the Great, restoring to order the estates of the Roman Church, re-established the old system in every particular.

[1] H. PIRENNE, *Le fisc royal de Tournai*, in MÉLANGES F. LOT, 1925, p. 641.
[2] See above, p. 48.   [3] GREGORY OF TOURS, *Hist. Franc.*, VI, 20.

The great domains of the Church were administered by *conductores*, who paid rent for them, so that the monks were able to devote themselves to spiritual matters exclusively.[1]

These *conductores*, like the *juniores* of the domains of the Bishop of Mans at Ardin[2] in Poitou, were laymen; they were responsible for the rents, which they paid in advance, and they kept accounts, so that they must have been able to write.

Prestations were nearly always paid in money, which shows that goods were circulating, that they were sold in the open market. There is no sign as yet of the closed economy of the mediaeval *curtes*.

In Provence, during the Merovingian epoch, the system of tenure was entirely Roman.[3] Here, it seems, there were only small estates, exploited by colonists. In the North, on the other hand, we see that the *terra indominicata* played a considerable part. The cartulary of Saint Vincent of Mâcon gives us, for the reign of King Gontram (561–592), a list of the *servientes* of this domain, which was exploited by slaves and by the *corvées* of the tenants.[4]

Great quantities of cereals were still moved from place to place. In 510 Theodoric sent quantities of corn to Provence on account of the ravages of war in that region,[5] and we know that Gregory the Great centralized the products of the domains of the Church.

The great estates, at this period, still yielded considerable revenues in money. In 593 Dinamius sent Gregory the Great 400 *solidi* from Provence; two years later the same Pope was awaiting the arrival of clothing and of Anglo-Saxon slaves, who were

---

[1] E. LESNE, *La propriété ecclesiastique en France aux époques remaine et mérovingienne*, Paris-Lille, 1910, p. 309. See also the text of Saint Caesar of Arles, cited in F. KIENER, *Verfassungsgeschichte der Provence*, p. 37, n. 84.

[2] Department of Deux-Sèvres, arrondissement of Niort, canton of Coulonges-sur-Autise.

[3] F. KIENER, *Verfassungsgeschichte der Provence*, Leipzig, 1900, pp. 34 *et seq.*; R. BUCHNER, *Die Provence in Merowingischer Zeit*, Stuttgart, 1933, p. 30, believes that agriculture was still well developed and remunerative.

[4] F. KIENER, *op. cit.*, p. 34.

[5] R. BUCHNER, *op. cit.*, p. 30, n. 1.

to be purchased in Provence with the revenues of his domains.[1] Similarly, in 557 Pope Pelagius was expecting supplies from Provence which were needed to relieve the distress of the Roman people.[2]

There was also a normal trade in corn. Despite his enormous resources, we find that Gregory the Great made purchases of grain.

We find that in 537-538 a *peregrinus acceptor* made important purchases in Istria; he must have been a corn-merchant.[3]

Africa, under the Vandals, must have retained the prosperity which was derived from the cultivation of cereals and the olive, since it was still prosperous when the Byzantines returned to it. It does not appear that the aspect of Gaul was in any way less civilized. It seems that the culture of the vine was continued wherever it existed in the time of the Romans. If we read Gregory of Tours we do not by any means obtain the impression of a country in a state of decadence; unless it had been prosperous the landowners could hardly have been so wealthy.

The retention of the Roman *libra* affords indirect proof of the stability of the economic situation.

As for the social classes, they were the same as before. The upper class consisted of freemen (*ingenui*),[4] and it included an aristocracy of great landowners (*senatores*).[5]

The class of free citizens properly so-called probably constituted a minority.

[1] GREGORY THE GREAT, *Registr.*, III, 33, ed. EWALD-HARTMANN, M.G.H. EPIST., vol. I, p. 191.

[2] *Ibid.*, VI, 10, pp. 388-389.

[3] CASSIODORUS, *Variae*, XII, 22, M.G.H. SS. ANTIQ., vol. XII, p. 378.

[4] We must not be tempted to underestimate the number of freemen, as some have done. Their essential characteristic was that they had to undertake military service. Cf. in the *Leges Visigothorum*, IX, 2, 9, M.G.H. LEGES, vol. I, ed. ZEUMER, p. 377, the law of Erviges, according to which each freeman had to bring to the army the tenth of his slaves. VERLINDEN, *L'esclavage dans le monde ibérique médiéval*, in ANUARIO DE HISTORIA DEL DERECHO ESPAÑOL, vol. XI, 1934, pp. 353-355.

[5] For the survival of the great families see, for example, the family of the Syagrii, mentioned by A. COVILLE in *Recherches sur l'histoire de Lyon du Vᵃ siècle au IXᵉ siècle*, pp. 5 et seq.

Beneath them were the colonists, especially numerous among the Visigoths, and the liberated slaves.[1]

There were still plenty of slaves. As we shall presently see, they were mostly alien Barbarians, Anglo-Saxon or others, prisoners of war.

There was also an urban population of which we shall say something presently.

On the large estates there were workshops in which the women spun yarn, and in which other workers, slaves or domainal serfs, practised various crafts. But these workshops had already existed during the later centuries of the Empire.[2]

The population had retained the form which had been impressed upon it by the fiscal organization, although this had been greatly diminished by the almost complete curtailment of the military and administrative expenditure. In this respect the Germanic conquest may perhaps have been beneficial to the people. On the whole, the great domain had remained the essential social and economic element. Thanks to the domain, the economic basis of the feudal system already existed. But the subordination of the greater part of the population to the great landowners was manifested as yet only in private law. The *senior* had not yet interposed himself between the king and his subjects. Moreover, although the constitution of society was predominantly agrarian, it was not exclusively so. Commerce and the cities still played a considerable part in the general economic, social, and intellectual life of the age.

2. *Navigation in the East. Syrians and Jews*

Of the two portions of the Empire, the Greek had always been marked by a more advanced civilization than the Latin. We need not insist upon this obvious fact.

This Greek portion of the Empire was in communication, by

---

[1] VERLINDEN, *op. cit.*, ANUARIO, vol. II, p. 347. According to Verlinden, the colonists can hardly have played an important part.

[2] GREGORY OF TOURS, *Hist. Franc.*, IX, 38, notes the existence of women's apartments. Cf. FUSTEL DE COULANGES, *L'alleu et le domain rural*, p. 375.

sea, with Venetia and the West. Syria, where the caravans arrived from China and Arabia, was particularly active.

The Syrians were then the great maritime carriers, as the Dutch were to be in the 17th century. It was in Syrian vessels that the spices of the East and the industrial products of the great Oriental cities—Antioch, Damascus, Alexandria, etc.—were exported. The Syrians were to be found in all the ports of the Mediterranean, but they also penetrated inland.

Under the Empire they had establishments in Alexandria, Rome, Spain, Gaul, and Great Britain, and even on the Danube, at Carnuntum.[1]

The invasions did not in any way alter the situation. Genseric, by his piracies, may have hindered navigation a little, but at all events it was as active as ever when he had disappeared.

Salvian (d. circa 484), doubtless generalizing from what he had seen at Marseilles, spoke of the *negociatorum et Syricorum omnium turbas quae majorem ferme civitatum universarum partem occupant*.[2]

This Syrian expansion is confirmed by the archaeologists, and the texts are even more significant.[3]

In the 6th century there were large numbers of Orientals in Southern Gaul. The life of Saint Caesar, Bishop of Arles (d. 542), states that he composed hymns in Greek and Latin for the people.[4] There were also many in the North, since Gregory of Tours speaks of the Greek merchants of Orleans, who advanced, singing,

---

[1] P. CHARLSWORTH, *Trade-routes and commerce of the Roman Empire,* Cambridge, 2nd ed., 1926, pp. 178, 202, 220, 238.

[2] Cf. in a general manner, P. SCHEFFER-BOICHORST, *Zur geschichte der Syrer im Abendlande,* in MITTEILUNGEN DES OESTERR. INSTIT. FÜR GESCHICHTSFORSCHUNG, vol. VI, 1885, pp. 521 *et seq.*; L. BREHIER, *Les colonies d'Orientaux en Occident au commencement du Moyen Age,* in BYZANT. ZEITSCHR., vol. XII, 1903, pp. i *et seq.*; FUSTEL DE COULANGES, *La monarchie franque,* p. 357; J. EBERSOLT, *Orient et Occident,* 1928–1929, 2 vols.

[3] GREGORY OF TOURS, *Hist. Franc.,* VII, 22; Cf. BREHIER, *L'art en France des invasions barbares a l'époque romane,* pp. 36 and 38.

[4] I, 19, SS.RER.MEROV., vol. III, p. 462.

to meet the king.[1] According to the life of Saint Genevieve (d. 512), Saint Simeon Stylites (d. 460) is said to have questioned the *negotiatores euntes ac redeuntes* concerning her.[2]

But in addition to these merchants, who travelled to and fro, there were many who had settled in Gaul.[3] They are mentioned in many inscriptions. There is one in the chapel of Saint Eloi in Eure,[4] near the mouth of the Seine. The Syrian to whom it relates was doubtless trading with Britain.

Among these merchants there were very wealthy individuals who settled in the country when they had made their fortune. Gregory of Tours mentions a *negotiator* of Bordeaux[5] who possessed a great house in which was a chapel containing relics, and he offered a hundred and then two hundred gold *solidi* in order that these should not be taken from him. Another such merchant was that Eusebius of Paris, *negotiator, genere Syrus*,[6] who purchased the episcopal dignity, and then, finding fault with his predecessor's *scola*, constituted one of his own, which comprised only Syrians. We see, then, that they abounded in Gaul, but more especially, of course, in the South.

The population of Narbonne in 589[7] consisted of Goths, Romans, Jews, Greeks and Syrians. It so happens that we have no information relating to the Syrians in Italy, Africa and Spain, but we can hardly suppose that what was true of Gaul was not also true of these other countries. There must have been Syrians and Greeks among the foreign traders (*transmarini negotiatores*) mentioned by Theodoric and the law of the Visigoths. We know from the *Vita*

---

[1] *Hist. Franc.*, VIII, 1.

[2] SS.RER.MEROV., vol. III, p. 226. KRUSCH, the editor of this text, regards this as *non credibile*!

[3] E. LEBLANT, *Inscriptions chrétiennes de la Gaule*, vol. I, pp. 207 and 328. Cf. Nos. 225 and 613a. Cf. HÉRON DE VILLEFOSSE, *Deux inscriptions chrétiennes trouvées à Carthage*, in COMPTES RENDUS DES SÉANCES DE L'ACADÉMIE DES INSCRIPTIONS ET BELLES LETTRES, 1916, p. 435.

[4] E. LEBLANT, *op. cit.*, vol. I, p. 205, no. 125.

[5] GREGORY OF TOURS, *Hist. Franc.*, VII, 31.　　　　　[6] *Ibid.*, X, 26.

[7] Council of Narbonne, MANSI, *Sacrocrum Conciliorum . . . Collectio*, vol. IX, circa 1015 and circa 1017.

Patrum emeritensium that Greek merchants arrived in Spain by sea from the East (*negociatores graecos in navibus de Orientibus advenisse* (*circa* 570).[1]

Procopius mentions the existence in Naples, in the time of Belisarius, of a great Syrian merchant, Antiochus, who was the leader of the Roman party in that city.[2]

We know, from other sources, that there were many of these Syrians in the neighbourhood of Paris.[3] Duchesne[4] mentions a Monophysite priest who was travelling in Gaul about the year 560, and was in communication with Saint Nizier, Bishop of Lyons (d. 573), who allowed himself to be persuaded by the Syrian that the Emperor was a Nestorian.

There were also Egyptian influences at work in Gaul: they explain the popularity in that country of certain Egyptian saints,[5] and also the fact that the churches of the Gauls enjoyed a right of asylum as extensive as that of the churches of Egypt; moreover, they doubtless explain the presence of a Stylites at Yvoy.[6]

But the Syrians and the Greeks were not the only Orientals in the West. There were also the Jews, who were almost as numerous. They too had penetrated everywhere before the invasions, and there they remained after the invasions.

In Naples, at the time when it was besieged by Belisarius, they

---

[1] A.A.S.S. BOL, Nov., vol. I, p. 323. P. DE MOREAU, *Les missions médiévales* (HISTOIRE GÉNÉRALE COMPARÉE DES MISSIONS, published by BARON DESCAMPS), 1932, p. 171, mentions the presence of Greeks at Cordova about 585. Justinian's reconquest in the 6th century contributed greatly to the increase of this navigation.

[2] PROCOPIUS, V, 8, 21, ed. DEWING, vol. III, 1919, p. 74.

[3] Review by R. DUSSAUD of P. PERDRIZET, *Le calendrier parisien à la fin du Moyen Age* (1933), in SYRIA, vol. XV, 1934, p. 210.

[4] Mgr. L. DUCHESNE, *L'Eglise au VIe siècle*, Paris, 1925, p. 191, n. 2.

[5] PERDRIZET, *Le calendrier parisien à la fin du Moyen Age*, 1933, pp. 35 and 287-289. ADAMNAN, the biographer of Saint Columban, relates that Irish monks used to go to Syria in order to study the architecture of the monasteries. J. BAUM, *Aufgaben der frühchristlichen Kunstforschung in Britannien und Irland*, 1934, cited by FORSCHUNGEN UND FORTSCHRITTE, vol. XI, 1935, *circa* 223.

[6] GREGORY OF TOURS, *Hist. Franc.*, VIII, 15.

formed a great part of the merchant population of the city.[1] But they were already numerous under Theodoric; in Rome, and in Ravenna, the people having destroyed their synagogue, the king intervened in their favour, and condemned the Catholics to repair the damage which they had caused.[2] Later there were Jews in Palermo (598),[3] Terracina (591),[4] and Cagliari in Sardinia (598); and they were numerous in these cities, for they had synagogues in all of them.

In Spain, too, there were Jews in Merida, and the bishop received them on an equal footing with the Christians.[5]

The *Lex Wisigothorum* makes mention of the Jews.[6] It confines itself to forbidding them to undertake propaganda. We see that their position was then the same as it had been under the Empire, since the Law of the Visigoths states that they were living under the Roman law.[7] Later on the laws concerning persecution show that their numbers were considerable. It was the same in Italy.[8] But naturally, thanks to Gregory of Tours, we are most fully informed in respect of Gaul. There were Jews in Clermont, Paris, Orleans, Tours, Bourges, Bordeaux and Arles.[9] Their centre was Marseilles. It was there that they took refuge when they were persecuted.[10] We obtain some idea of their numbers when we consider that no fewer that five hundred were converted in Clermont.[11] After the 6th century their position was the same. In the middle of the 7th century the *Vita Sancti Sulpicii*[12] speaks of their presence in Bourges.

Even if they were disliked by the people,[13] they were not at first

---

[1] HARTMANN, *op. cit.*, vol. I, p. 262.   [2] *Ibid.*, vol. I, p. 222.

[3] JAFFÉ-WATTENBACH, *Regesta*, No. 1564.   [4] *Ibid.*, No. 1104.

[5] *Vita patrum Emeritensium*, MIGNE, *Patr. Lat.*, vol. 80, col. 139.

[6] XII, 2, 14, M.G.H. LEGES, vol. I, ed. K. ZEUMER, p. 420.

[7] XII, 2, 13, ed. ZEUMER, *loc. cit.*, p. 419.

[8] JAFFÉ-WATTENBACH, *Regesta*, No. 1157.

[9] F. KIENER, *op. cit.*, p. 28; F. VERCAUTEREN, *Étude sur les Civitates de la Belgique Seconde*, 1934, p. 446.

[10] GREGORY OF TOURS, *Hist. Franc.*, V, 11.   [11] *Ibid.*

[12] M.G.H.SS.RER.MÉROV., vol. IV, pp. 374-375.

[13] GREGORY OF TOURS, *Hist. Franc.*, V, 11.

molested by the authorities. In 582, however, in Gaul, the king had them converted by force.[1] Heraclius is said to have asked Dagobert to have them baptized.[2] Some allowed themselves to be converted,[3] but others fled to Marseilles, where they were not molested. They were sometimes accused of sacrilege.[4] At Bourges, in the first half of the 7th century, Saint Sulpicius caused large numbers of them to be baptized.[5] At Clermont Bishop Avitus had many Jews baptized, without, however, subjecting them to constraint.[6] Chilperic also caused some Jews to be baptized,[7] and one of these, having refused, was imprisoned; but Gregory the Great, in 591, reprimanded the laity of Arles and Marseilles, who were forcing baptism upon the Jews;[8] he also rebuked the Bishop of Terracina, who had expelled the Jews from their synagogues. They must, he said, be led by kindness.[9] He would not even allow the Bishop of Naples to prevent the Jews from working on feast days and holy days.[10] The only restriction which he sought to impose upon them was in respect of owning Christian slaves.[11] He requested Brunehaut to promulgate a law forbidding them to own such slaves.[12]

Certain Councils, like the Council of Clermont, in 535, enacted that Jews must not become judges.[13] The Merovingian Councils made many stipulations prohibiting marriage between Jews and Christians, forbidding Christians to attend the banquets of Jews, and Jews were forbidden to own *mancipia Christiana*. An edict of 614 forbade them to bring public actions against Christians.[14]

In Spain, after the conversion of Reccared, the laws against the

[1] GREGORY OF TOURS, *Hist. Franc.*, VI, 17.

[2] *Chronique du pseudo-Frédégaire*, IV, 65, M.G.H.SS.RER.MEROV., vol. II, p. 153. [3] GREGORY OF TOURS, *Hist. Franc.*, V, 11.

[4] GREGORY OF TOURS, *Liber in Gloria Martyrum*, ch. 21, ed. KRUSCH, M.G.H.SS.RER.MEROV., vol. I, p. 501. [5] See above, p. 65, n. 12.

[6] GREGORY OF TOURS, *Hist. Franc.*, V, 11. Concerning the Jews of Lyons, see COVILLE, *op. cit.*, pp. 538 *et seq.*

[7] GREGORY OF TOURS, *Hist. Franc.*, VI, 17.

[8] JAFFÉ-WATTENBACH, *Regesta*, No. 1115. [9] *Ibid.*, No. 1104.

[10] *Ibid.*, No. 1879. [11] *Ibid.*, No. 1157.

[12] *Ibid.*, Nos. 1743–1744. [13] M.G.H.CONCILIA, ed. MAASEN, vol. I, p. 67.

[14] M.G.H.CAPIT., ed. BORETIUS-KRAUSE, vol. I, p. 22.

Jews became severe. Sisebut (612–631) compelled certain Jews to become Christians, for which he was blamed by Isidore.[1] Chrutela (636–640) ordained that there should no longer be any but Catholics in the kingdom. Reccesvinth (649–672) prohibited circumcision, the celebration of the Sabbath, and the Jewish festivals. Ervigus (680–687) commanded the Jews to abjure their religion within the year under penalty of confiscation and exile. Egica (687–702) forbade them to trade with foreigners or with Christians. A popular revolt against the Jews broke out, and the upshot was that all Jews were declared to be slaves of the Christians (696). Isidore of Seville composed a *contra Judaeos*[2] against them. They offered money to Reccared, who refused it.[3] At the time of Sisebut's persecution numbers of Jews took refuge in Gaul.[4]

Certain Jews were sailors, or at all events shipowners;[5] others owned land which was cultivated by colonists or *originarii*;[6] others again were physicians.[7] But the immense majority were engaged in commerce, and above all in lending money at interest. Many of them were slave-merchants; for example, at Narbonne.[8] Some were engaged in maritime commerce.[9] Gregory of Tours mentions several who sold spices at Tours at unduly high prices, with the complicity of the bishop.[10] In Paris, the Jew Priscus, *familiaris* of King Chilperic, furnished him with spices,[11] unless indeed he was his banker, for certainly the word *species* which Gregory employs seems, in a certain passage, to denote money.[12] The *Gesta Dagoberti*[13]

---

[1] ZIEGLER, *Church and State in Visigothic Spain*, 1930, p. 189.

[2] A. EBERT, *op. cit.*, French translation. AYMERIC and CONDAMIN, vol. I, 1883, p. 631.   [3] JAFFÉ-WATTENBACH, *Regesta*, No. 1757.

[4] J. ARONIUS, *Regesten zur Geschichte der Juden*, p. 21, No. 59.

[5] JAFFÉ-WATTENBACH, *op. cit.*, No. 1564.   [6] *Ibid.*, No. 1293.

[7] GREGORY OF TOURS, *Hist. Franc.*, V, 6.

[8] ARONIUS, *Regesten zur Geschichte der Juden*, p. 19, No. 53.

[9] GREGORY OF TOURS, *Liber in Gloria Confessorum, circa* 95, ed. KRUSCH, M.G.H.SS.RER.MEROV., vol. I, p. 809.

[10] GREGORY OF TOURS, *Hist. Franc.*, IV, 12.   [11] *Ibid.*, VI, 5.

[12] *Ibid.*, IV, 35. It will be noted that in the French language this word has given rise to the words "épices" and "espèces."

[13] Ed. KRUSCH, M.G.H.SS.RER.MEROV., vol. II, p. 413. It should be noted, however, that these *Gesta* were not written until the 19th century.

speak of a *negotiator*, Salomon, who was a Jew. But many of the Jews—doubtless the majority—were engaged in banking, and of these a large number seem to have been very wealthy.

Besides the Syrians and the Jews, there were doubtless Africans among the *transmarini negotiatores* mentioned by Cassiodorus and the law of the Visigoths. Carthage was a great city, an *étape* for vessels sailing to the East, and the camels utilized as beasts of burden in Gaul[1] probably came from Carthage.

While navigation was especially active in the Mediterranean, Bordeaux and Nantes were likewise busy ports, whose vessels crossed the Atlantic to the British Isles—from which they brought Saxon slaves—and to Galicia.[2] The navigation of Belgium, so active under the Romans,[3] must have suffered greatly when England was invaded by the Anglo-Saxons. But it still survived. Tiel, Duurstede and Quentovic were still centres of maritime traffic, which may have been fed by the Flemish cloth trade.[4] But here, apparently the trade was in local hands.[5] Gaul had several ports on the Mediterranean. In addition to Marseilles, there were Fos,[6] Narbonne, Agde, and Nice.

The Roman organization appears to have been retained. Along the quays—*cataplus*[7]—a sort of market or exchange seems to have been held. At Fos, for example, there was a magazine of the fisc on the quays. We know that in Italy, during the reign of Theodoric, there were all sorts of officials who were occupied in the regulation

---

[1] GREGORY OF TOURS, *Hist. Franc.*, VII, 35; *Vita S. Eligii*, SS.RER.MEROV., vol. IV, p. 702.

[2] VENANTIUS FORTUNATUS, *Vita Sancti Germani*, circa 47, M.G.H.SS.RER. MEROV., vol. VII, pp. 401–402.

[3] FR. CUMONT, *Comment la Belgique fut romanisée*, 2nd ed., Brussels, 1919, pp. 25–29.

[4] H. PIRENNE, *Draps de Frise ou draps de Flandre?* in VIERTELJAHRSCHR. FÜR SOZ. UND WIRTSCHAFTSGESCHICHTE, vol. VI, 1909, p. 313.

[5] The rare pieces of Anglo-Saxon gold struck in the South bear witness to a certain commercial activity.

[6] PAULY-WISSOWA, *Real-Encyclopadie*, vol. VII, circa 75, No. 12.

[7] F. VERCAUTEREN, *Cataplus et Catabolus*, in BULLETIN DUCANGE, vol. II, 1925, p. 98.

of commerce.[1] Similarly, in Spain there were *thelonearii* for the benefit of the *transmarini negociatores*. The Byzantine "commerciaries" introduced at Carthage after the reconquest[2] must have exercised a certain amount of influence throughout the Tyrrhenian Sea. All these references show that it would be a mistake to imagine that this commerce was concerned only with luxuries. Archaeology, of course, has preserved for us only the *objets de luxe*, and the *Liber Judiciorum* of the Visigoths speaks of the *transmarinus negociator* who imported gold, silver, clothing, and all sorts of *objets de luxe*.[3] We have knowledge, too, of many other kinds of merchandise: of the ivories from Egypt, which are represented in our museums,[4] the decorated liturgical tunic of Saqqesara,[5] the purses from Phoenicia,[6] which, according to Gregory, were in common use among the merchants, and the Oriental curtains with which the altars were decorated.[7] Undoubtedly the more expensive luxuries were entirely Oriental, and the fashions of Constantinople set the *ton*, just as those of Paris do today; we know that there was very great luxury among the Merovingians.[8] There are numbers of texts which tell us that silk was worn by the men as frequently as by the women.[9] And where could this silk have come from, if

---

[1] CASSIODORUS, *Variae*, V, 39, publishes a regulation concerning the market tolls for the *transmarini*, ed. MOMMSEN, M.G.H.SS.ANTIQ., vol. XII, p. 164.

[2] DIEHL, *L'Afrique byzantine*, p. 500; G. MILLET, *Sur les sceaux des commerciaires byzantins*, in MÉLANGES G. SCHLUMBERGER, vol. II, 1924, pp. 324-326.

[3] "Si quis transmarinus negociator aurum, argentum, vestimenta vel quelibet ornamenta . . . vendiderit," *Lex Visigothorum*, XI, 3, 1, ed. K. ZEUMER, M.G.H. LEGES, vol. I, p. 404.

[4] M. LAURENT, *Les ivoires prégothiques conservés en Belgique*, 1912, pp. 9, 17, 20, 84.

[5] *Cooperturium Sarmaticum*. GREGORY OF TOURS, *Liber Vitae Patrum*, circa 11, ed. KRUSCH, SS.RER.MEROV., vol. I, p. 701.

[6] GREGORY OF TOURS, *Liber in gloria Confess.*, circa 110, ed. KRUSCH, *loc. cit.*, p. 819.

[7] FUSTEL DE COULANGES, *La monarchie franque*, p. 257.

[8] Concerning the luxury of the Merovingians, see *Vita S. Eligii episcopi Noviomagensis*, I, 12, ed. KRUSCH, M.G.H.SS.RER.MEROV., vol. IV, p. 678.

[9] GREGORY OF TOURS, *Hist. Franc.*, VI, 10; VI, 35; X, 16; *Liber in gloria martyrum*, SS.RER.MEROV., vol. I, pp. 491, 535, 549; *Liber de virtutibus S. Martini*, I, II; *ibid.*, p. 595; II, 23, *ibid.*, p. 617.

not from the East? It was brought from China, until Justinian established the manufacture of silk in the Empire.

The luxuries of the table were also supplied by the East. Gregory[1] speaks of the wines of Syria which were exported from Gaza.[2] They were to be found everywhere, and in great quantities. Gregory of Tours tells us that a widow of Lyons used to take two gallons of Syrian wine to her husband's tomb every day,[3] and he mentions elsewhere that at Tours he sent to a wine-shop in order to obtain some Syrian wine for a guest.[4] It was therefore a usual article of commerce. It is perhaps this wine that is mentioned in a letter from Didier of Cahors to Paul, Bishop of Verdun, in which he states that he is sending the bishop ten casks of Falerno;[5] which shows, by the way, that there was a good deal of inland traffic.[6]

There is also mention of other choice liquors. In 597 Gregory the Great wrote to the Bishop of Alexandria respecting a liquor known as *Cognidium*;[7] this was exported by merchants who must have been established in Alexandria, since the recipient of the letter was living there.

Doubtless, also, foodstuffs were imported from the East. At all events, during Lent the ascetics used to eat bitter herbs imported from Egypt. Gregory of Tours speaks of the hermit in the neighbourhood of Nice who ate nothing but roots which were brought him from Alexandria.[8]

This speaks of a trade which went beyond the mere importation of jewels and articles of clothing; but the really important branch of Oriental commerce, by which it was actually related to every-

[1] GREGORY OF TOURS, *Hist. Franc.*, VII, 29.

[2] Concerning these wines, see the *Vie de Porphyre, évêque de Gaza*, by MARC LE DIACRE, published by H. GRÉGOIRE and M. A. KUGENER, Paris, 1930, pp. 124–126.

[3] GREGORY OF TOURS, *Liber in gloria Confessorum, circa* 64, ed. KRUSCH, *loc. cit.*, p. 785.

[4] GREGORY OF TOURS, *Hist. Franc.*, VII, 29.

[5] M.G.H.EPIST.MEROV., vol. I, p. 209, about 630–647.

[6] FORTUNATUS also mentions the wine of Gaza. *Vita S. Martini*, II, 81, ed. LEO, M.G.H.SS.ANTIQ., vol. IV[2], p. 316.

[7] JAFFÉ-WATTENBACH, *Regesta*, No. 1483.   [8] *Hist. Franc.*, VI, 6.

day life, was the importation of spices.[1] One cannot insist too strongly on the importance of this trade. The Roman Empire had received all sorts of spices from India, China, Arabia. It was the trade in spices that built up the prosperity of Palmyra and Apamea. Pliny the Elder estimates that the Empire spent every year at least one hundred millions of our francs on spices imported from India and China and Arabia. Their diffusion throughout the Roman Empire was not interrupted by the invasions. They continued, after the invasions, as before them, to form a constituent of the everyday diet.[2]

We are able to obtain some notion of this trade from the treatise of Anthimus, a Greek physician who was banished from Byzantium in 478, and whom Theodoric sent as Ambassador to Thierry I, King of Austrasia (511–534).[3]

A diploma granted to the Abbot of Corbie on April 29th, 716, by Chilperic II casts a revealing light on this branch of commerce.[4] This confirms documents of a similar nature which were granted to Corbie by Clotair III (657–673) and Chilperic II (673–675). The sovereign gave this church an authorization to levy merchandise from the *cellarium fisci* of Fos. In it I find the following list:

> 10,000 pounds of oil.
> 30 hogsheads of *garum* (a sort of condiment).[5]
> 30 pounds of pepper.
> 150 pounds of cummin.
> 2 pounds of cloves.
> 1 pound of cinnamon.
> 2 pounds of nard.
> 30 pounds of *costum* (an aromatic herb).[6]

[1] F. CUMONT, *Fouilles de Doura-Europos*, 1926, p. xxxiii.

[2] LOT, PFISTER and GANSHOF, *Hist. du Moyen Age*, vol. I, p. 356, considered that they were employed only at court and by the aristocracy.

[3] *Epistula de observatione ciborum*, ed. ED. LIECHTENHAN, 1928 (*Corpus Medicorum Latinorum*, vol. VIII¹).

[4] L. LEVILLAIN, *Examen critique des chartes . . . de Corbie*, 1902, p. 235, No. 15.

[5] DUCANGE, *Glossarium*, verbo garum.

[6] E. JEANSELME, *Sur un aide-mémoire de thérapeutique byzantin*, in MÉLANGES CH. DIEHL, vol. I, 1930, p. 150, No. 12; DUCANGE, *op. cit.*, costum, mulled wine.

50 pounds of dates.

100 pounds of figs.

100 pounds of almonds.

30 pounds of pistachios.

100 pounds of olives.

50 pounds of *hidrio* (a kind of spice).[1]

150 pounds of chick-peas.

20 pounds of rice.

10 pounds of *auro pimento*.

20 skins (*seoda*—skins dressed with oil?).[2]

10 skins of Cordova leather.

50 quires of papyrus.

Of course, all these goods—the oil, for example—were not spices imported from the East. But the majority were. And the document enables us to draw various conclusions. First, that the cellar of the fisc was always abundantly furnished with these spices, since the permission granted to the monks does not specify any particular date: they could go to the cellar when they wished. Again, we can hardly suppose that this document records an instance of generosity by which only the monastery of Corbie profited. But even if this were the case, we should still have to deduce that spices were so generally employed that even a monastery kitchen could not dispense with them.

As a matter of fact, they were in such general use that the king provided for the consumption, by the *missi* of the monastery at Fos, of a pound of *garum*, an ounce of pepper, and two ounces of cummin. Thus even these poor fellows found pepper as necessary as salt. These prestations to the *missi* had to be made at every stopping-place, or perhaps we should say at every posting-house, going and returning, which amounts to saying that they were obtainable everywhere.

We shall find similar data recorded in the *tractoria* which Marculf has preserved for us.[3] Practically the same spices are mentioned as

---

[1] DUCANGE, *verbo* hidrio. We do not find this word elsewhere; perhaps it is an erroneous reading?

[2] DUCANGE, *sub verbo seoda*.   [3] *Formulae*, I, II, ed. EXUMER, p. 49.

in the Corbie document. I know that Krusch[1] claims that Marculf's formula is simply copied from the Corbie diploma. He says, in a jesting tone, that the royal officials never ate all that, and no doubt he is right.[2] On the other hand, we cannot suppose that Marculf would have included a list containing all these spices in his formula if such condiments had been rare. He must have regarded them as condiments in general use, and this is all the more significant, as he was writing in the North. Moreover, is it the fact that Marculf merely copied the Corbie diploma?[3] It will be noted that he includes supplies of meat as well as the goods that figure in the Corbie document. And if he had merely copied the latter, why should he have omitted any mention of papyrus?[4]

In any case, the Corbie diploma and the conclusions to be derived from it suffice to emphasize the essential importance of the traffic in spices during the Merovingian epoch. And doubtless what is true for Gaul is also true of the other shores of the Tyrrhenian Sea.

Papyrus was another thing that came from the East, and of which great quantities were consumed.[5] Egypt had the monopoly of furnishing the whole Empire with the writing material in general use, parchment being reserved for special purposes. Now, both after and before the invasions the art of writing was practised throughout the West. It was a necessary constituent of social life. The juridical and administrative life of the Empire, the very

[1] KRUSCH, *Ursprung und Text von Markulfs Formelsammlung*, NACHRICHTEN VON DER GESELLSCHAFT DER WISSENSCHAFTEN ZU GÖTTINGEN, 1916, p. 256.

[2] On the other hand, no spices are provided for in the diet of officials in the Carolingian period. G. WAITZ, *Deutsche Verfassungsgeschichte*, vol. IV, 2nd ed., p. 23.

[3] SPROEMBERG, *Marculf und die Fränkische Reichskanzlei*, NEUES ARCHIV., vol. 47, 1927, p. 89, accepts KRUSCH's point of view.

[4] As far as spices are concerned, the commerce of the Merovingian epoch bears a resemblance to the trade of the Italian cities from the 12th century onwards. GREGORY OF TOURS mentions that spices were sold by the merchants of Paris. *Hist. Franc.*, VI, 32.

[5] H. PIRENNE, *Le commerce du papyrus dans la Gaule mérovingienne*, COMPTES RENDUS DES SÉANCES DE L'ACADÉMIE DES INSCRIPTIONS ET BELLES LETTRES, 928, pp. 178-191.

functioning of the State, necessitated the practice of the art, and the same may be said of social relations. The merchants had their clerks, *mercenarii litterati*. Masses of papyrus must have been required by those who kept the registers of the fisc, by the notaries of the tribunals, by private correspondents, and by the monasteries. The monastery of Corbie, as we have seen, consumed, every year, fifty quires (*tomi*) of papyrus, drawn from the *cellarium fisci* of Fos. Whole cargoes of this commodity must have been unloaded upon the quays of the seaports.

Gregory's reproach to his colleagues of Nantes, whose insults could not have been inscribed upon all the papyrus discharged in the port of Marseilles,[1] affords striking proof of the frequencies of such cargoes. Moreover, papyrus was used in the manufacture of wicks for candles, and also, apparently, oiled papyrus was used instead of glass in the lights of lanterns.[2] The fact that papyrus could be bought in the shops in Cambrai means that it could be obtained throughout the country.[3] It was therefore an article of general consumption, and there was consequently a wholesale trade in papyrus, radiating from Alexandria to all parts of the Mediterranean. We have the material proof of this in the handsome royal diplomas preserved in the Archives Nationales of Paris[4] and in certain fragments of private charters; the débris of the innumerable *scrinia* in which private persons kept their business papers and their correspondence, just as the cities preserved the acts inserted in the *gesta municipalia*.

The fragility of papyrus in the northern climate explains why so little is left; but we must be under no illusion as to the quantity

---

[1] GREGORY OF TOURS, *Hist. Franc.*, V, 5: *O si te habuisset Massilia sacerdotem! Numquam naves oleum aut reliquas species detulissent, nisi cartam tantum, quo majorem opportunitatem scribendi ad bonos infamandos haberes. Sed paupertas carta finem imponit verbositati.*

[2] GREGORY OF TOURS, *Liber in gloria martyrum*, M.G.H.SS.RER. MEROV., vol. I, p. 558; *Liber de virtutibus S. Martini, ibid.*, p. 644; *Liber Vitae Patrum, ibid.*, p. 698.

[3] F. VERCAUTEREN, *Étude sur les Civitates*, pp. 211-212.

[4] LAUER and SAMARAN, *Les diplômes originaux des Mérovingiens*, Paris, 1908.

which was formerly employed. And the wealth of information which we possess concerning Gaul, thanks to Gregory of Tours, should not make us forget the fact that still more papyrus must have been used in Italy and Spain, and that this must have necessitated an exceptionally active import trade.

Another article of consumption figured very largely in the commerce of the period. This was oil. There was a demand for it everywhere; in the first place for alimentary purposes, for it seems that in Southern Gaul nearly everything was cooked in oil, as in Spain and Italy. The native olive trees did not suffice to meet the demand. It was necessary to import oil from abroad; all the more necessary inasmuch as the lighting of the churches at this period—doubtless precisely because oil was so abundant—was effected not by means of wax candles, as it was at a later date, but by means of oil-fed lamps. Now Africa was the greatest oil-producing country in the Empire, and was to remain so until the Musulman conquest. It was exported from Africa in *orcae*. Theodoric, between 509 and 511, wrote to the Bishop of Salona[1] on behalf of the merchant Johannes, who had furnished this bishop with *sexaginta orcas olei ad implenda luminaria*, and who wanted to be paid. The rest of the letter shows this was merely a *parvitas*, that is to say, a bagatelle. Gregory of Tours tells us something about the oil trade at Marseilles;[2] he speaks of a merchant who had seventy *orcae* of oil stolen on the quay.[3] A diploma granted by Clovis III, in 692, and renewed in 716, but which really dated back to Dagobert I (d. 639) granted the monastery of Saint-Denis an annual subsidy of a hundred *solidi*, with which the *actores regii* were to buy oil from the *cellarium fisci*, in accordance with the *ordo cataboli*.[4] A formula of Marculf's mentions Marseilles as the port where the oil for the *luminaria* was generally purchased.[5]

This oil therefore found its way even into the North. The

---

[1] CASSIODORUS, *Variae*, III, 7, ed. MOMMSEN, M.G.H.SS.ANTIQ., vol. XII p. 83. This text was kindly communicated to me by M. KUGENER.

[2] BUCHNER, *Die Provence*, pp. 44–45. He bases his remarks principally upon GREGORY OF TOURS, *Hist. Franc.*, V, 5.   [3] *Ibid.*, IV, 43.

[4] *Ibid.*, pp. 44–45.   [5] MARCULF, *Supplementum*, I, ed. ZEUMER, p. 107.

Corbie diploma of 716, which mentions 10,000 pounds of oil, is further proof of this. It must not be supposed that this was oil from Provence, for it was deposited in the *cellarium fisci*.[1] A tax which refers to the exportation of oil from Bordeaux gives us reason to believe that this oil was forwarded from Marseilles.[2]

All this affords proof of active trade relations with Africa. But the very curious fact that camels were employed as pack-animals in Spain and Gaul throws a vivid light on these relations. For these camels can only have come from Africa, where they were introduced by Rome in the 2nd century. They must evidently have been employed on this side of the Mediterranean before the invasions. Gregory of Tours[3] speaks of the camels and horses loaded *cum ingenti pondere auri atque argenti* and abandoned by the army of Gondevald during its retreat. Moreover, Brunehaut, before her execution,[4] was paraded before the army on a camel. And this, it would seem, if we compare it with the preceding text, proves that the armies used to transport their baggage on the backs of camels. The *Vita Sancti Eligii*[5] speaks of a camel which accompanied the bishop on his travels. In Spain, King Wamba had the rebel Paulus brought to Toledo *abrasis barbis pedibusque nudatis, subsqualentibus veste vel habitu induti, camelorum vehiculis imponuntur*.[6]

The foregoing clearly proves the existence of extremely active navigation on the Tyrrhenian Sea, to the East and to the coast of Africa. Carthage seems to have been a sort of half-way

---

[1] BUCHNER's calculation, *op. cit.*, p. 45, according to which the imports of oil into Fos amounted to 200,000 pounds per annum, need not be taken seriously.

[2] *Vita S. Filiberti abbatis Gemeticensis*, M.G.H.SS.RER.MEROV., vol. V, p. 602.

[3] GREGORY OF TOURS, *Hist. Franc.*, VII, 35.

[4] PSEUDO-FREDEGARIUS, *Chronica*, IV, 42, SS.RER.MEROV., vol. II, p. 141; *Vita Columbani*, I, 29, *ibid.*, vol. IV, p. 106; *Liber Historiae Francorum, circa* 40, *ibid.*, vol. II, p. 310.

[5] *Vita S. Eligii*, II, 13, M.G.H.SS.RER.MEROV., vol. IV, p. 702.

[6] JULIAN OF TOLEDO, *Historia Wambae*, SS. RER. MEROV., vol. V, p. 525. DUCANGE, *sub verbo* Camelus, cites a text of the *Vita SS. Voti et Felicis* relating to Spain, in which we must read *Camelus* and not correct this into *rupicapra* (chamois) as DUCANGE has done.

station for the Oriental trade. There was also a coasting trade along the shores of Italy, Provence, and Spain. People travelling to Rome from the North embarked at Marseilles for Porto, at the mouth of the Tiber.[1] Travellers going to Constantinople went by sea. The land-route by way of the Danube, encumbered with Barbarians, was seldom used.[2] There was another route by way of Ravenna and Bari. There may have been regular sailings between Marseilles and Spain, like those of our cargo vessels. We may conclude as much from the expression *negotio solito* employed by Gregory of Tours.[3] I think we may say that navigation was at least as active as under the Empire. After Genseric we hear no further mention of piracy, and it is clear that the trade which was carried on was wholesale trade on a very large scale. We can no longer doubt this when we consider the nature of the imports, their regularity, and the wealth amassed by the merchants.

The only port concerning which we have plenty of information, Marseilles, appears to have been, definitely, a great seaport. It was a cosmopolitan city. Its importance may be deduced from the anxiety displayed by the king to obtain possession of the city when the kingdom was divided.[4] There were many Jews and Syrians there, to say nothing of Greeks, and there must have been Goths also. The *Annales Petaviani*[5] speak of an Anglo-Saxon *negotiator*, Botto, who, since his son died in 790, must have been established there in the early part of the 8th century—that is, at a time when the decadence was setting in. The city must have been very populous, and it would still have contained some of those great many-storied houses like those of which the ruins may be seen at Ostia. Gregory of Tours[6] speaks of eight persons having died in one house, from which we may conclude that it was a sort of lodging-house. One may arrive at the same con-

[1] R. BUCHNER, *op. cit.*, p. 32.   [2] *Ibid.*, p. 33.
[3] GREGORY OF TOURS, *Hist. Franc.*, IX, 22.
[4] LOT, PFISTER and GANSHOF, *Hist. du Moyen Age*, vol. I, pp. 258 and 259.
[5] *Annales Petaviani*, M.G.H. SS., vol. I, p. 17.
[6] GREGORY OF TOURS, *Hist. Franc.*, IX, 22.

clusion if one notes the frequency of epidemics in this maritime city under Bishop Theodore (*circa* 566–591). A ship coming from Spain brought an epidemic which continued for two months.[1] It spread through the hinterland as far as the neighbourhood of Lyons.[2] There is frequent mention of other epidemics[3] in Provence, at Narbonne. Fredegarius describes an epidemic in 598–599 which reminds us of the Black Death.[4]

3. *Inland Commerce*

Naturally, we cannot suppose that the Oriental merchants, Jews and others, restricted themselves to an import trade in the Mediterranean basin, without exporting anything. Their vessels would, of course, have carried some return freight. The principal cargo may have consisted of slaves. We know that household and agricultural slavery was still very widespread after the 5th century. For my own part, I am rather inclined to believe that the Germanic invasions may have revived the prosperity of the slave trade. The Germans were as familiar with the institution of slavery as the Romans, and must have brought plenty of slaves with them. Their wars against the Barbarians beyond the Rhine, and against the Lombards, must have added to the numbers of their slaves.

On the other hand, while the Church, by admitting the slave to the Sacraments, and recognizing his right, or rather his obligation to contract matrimony, had improved his condition, it had neither condemned nor attacked the institution of slavery on principle.[5] *Mancipia* were consequently to be found everywhere, not only in the great domains, but in the service of all private persons

---

[1] GREGORY OF TOURS, *Hist. Franc.*, IX, 21 and 22.   [2] *Ibid.*, X, 25.

[3] *Ibid.*, VIII, 39, and VI, 14.

[4] *Chronica*, IV, 18, SS.RER.MEROV., vol. II, p. 128: *Eo anno cladis glandolaria marsilia et reliquas Provinciae civitates graviter vastavit.*

[5] The Church's point of view was absolutely the same as under the Roman Empire. Cf. VERLINDEN, *op. cit.*, ANUARIO DE HISTORIA DEL DERECHO ESPAÑOL, vol. XI (1934), p. 312.

who were at all prosperous. The liberation of slaves did nothing to reduce their numbers; there were still slaves everywhere, and their numbers were increased by constant fresh arrivals.[1]

The Barbarian peoples constituted the great source of slaves. That Samo of whom Fredegarius[2] records that he arrived in the country of the Wends at the head of a troop of merchant adventurers, in 623–624, was certainly a slave-dealer. These merchants went into the country of the Wends as the Varangians of the 9th century entered Russia, in order to raid the country for slaves, and also, doubtless, in order to bring back furs. The Wends, being pagans, could be bought and sold without scruple, for the Councils only sought to hinder the sale of Christian slaves to persons outside the kingdom, which proves that slaves were sold to foreigners.[3]

Samo was not the only merchant of this character, for on becoming king of the Wends he had some Frankish merchants massacred, which led to war between him and Dagobert. His accession to the monarchy is a striking point of similarity between him and the Varangians. On the other hand, we may guess that he himself sold arms to the Barbarians, as did the contraband merchants on the frontier, against whom so many of the capitularies legislated. For the rest, although Fredegarius called Samo *negucians*, and his companions *negutiantes*, we cannot regard him as a professional merchant, but very definitely as an adventurer.

---

[1] The *Lex Visigothorum*, III, 4, 17, ed. ZEUMER, M.G.H. LEGES, vol. I, p. 157, even makes mention of slaves in the houses of *pauperes*. As a matter of fact, relapsed prostitutes were given to such masters in order that they might be *in gravi servitio*.

[2] FREDEGARIUS, *op. cit.*, IV, 48, M.G.H. SS. RER. MEROV., vol. II, p. 144. Cf. CH. VERLINDEN, *Le Franc Samo*, REVUE BELGE DE PHILOLOGIE ET D'HISTOIRE, vol. XII, 1933, pp. 1090–1095. FUSTEL DE COULANGES, *La monarchie franque*, p. 258, compares Samo with the head of a great commercial company!

[3] The Council of Châlon, 639–654, M.G.H. CONCILIA, ed. MAASEN, vol. I, p. 210, prohibited the sale of slaves to persons outside the Frankish kingdom.

Moorish slaves also were sold in Gaul; other slaves came from Thuringia, and yet others from England.[1]

There were many English slaves for sale in the market of Marseilles, where Gregory the Great, in 595, had some purchased in order that they might be sent to Rome to be converted.[2] Probably these were prisoners taken during the wars between the Britons and the Saxons, and sent overseas into Gaul. Possibly the captives whom Saint Amand (d. 674–675) ransomed in Gand were some of these prisoners.[3] Undoubtedly the slaves whom a certain merchant brought into the neighbourhood of Cambrai, and of whom we read in the *Vita Gaugerici*, were also from the North.[4]

Slaves could be bought in all parts of the country. Gregory of Tours[5] speaks of Saxon slaves belonging to a merchant of the Orleanais.

Fredegarius relates[6] that Bilichildis, who became the wife of Theudebert, was purchased from some *negotiatores* by Brunehaut, no doubt on account of her beauty.

The *tonlieux* of Arras and Tournai also furnish evidence of the transit of slaves, for whom the merchants had to pay dues.[7]

---

[1] *Vita S. Eligii*, M.G.H. SS. RER. MEROV., vol. IV, p. 676, VERLINDEN, *op. cit.*, p. 379, thinks it probable that slaves were sold also in Spain. Saint Bathild had been *de partibus transmarinis . . . vili pretio venundata*. SS. RER. MEROV., vol. II, p. 482, cf. LESNE, *La prorpiété ecclésiastique en France*, I, 1910, p. 359. At Clermont, Sigivaldus had as slave (*in cugus servitio erat adolescens quidam nomine Brachio*) a Thuringian who was employed in hunting the boar. GREGORY OF TOURS, *Liber Vitae Patrum*, M.G.H. S.S. RER. MEROV., vol. I, p. 712. GUILHIERMOZ, *Essai sur l'origine de la noblesse en France au Moyen Age*, 1902, p. 74, is certainly mistaken in regarding him as a private soldier.

[2] JAFFÉ-WATTENBACH, *Regesta*, No. 1386.

[3] DE MOREAU, *Saint-Amand*, 1927, p. 133. Concerning the sale of captives, see LESNE, *op. cit.*, pp. 357 and 369.

[4] *Vita S. Gaugerici*, ed. KRUSCH, M.G.H. SS. RER. MEROV., vol. III, p. 656. Cf. VERCAUTEREN, *Etude sur les Civitates*, p. 213.

[5] GREGORY OF TOURS, *Hist. Franc.*, VII, 46.

[6] *Op. cit.*, M.G.H. SS. RER. MEROV., vol. II, pp. 134 and 135.

[7] The market tariff of Arras, which figures in the *Cartulaire de Saint-Vaast*, GUIMAN, ed. VAN DRIVAL, p. 167, betrays the old Merovingian basis under its 12th-century veneer. The text attributes it to a *rex Theodericus* (165). Now the sale of the *servus* and the *ancilla* is mentioned in the paragraph entitled *De Bestiis*. The same thing may be observed in the tariff of the Tournai market tolls: see *servus vel ancilla vel auri uncia vendantur . . .* P. ROLLAND, *Deux tarifs du tonlieu de Tournai*, Lille, 1935, p. 17.

All the slaves captured on raids[1] by traders like Samo, or procured in Britain, were despatched to the Mediterranean ports.[2]
We read of their being offered for sale at Narbonne.[3] There is
mention of them also in Naples,[4] whence they came, no doubt,
from Marseilles, which was the great slave-market.[5]

Many merchants were engaged in the slave-trade.[6] They seem
to have been principally Jews. The Council of Mâcon, 583, permitted Christians to ransom slaves from the Jews for twelve *solidi*,
either to set them free, or to take them into their service. There
is mention of Jewish slave-merchants at Narbonne[7] and in Naples.[8]

We may conclude from all this that there was a trade in slaves
of considerable importance on the shores of the Tyrrhenian Sea;
and there seems no doubt that the ships which brought spices, silk,
and papyrus to the West carried slaves to the East as return cargo.

For that matter, Gaul seems to have sent to the East not only
slaves, but clothing, textile fabrics, timber for building, and possibly
madder. Gregory the Great bought clothing at Marseilles and at

---

[1] PAULUS DIACONUS, *Historia Langobardorum*, ed. BETHMANN and G. WAITZ,
I, I, M.G.H. SS. RER. LANGOB. ET ITAL., p. 48, says that many Barbarians were
brought from populous Germany to be sold to the peoples of the South.

[2] Concerning the sale of slaves at Marseilles, see *Vita Boniti*, M.G.H., SS.
RER. MEROV., vol. VI, p. 121. For the slave-trade see A. DOPSCH, *Wirtschaftliche
und soziale Grundlagen der Europäischen Kulturentwicklung* Vienna, 2nd ed., 1924,
vol. II, p. 175; BR. HAHN, *Die Wirtschaftliche Tätigkeit der Juden im Fränkischen
und Deutschen Reich bis zum zweiten Kreuzzug*, Fribourg, 1911, p. 23; FUSTEL
DE COULANGES, *L'alleu et le domaine rural*, p. 279.

[3] JAFFÉ-WATTENBACH, *Regesta*, No. 1467.   [4] *Ibid.*, No. 1409.

[5] The *Vita S. Eligii*, I, 10, M.G.H. SS. RER. MEROV., vol. IV, p. 677, speaks
of captives liberated by Saint Eloi, sometimes twenty or thirty in number,
sometimes fifty: *nonnumquam vero agmen integrum et usque ad centum animas,
cum navem egrederentur utriusque sexus, ex diversis gentibus venientes, pariter
liberabat Romanorum scilicet, Gallorum atque Brittanorum necnon et Maurorum,
sed praecipue ex genere Saxonorum, qui abunde eo tempore veluti greges a sedibus
propriis evulsi in diversa distrahebantur.* Cf. BUCHNER, *op. cit.*, p. 47.

[6] A formula from Sens, M.G.H. FORMULAE, ed. ZEUMER, p. 189, No. 9,
relates to the purchase of a slave by an *homo negotiens.*

A formula from Angers, *ibid.*, p. 22, No. 51, is a search-warrant for the
fugitive slave of a *negociens.*   [7] JAFFÉ-WATTENBACH, *Regesta*, No. 1467.

[8] JAFFÉ-WATTENBACH, *op. cit.*, No. 1629, and also Nos. 1409 and 1242
of the year 593, in which there is once more mention of the purchase
of Christian slaves by a Jew.

Arles, and had timber sent to Alexandria, which was purchased in Gaul.[1]

In any case, the abundant circulation of gold compels us to conclude that there was a very considerable export trade.

Besides this international commerce, which was largely if not exclusively in the hands of foreigners, the inland trade filled an important role in the economic life of the West. Here a different picture presents itself. Of course, as we have seen, the Jews played a prominent part in this trade, and the same may certainly be said of the Syrians established in the country, of whom we have already spoken. But in addition to these the native merchants were much to the fore. It is evident that there were not only shop-keepers among them, but also merchants by profession.[2]

The anecdote that Gregory of Tours relates of the merchants of Verdun[3] is characteristic in this respect: the city being afflicted by poverty under the Bishop Desideratus (first half of the 6th century), the latter borrowed 7,000 *aurei* from King Theodebert and distributed them among the citizens "*at illi negotia exercentes divites per hoc effecti sunt et usque hodie magni habentur.*" Here we have indubitable proof of great commercial activity.[4] And it is a remarkable fact that the bishop spoke to the king reviving the trade of his city *sicut reliquae habent*; from which we may conclude that commercial activity was a feature of all the cities.[5]

Gregory of Tours[6] relates, among other things, a detail that

---

[1] *Registr.*, VI, 10, M.G.H. EPIST., vol. I, p. 388. LYDUS, *de Magistratibus*, I, 17, ed. WUENSCH, Teubner, 1903, p. 21, mentions also the textiles of Arras. See, however, certain reservations made by F. VERCAUTEREN, *Etude sur les Civitates*, p. 183.

[2] A. DOPSCH, *Wirtschaftliche Grundlagen*, vol. II, 2nd ed., p. 439, refutes the notion that there were only foreign merchants.

[3] GREGORY OF TOURS, *Hist. Franc.*, III, 34.

[4] The bishops engaged in commerce at Nantes. Bishop Felix enlarged the port: VENANTIUS FORTUNATUS, *Carmina*, III, 10, M.G.H. SS. ANTIQ., vol. IV[1], p. 62.

[5] LOT, in LOT, PFISTER and GANSHOF, *Histoire du Moyen Age*, vol. I, p. 365, cites this very example of Verdun in order to prove the insignificant development of capitalism. If we draw similar comparisons between our own epoch and the 13th century we shall come to identical conclusions in respect of this latter period. It is quite certain, however, that the persons in question here were retail merchants, and therefore very active retailers.

[6] GREGORY OF TOURS, *Hist. Franc.*, VII, 46.

sheds a vivid light on the commercial life of the period: "During a time of scarcity, the merchant Christoforus of Tours learned that a great stock of wine had just arrived in Orleans. He set off immediately, well furnished with money by his father-in-law, doubtless a merchant like himself, bought the wine, and had it placed aboard some boats. He then proceeded to return homewards on horseback, but was killed on the way by two Saxon slaves who accompanied him." Here is an example of mercantile speculation which has nothing mediaeval about it. This Christoforus was evidently a great merchant, that is to say, a wholesale merchant who wanted to do a good stroke of business by snapping up all the wine on the market. And it should be noted that he acted alone. There was nothing in this transaction to recall the guilds or commercial exchanges; it was an instance of individualistic commerce of the Roman type.[1] And Gregory of Tours mentions that other merchants made similar speculations.[2]

There was also a good deal of fraud. Gregory of Tours[3] tells us of a merchant who with a *trians* made 100 *solidi* by adulterating his wine. He, no doubt, was a retail merchant.

There were certainly also professional merchants in Italy; of this we have sufficient proof in the mentions of Lombard merchants who served in the army. They constituted, therefore, an independent social class, living by purchase and sale. That they were very numerous is proved by the fact that there was a special regulation effecting their military service.[4]

---

[1] There were also merchants who travelled in companies in the 6th century; see the reference to Wado on the following page.

[2] GREGORY OF TOURS, *Hist. Franc.*, VII, 45.

[3] GREGORY OF TOURS, *Liber in Gloria Confessorum*, circa 110, SS. RER. MEROV., vol. I, p. 819.

[4] *Leges Ahistulfi regis*, ed. F. BLUHME, M.G.H. LEGES, vol. III, in-f°, p. 196, aᵘ 750. These merchants were evidently the successors of those for whose benefit Theodoric legislated in 507–511 "*ne genus hominum, quod vivit lucris, ad necem possit pervenire dispendiis.*" CASSIODORUS, *op. cit.*, II,26, M.G.H. SS. ANTIQ., vol. XII, p. 61. Cf. A. DOPSCH, *Wirtschaftliche Grundlagen*, vol. II, 2nd ed., p. 437; DOREN, *Italienische Wirtschaftsgeschichte*, 1934, p. 122, makes the observation that these laws of Ataulf must be traceable to more ancient texts, for in them the merchants are already divided into several categories.

There is no doubt that commerce was extremely profitable. It seems that the booty taken in Poitou from some merchants pillaged by the sons of Waddo was very considerable.[1]

But we have more certain evidence than this. The epitaph of a merchant of Lyons says that he was "the consolation of the afflicted and the refuge of the poor"; he must therefore have been very wealthy.[2]

In 626 the merchant John bequeathed certain properties to the Abbot of Saint Denis and to various churches in the diocese of Paris.[3] As this donation was confirmed by the king the properties must have been very considerable. Fortunatus wrote an epitaph for the merchant Julianus, famous for his lavish alms.[4] In 651 Leodebode, Abbot of Saint Aigan at Orleans, bequeathed to the Abbey of Saint Pierre at Fleury-sur-Loire some urban properties which he had formerly bought from a merchant; so that the latter must have been the owner of house property in the city.[5]

The *Rodulfus negotiens*, whose name we find inscribed in a Roman book, was certainly a Merovingian merchant.[6] Gregory of Tours speaks also of a merchant of Comminges, whom I am inclined to believe was the owner of various shops.[7]

We hear also of a merchant of Poitiers who used to travel to Trèves and to Metz,[8] where he met another merchant who bought and sold salt and made journeys by boat on the Moselle. There is

---

[1] GREGORY OF TOURS, *Hist. Franc.*, X, 21.

[2] LEBLANT, *Inscriptions*, vol. I, p. 41. Cf. COVILLE, *op. cit.*, p. 534.

[3] J. HAVET, *Œuvres*, vol. I, 1896, p. 229 (definitive text).

[4] LEBLANT, *Inscriptions*, vol. II, p. 520, No. 645.

[5] "*Quod de heredibus Pauloni negociatoris, quondam visus sum comparasse, areas scilicet in oppido civitatis Aurelianensium cum domibus desuper positis, acolabus ibidem residentibus.*" PROU and VIDIER, *Recueil des chartes de Saint-Benoît-sur-Loire*, vol. I, 1900, p. 7. Concerning the same merchant, see FUSTEL DE COULANGES, *La monarchie franque*, p. 256, No. 5.

[6] M. PROU, *Catalogue des monnaies carolingiennes de la Bibliothèque Nationale*, Paris, 1896, p. xxxviii.

[7] GREGORY OF TOURS, *Hist. Franc.*, VII, 37: "*Chariulfus valde dives ac praepotens, cujus adpotecis ac prumtuariis urbi valde referta erant.*"

[8] GREGORY OF TOURS, *Liber de virtutibus S. Martini*, IV, 29, M.G.H. SS. RER. MEROV., vol. I, p. 656.

here sufficient evidence to permit of our asserting that until the end of the 7th century there were certainly many native merchants in addition to the Jewish and Oriental merchants; some of them were assuredly very wealthy; and it is a very long time before we hear of such wealthy merchants again.

The commerce of the Empire, as it existed before the invasions, was therefore most certainly carried on after the invasions.

Where was it carried on? Obviously in the cities. According to all the information that has come down to us, it was there that the *negotiatores* resided. They were installed within the walls, in the *oppidum civitatis*.[1]

The cities were both ecclesiastical and commercial in character. Even in the cities of the North, such as Meaux, there were streets with arcades which were sometimes prolonged into the suburb.[2] These arcaded houses must have given the cities an Italian appearance, even in the north. They doubtless served to shelter the shops, which were generally grouped together; according to Gregory of Tours, this was especially the case in Paris.[3]

In these cities, besides the merchants, lived the artisans, concerning whom we have very little information. Saint Caesarius speaks of their presence at Arles, in the 6th century.[4] The glass industry seems to have been important; the Merovingian tombs contain many objects made of glass.

The *curator civitatis* and the *defensor civitatis* saw to the policing of the markets and the protection of goods.[5] At Ravenna some relics of the ancient colleges of artisans seem to have been preserved.

Is it possible to estimate the size of the cities after the invasions?

[1] J. HAVET, *Œuvres*, vol. I, p. 230, and the text cited on p. 84, No. 6.

[2] At Meaux Saint Faron inherited *casas cum areis, tam infra muros quam extra muros civitatis,* PARDESSUS, *Diplomata,* col. II, p. 16, No. cclvii.

[3] GREGORY OF TOURS, *Hist. Franc.,* VII, 37, speaks of the *apotecae* and the *prumptuaria* of Comminges. In Paris, GREGORY OF TOURS, *Hist. Franc.,* describes Leudaste: *domus negutiantum circumiens, species rimatur, argentum pensat atque diversa ornamenta prospicit.* He also speaks of these *domus necutiantum, ibid.,* VIII, 33, which seem to have been set in a row.

[4] Cited by F. KIENER, *op. cit.,* p. 29, No. 38: *sutores, aurifices, fabri vel reliqui artifices.*　　[5] KIENER, *op. cit.,* p. 15.

We have only sporadic information on this subject. In Gaul the walled portions of the cities were by no means extensive. Vercauteren[1] estimates their population at 6,000 and often very much less.

This population, however, must have been very close packed, and it is possible that large houses like those of Marseilles were not uncommon;[2] while in Paris there were houses built on the bridges.[3]

The cities of the South were larger. At Fréjus, judging from the ruins, the ancient city must have been five times the size of the modern town. Nîmes covered an area of about 320 hectares.[4] The Roman wall of Toulouse is said to have had a circumference of 3 kilometres.[5] And Hartmann estimates that in Theodoric's time the population of Milan must have been 30,000.[6]

The cities had, of course, suffered from the invasions. Bridges had broken down and had been replaced by bridges of boats. But all the cities still existed; moreover, the bishops had restored them. And there is no doubt that just as they were the centres of civil and religious administration, they were also the permanent commercial centres of the country. Here again the ancient economy was continued. We find nothing resembling the great fairs of the Middle Ages—such as those of Champagne.

There were, however, fairs, but they were doubtless local ones.[7] New fairs were established in the North: that of Saint Denis is

[1] F. VERCAUTEREN, *Étude sur les Civitates de la Belgique Seconde*, Brussels, 1934, pp. 354 and 359.

[2] Cf. for Angers, GREGORY OF TOURS, *Hist. Franc.*, VIII, 42.

[3] *Vita S. Leobini, circa* 62, ed. KRUSCH, SS. ANTIQ., vol. IV², p. 79.

[4] BLANCHET, *Les enceintes romaines de la Gaule*, Paris, 1907, pp. 211 and 208.

[5] *Ibid.*, p. 202, No. 3.

[6] We see from the *Lex Visigothorum*, III, 4, 17, ed. ZEUMER, M.G.H. LEGES, p. 157, that professional prostitutes, both free and slaves, were very numerous in the Spanish cities.

[7] A letter addressed about 630–635 to Didier, Bishop of Cahors, M.G.H. EPIST., vol. III, p. 214, speaks of "*istas ferias in Rutenico vel vicinas urbes*"; that is to say, of the fairs of Rodez, which the inhabitants of Cahors were forbidden to frequent on account of the plague which was then prevalent in Marseilles.

mentioned for the first time in 709.[1] But these played only a secondary part. According to L. de Valdeavellano,[2] there were no fairs in Spain. And in any case, we find no mention anywhere of those little markets which were so numerous in the Carolingian period. But we must not regard this as a proof of a commercial backwardness. On the contrary. Markets were not an essential element in cities where there were professional merchants, and which were permanent commercial centres. It was when commerce had disappeared that all these small economic centres of replenishment were organized, serving a restricted area and frequented only by occasional merchants. On reading Gregory of Tours, on the other hand, we obtain the impression of a period of urban commerce. The *conventus* of the merchants were held in the cities.[3] We hear of none in the countryside. It is certainly an error, as Waitz[4] has already pointed out, to regard the innumerable localities whose names were impressed by the *monetarii* on the Merovingian coins as the sites of markets. What we do find existing in the Merovingian period, as in antiquity, are *portus*—that is to say, *étapes* and wharves or landing-places, but not markets. The king levied market-tolls (*tonlieux*) in the cities and in the *portus*.[5] These were the ancient Roman market-tolls, payable in the same places.[6] Of course, abuses were already creeping in. Some of the

---

[1] VERCAUTEREN, *op. cit.*, p. 450. According to LEVILLAIN this fair was instituted in 634 or 635. *Étude sur l'abbaye de Saint-Denis*, BIBL. DE L'ÉCOLE DES CHARTES, vol. XCI, 1930, p. 14.

[2] L. G. DE VALDEAVELLANO, *El mercado. Apuntes para su estudio en Léon y Castilla durante la Edad Media*, ANUARIO DE HISTORIA DEL DERECHO ESPAÑOL, vol. VIII, 1931, p. 225.

[3] *Lex Visigothorum*, IX, 2, 4, ed. ZEUMER, M.G.H. LEGES, vol. I, in-4°, p. 368.

[4] G. WAITZ, *op. cit.*, vol. II, part 2, 3rd ed., p. 309.

[5] Levied, according to the diplomas, *per civitates seu seu per castella per portus seu per trexitus*, M.G.H. DIPLOMATA, in-f°, ed. PERTZ, p. 46, No. 51. For another mention of *portus*, see *Recueil des chartes de Stavelot-Malmédy*, ed. J. HALKIN and ROLAND, vol. I, p. 13, No. 4. We see from this same text (diploma of Sigebert III, 652), that there was a *negotiantum commertia* and that the king had *telonearii*.

[6] Formula No. 1 of the supplement of Marculf, ed. ZEUMER, M.G.H. FORMULAE, p. 107, enumerates the *tonlieux* of the Rhône basin: Marseilles, Toulon, Fos, Arles, Avignon, Soyon, Valence, Vienne, Lyons and Châlon-sur-Saône.

Counts attempted to establish new tolls for their own benefit, upon which Clotair II, in 614, intervened, ordaining that the tolls should remain as they had been under his predecessor.[1]

Theodoric wrote to the same effect to his agents in Spain, in order to prevent the imposition of fraudulent market tolls to the detriment of the *transmarini*.[2]

The market tolls or *tonlieux* comprised all sorts of taxes: *portaticum, rotaticum, pulveraticum*, etc. Their character was clearly fiscal and not economic. They seem to have been levied exclusively in money.[3] The king could allow remission of the tax in the case of the abbeys, but he did not, except during the period of decadence, cede it to anyone else. The *tonlieu* was a tax imposed for the benefit of the king. Its yield was very great. We have proof of this in the magnitude of the annuities assigned by the king—more particularly to certain abbeys—to be drawn from the *cellarium fisci*.

The collection of these taxes was still possible because the king had at his disposal agents who were able to read and write, the *telonearii*, They doubtless farmed the taxes, and this is probably why the Jews, despite the disapproval of the Councils, were granted the right of collecting them.[4]

In the great seaports there were magazines or warehouses,[5] and officials stationed in the ports, as we learn from the laws of Theodoric.

As for the post, it still existed throughout the basin of the Tyrrhenian Sea. Traffic followed the Roman roads. Bridges of boats had replaced such of the old Roman bridges as were broken down. The competent authorities insisted that the banks of water-

[1] Edict of Clotair II, October 18th, 614, M.G.H. CAPIT., vol. I, p. 22.

[2] CASSIODORUS, *Variae*, V, 39, M.G.H. SS. ANTIQ., vol. XII, p. 165.

[3] G. WAITZ, *op. cit.*, vol. II, part 2, 3rd ed., p. 301, states, for reasons which I believe are erroneous, that it was levied in kind.

[4] We have such a collector in the *negotiator Salomon*, assuredly a Jew, who was Dagobert's *Hoflieferant*, and to whom Dagobert ceded the tolls collected at one of the gates of Paris. *Gesta Dagoberti, circa* 33, ed. KRUSCH, M.G.H. SS. RER. MEROV., vol. II, p. 413.

[5] Cf. what has been said earlier concerning the *cellarium fisci*.

courses must be left clear for the space of at least a *pertica legalis* on either side, in order to permit of the hauling of barges.

4. *Money and the Monetary Circulation*

The Roman gold *solidus*, adjusted by Constantine, was the monetary unit throughout the Empire at the time of the invasions.[1] This monetary system, which had long been known to the Barbarians, thanks to the subsidies which they had received from the Empire, was preserved by them unchanged.

In none of the countries occupied by them do we find that there was at first any change whatever in the currency. Indeed, the Germanic kings continued to strike coins bearing the effigies of the Emperors.[2]

Nothing attests more clearly the persistence of the economic unity of the Empire. It was impossible to deprive it of the benefit of monetary unity. Until the cataclysm which occurred in the time of the Carolingians, the Greek Orient, like the Occident conquered by the Germans, adhered as a whole to the gold monometallism which had been that of the Empire. The Syrian navigators, on disembarking in the ports of the Tyrrhenian Sea, found there the currency to which they had been accustomed in the ports of the Aegean Sea. What is more, the new Barbarian kingdoms adopted, in their coinage, the changes introduced in the Byzantine currency.[3]

There were, of course, bronze and silver coins, but we cannot agree with Dopsch[4] that their existence is evidence of the intro-

---

[1] The gold *solidus* of Constantine weighed 4.48 gr.; 72 went to the pound. The gold value of the *solidus* was 15 fr.43. E. STEIN, *Geschichte des Spätrömischen Reiches*, Vienna, 1928, vol. I, p. 177.

[2] GUNNAR MICKWITZ, *Geld und Wirtschaft im Römischen Reich des IV. Jahrhunderts nach Christi*, Helsingfors, 1932, concludes, p. 190, that it is impossible to regard the 4th century as a century of *Naturalwirtschaft*.

[3] When at the end of the 6th century the Cross replaced the Victory on the Imperial coins, the mints of Marseilles, and then the other mints, followed this example. M. PROU, *Catalogue des monnaies mérovingiennes de la Bibliothèque Nationale*, Paris, 1892, p. lxxxv.

[4] A. DOPSCH, *Die Wirtschaftsentwicklung der Karolingerzeit, vornehmlich in Deutschland*, vol. II, 2nd ed., 1922, p. 300.

duction of bimetallism. Gold alone was the official currency. The monetary system of the Barbarians was that of Rome. The Carolingian system, which was silver monometallism, was that of the Middle Ages.

The Anglo-Saxons constituted the only exception; among them silver was the principal metal employed. However, a few gold coins were struck in the southern parts of Britain—that is to say, in those parts which maintained commercial relations with Gaul—and there is reason to believe that these coins were the work of Merovingian minters.[1]

In the kingdom of Mercia, which was more remote from Gaul, only silver coins have been found, some of which bear runic legends.[2] The Merovingian kings struck pseudo-Imperial coins, the series of which closes with the reign of Heraclius (610–641), the first Emperor to come into hostile contact with the Arabs.[3]

As a rule, they can be distinguished at a glance from the Imperial currency. On the other hand, they bear a close resemblance to one another. It is rarely possible to say whether they were struck by the Visigoths, the Burgundi or the Franks.[4] It was economic necessity that caused the Barbarians to retain the Roman currency.[5] This is proved by the fact that the imitation of Roman coins was continued in Marseilles and the neighbouring regions longer than elsewhere.[6] It is rare to find the name of a Frankish king on a coin. Such a name appeared for the first time, to the great dismay of Procopius, while Theodebert I was making war in Italy against Justinian, in 539–540. These coins also bear the word "Victor," which is exceptional in Roman numismatics.[7] They are so much finer than any other Frankish coins that Prou[8] supposes that Theodebert had them struck during his Italian expedition, or rather, they were struck in the regions which he retained for some

[1] ENGEL and SERRURE, *Traité de numismatique du Moyen Age*, vol. I, Paris 1891, p. 177. [2] *Ibid.*, pp. 179–180.

[3] M. PROU, *Catalogue des monnaies mérovingiennes*, pp. xxvii and xxviii.

[4] PROU, *op. cit.*, p. xvi. [5] *Ibid.*, p. xv.

[6] *Ibid.*, p. xxvi. [7] *Ibid.*, p. xxxii.

[8] *Ibid.*, pp. xxxiv and xxxv.

time after the expedition. It was only from the reign of Clotair II (584–629/630) that the name of the king replaced the name of the Emperor in the mints of Marseille, Viviers, Valence, Arles and Uzès. The formula *Victoria Augustorum* was replaced by *Victoria Chlotarii*.[1]

In Gaul, under Justin II (565–578), the mints, at first in Provence, adopted the weight of 21 siliquae instead of 24 for the gold *solidus*. These were perhaps the *solidi Gallicani* of which Gregory the Great seems to say, in a letter, that they were not current in Italy.[2]

The gold coins of the Barbarians were especially abundant among the Franks and the Visigoths. The Vandals had no gold coins; the Ostrogoths had hardly any but those of Theodoric. This is doubtless explained by the fact that Roman gold must have been widely diffused among them; for in the case of the Vandals, at all events, we know that their country was very wealthy.

The minting of money naturally retained its royal character, but the organization of the mints was, so to speak, decentralized. The Visigoth kings established mints in various different cities.[3]

Among the Franks, there was a mint in the palace and others in various cities. But coins were also struck by the churches, and by an enormous number of *monetarii*. No doubt this diversity in the coinage resulted from the method of collecting the impost.

"It was convenient to authorize the collector of a particular tax, the farmer of a salt-pan, the steward of a royal domain, the treasurer of a monastery, etc., to receive in payment, at need, prestations in kind, foreign or ancient coins, or metals by weight, and to render the amount of his receipts or the revenues of his

---

[1] PROU, *op. cit.*, p. xxxix.   [2] *Ibid.*, p. lxiv.

[3] ENGEL and SERRURE, *op. cit.*, vol. I, p. 50. There were four mints in Gaul during the Roman period: Trèves, Arles, Lyons and Narbonne, UPRO. *Catalogue des monnaies mérovingiennes*, p. lxv. F. LOT, *Un grand domaine à l'époque franque. Ardin en Poitou, Cinquantenaire de l'École pratiques de Hautes Études*, BIBL. DE L'ÉCOLE DES HAUTES ÉTUDES, fasc. 230, Paris, 1921, p. 127, says that the gold *solidi* derived from the tax were converted on the spot into ingots by the moneyers. This practice was already followed in the Roman epoch. See *Codex Theodosianus*, XII, 6, 13, law of 367.

farming in coins minted on the spot, and bearing a signature which served as a guarantee of their standard and value, and a place-name which recorded their place of origin."[1]

Luschin[2] considers that we may regard this minting of the gold furnished by the impost as a Roman custom. According to him, the moneyers were not small artisans, but the farmers of the tax.

We must suppose, with Luschin, that some control was exercised over the striking of these coins, for this diversity did not result in confusion like that of the feudal currencies of the Middle Ages.

According to Prou[3] the moneyers were artisans who had escaped from the old Imperial mints, after which they worked for the public.

We read upon some of the coins struck by some of the moneyers the words *ratio fisci* or *ratio domini*,[4] which appears to indicate that the money was struck under the control of the fisc. The fact that coins were minted not only in a great number of cities, but in *vici, castra, villae*, seems, on the other hand, to confirm the hypo-thesis that they were struck on the occasion of collecting the impost. It is impossible to believe, with Prou,[5] that there can have been mints in all these places. And he himself acknowledges that the moneyers were not public officials.[6] Very rare after Pippin's reign, they finally disappeared in 781;[7] that is to say, at the very time when the Roman impost disappeared.

There were no concessions of the right to mint coins in the Merovingian epoch.[8] According to Mgr. Lesne, the churches would have minted money simply in order to mobilize their

---

[1] ENGEL and SERRURE, *op. cit.*, vol. I, p. 97.

[2] A. LUSCHIN VON EBENGREUTH, *Allgemeine Münzkunde und Geldgeschichte*, 2nd ed., 1926, p. 97.

[3] PROU, *Catalogue des monnaies mérovingiennes*, p. lxxxi. I think this agrees very well with the text of the *Vita Eligii*, I, 15. M.G.H. SS. RER. MEROV., vol. IV, p. 681.　　　　　　　　　　　　　　　　　　　　　[4] PROU, *op. cit.*, p. li.

[5] *Ibid.*, pp. lxx and lxxxii.　　　　　　　　　　　　　[6] *Ibid.*, p. lxxxi.

[7] PROU, *Catalogue des monnaies carolingiennes*, p. xlvii.

[8] PROU, however, doubts this.

resources. "The ecclesiastical mintage," he writes, "seems to have been less the exercise of a royal privilege than of the option which was granted to the clergy and the monks of transforming their savings . . . into ready money."[1]

These constant mintages, and what we know from other sources concerning the kings' wealth in gold,[2] and the wealth of the Church and of private individuals,[3] proves that there was a very considerable stock of gold in the West; and yet there were no gold mines, and we cannot suppose that much gold can have been derived from auriferous sands and gravels. How then can we speak of "natural economy" in the presence of these large amounts of liquid treasure?

In this connection, how many characteristic data have come down to us![4] Bishop Baldwin of Tours distributed 20,000 gold *solidi* to the poor. Gold was profusely employed in the decoration of garments; and there was much gold in the possession of private persons, as is proved by the continual confiscations of gold by the king.[5]

The royal treasury, fed by the taxes, was also increased by the large subsidies paid by the Emperors, who sometimes sent as much as 50,000 gold *solidi*. It was a formidable suction-pump, but it was also a force-pump, for the king's gold did not stagnate in his coffers. It provided opulent annuities, dowries for his daughters, gifts to his friends, and lavish alms to the poor; it enabled him

---

[1] LESNE, *op. cit.*, p. 273.

[2] Cf. the golden crowns found at Guarrazar, near Toledo (7th century). They are evidence of the wealth of the royal treasury, at this period at all events. Cf. A. RIEGL, *Spätrömische Kunstindustrie*, 1927, p. 381.

[3] Concerning the wealth of private persons in gold and precious stones, see GREGORY OF TOURS, *Hist. Franc.*, X, 21, and above all IX, 9. The treasure of the wife of Duke Rauching was equal to that of the king.

[4] KLOSS, *Goldvorrat und Geldverkehr im Merowingerreich*, 1929, does not take into account the texts cited by LESNE, *op. cit.*, p. 200.

[5] Concerning the wealth of the Church, see LESNE, *op. cit.*, p. 200. The treasures of the churches, in case of need, were turned into money. We find an example in GREGORY OF TOURS, *Hist. Franc.*, VII, 24, of a bishop who had a golden chalice turned into money in order to ransom his city, which was threatened with pillage.

also to lend money at interest, as we find him lending it to the Bishop of Verdun; to pay pensions, as we might pay them by cheques on a current account, to needy ecclesiastics; to provide Saint Amand with money when he went forth to convert the Franks; to buy peace from the Barbarians, as did Brunehaut;[1] or to cover the apse of Saint Denis with silver, as Dagobert did; to purchase *missoria* from Constantinople; to defray the expenses of the chancellery and the *scola*, etc. etc. I agree that some part of these immense resources may have been furnished by the booty taken from conquered Germans and Slavs, by the Byzantine subsidies, and by the tribute paid by the Goths after Theodoric's time, and later still by the Lombards,[2] but even all this does not suffice to explain their abundance. In my opinion, commerce alone could have brought this continual stream of gold into the West. We must therefore conclude that it was very much more important than has hitherto been believed, and above all we must refuse to admit that it can have been restricted to the importation of goods against cash.

Some have attempted to explain the accumulation of gold in the kings' treasuries by supposing that all the gold in the country came into their possession. Prou,[3] in support of this theory, cites a law of the Emperors Gratian, Valentinian and Theodosius, which prohibited the payment of gold to the Barbarians. But it is evident that this law could not have been enforced in the case of Barbarians who were independent of the Emperor. According to Luschin, the stock of gold in the possession of the Barbarian kings would have consisted of Roman coins and goldsmiths' work. If this had been the case, we may be certain that the gold reserve of Gaul could not have been maintained from the time of Clovis to that

---

[1] G. RICHTER, *Annalen des Fränkischen Reichs im Zeitalter der Merovinger*, 1873, p. 98.

[2] We see also that in 631 the pretender Sisenand offered 200,000 gold *solidi* to Dagobert. G. RICHTER, *Annalen*, p. 161.

[3] PROU, *Catalogue des monnaies mérovingiennes*, pp. xi and cv. M. LOT also believes that gold was drained from the country in this way. LOT, PFISTER and GANDHOF, *op. cit.*, p. 358.

of Charles Martel—that is, for two and a half centuries.[1] Gold must have been pouring into the country. What brought it? Obviously commerce. Moreover, the Barbarian kings imported gold. The Law of the Visigoths proves that they did so.[2] Gregory of Tours shows us the king buying gold in Constantinople,[3] and his account of a shipwreck off Agde proves that gold was carried by sea. Moreover, the sale of corn certainly brought gold into the country.[4] The transport of gold, like that of slaves, is mentioned in the tariffs of the *tonlieux*.[5]

We have already cited the text which shows Pope Gregory the Great instructing the priest Candidas to buy clothing and Anglo-Saxon slaves in Provence with Gaulish gold, which was not current in Rome, and which the Pope remitted to him.

It is true that we have very few texts to go by, but if the historians had depended solely on the literary sources of the Middle Ages what could they have learned of the great commercial development of the epoch? This was made apparent only by the archives. Now, as regards the Merovingian period, apart from a few royal diplomas and a very few private charters all the archives have disappeared. We have therefore to argue from analogy.

The presence of this great stock of gold has to be explained in some way. If it had gradually been drained away by foreign trade

---

[1] M. BLOCH, *Le problème de l'or au Moyen Age*, in ANNALES D'HISTOIRE ÉCONOMIQUE ET SOCIALE, vol. V, 1933, pp. 1 *et seq.*; SOETBEER, *Beiträge zur Geschichte des Geld-und Münzwesens in Deutschland*, FORSCHUNGEN ZUR DEUTSCHEN GESCHICHTE, vol. II, 1862, p. 307; A. LUSCHIN VON EBENGREUTH, *Allgemeine Münzkunde und Geldgeschichte des Mittelalters und der Neueren Zeit*, Munich and Berlin, 2nd ed., 1936, p. 41.

[2] *Lex Visigothorum*, XI, 3, 1, ed. ZEUMER, M.G.H. LEGES, vol. I, p. 404: *Si quis transmarinus negotiator aurum, argentum, vestimenta, vel quelibet ornamenta provincialibus nostris vendiderit, et conpetenti pretio fuerint venundata . . .*

[3] GREGORY OF TOURS, *Hist. Franc.*, VI, 2.

[4] CASSIODORUS, *Variae*, XII, 22, M.G.H. ANTIQ., vol. XII, p. 378: Theodoric, addressing the people of Istria, tells them that if they have no corn to sell they cannot receive any gold.

[5] GUIMAN, *Cartulaire de Saint-Vaast d'Arras*, p. 167, and P. ROLLAND, *Deux tarifs du tonlieu de Tournai*, 1935, p. 37.

we should find that it diminished as time went on. But we do not find anything of the sort.

One thing is certain—that there was an active circulation of money. We must repudiate the idea that the people of the Merovingian epoch lived under a system of natural economy. Lot,[1] in support of this point of view, cites the example of the city of Clermont, which paid the impost in cereals and wine. But this very impost in kind was transformed into a money tax at the request of the bishop. We must add that this instance, related by Gregory of Tours, refers to the 4th century; that is, to the Imperial epoch. Gregory confines himself to recalling the case, stressing the point that the intervention of the bishop was an act of kindness, which proves that in his time the tax was still normally paid in money. Nowhere else in Gregory of Tours is there any mention of payments made otherwise than in money, and we have already seen that all the payments of taxes to the king were made in gold.

Moreover, there were certainly great quantities of currency in circulation, and people sought to invest it to advantage. Otherwise it would be impossible to explain how it was that many ambitious men offered the king considerable sums of money in order that they might be appointed bishops. The custom of farming out the collectorship of the taxes proves the same thing.[2] An anecdote related by Gregory of Tours[3] clearly illustrates the importance of the trade in money. The Jew Armentarius, with a co-religionist and two Christians, came to Tours in order to demand the securities which they had advanced, doubtless as tax farmers (*propter tributa publica*), to the *vicarius* Injuriosus and the Count Eonomius, who had promised to repay the amounts with interest (*cum usuris*). These tax-farmers had also lent money to the *tribunus* Medard. And they requested that he also would repay his debt. These influential debtors could think of nothing better to do than to

---

[1] F. LOT, *Un grand domaine a l'époque franque*, BIBLIOTHÈQUE DE L'ÉCOLE DES HAUTES ÉTUDES, fasc. 230, p. 123. He gives as his source GREGORY OF TOURS, *Liber vitae Patrum*, M.G.H. SS. RER. MEROV., vol. I, p. 669.

[2] *Ibid,*, p. 125. [3] GREGORY OF TOURS, *Hist. Franc.*, VII, 23.

invite their creditors to a banquet, in the course of which they had them assassinated.

To all appearances, these Jewish and Christian associates, who were the creditors of these high officials, had accumulated their capital by means of commerce. And it should be noted that they lent their money at interest: *cum usuris*. This is a proof, and a proof of great importance, of the fact that under the Merovingians interest was regarded as lawful. Everybody lent money at interest, even the king, who authorized a loan, at interest, to the city of Verdun.[1]

According to a formula of Marculf's,[2] the interest charged was one *trians* per *solidus*, which would represent 33.5 per cent. According to the Breviary of Alaric it should have been only 12.5 per cent.[3] Perhaps we ought to conclude that there was a shrinkage of capital between these two dates. But can we be quite certain that we are dealing here with commercial rates of interest?

The Church, it is true, constantly forbade clerics, and even laymen, to charge usurious interest, which certainly seems to indicate that the rate of interest was tending to increase.[4] Those who engaged in this money trade were mostly Jews.[5] We have already mentioned that there were Jews among the collectors of the market tolls, and it even seems that there must have been a great many of them, since the Councils protested concerning their number.[6] There were also Jews among the moneyers, and we find the names of some of them on the coins which they struck.[7] Their

---

[1] GREGORY OF TOURS *Hist. Franc.*, III, 34.

[2] MARCULF, II, 26, M.G.H. FORMULAE, ed. ZEUMER, p. 92.

[3] *Lex romana Visigothorum*, II, 33, ed. HAENEL, pp. 68–70.

[4] Council of Orleans, 538, *c.* 30. M.G.H. CONCILIA, vol. I, ed. MAASEN, p. 82, Council of Clichy, 626–627, *c.* 1, *ibid.*, p. 197.

[5] At Clermont the priest Eufrasius, the son of a Senator, offered the king, in order that he might be appointed bishop, the money which he had borrowed from the Jews: "*Susceptas a Judaeis species magnas,*" GREGORY OF TOURS, *Hist. Franc.*, IV, 35. The Bishop Cautinus was "*Judaeis valde carus ac subditus . . .*" because he had borrowed money from them or purchased *objets de luxe.* GREGORY OF TOURS, *Hist. Franc.*, IV, 12.

[6] M.G.H. CONCILIA, vol. I, p. 67, *a°* 535 and p. 158, *a°* 583.

[7] A. LUSCHIN, *op. cit.*,., p. 83; PROU, *op. cit.*, p. lxxvi.

clientèle, like that of the money-lenders in general, must have been very considerable. In addition to the tax-collectors, it must also have included the *locatores* of the domains of the Church, who likewise farmed their offices. Commerce also must have depended largely on credit. Sidonius[1] tells the story of a clerk (*lector*) of Clermont who went to Marseilles to make wholesale purchases of the importers there by means of borrowed money; he sold the goods retail at Clermont, repaid his creditor, and still made a handsome profit.

This was doubtless an example of that *turpe lucrum* with which the Councils forbade the clergy to meddle.[2]

All this clearly proves that the economic life of the Roman Empire was continued into the Merovingian epoch throughout the Tyrrhennian basin; for there is no doubt that what was happening in Gaul happened also in Africa and in Spain.

All the features of the old economic life were there: the preponderance of Oriental navigation, the importation of Oriental products, the organization of the ports, of the *tonlieu* and the impost, the circulation and the minting of money, the lending of money at interest, the absence of small markets, and the persistence of a constant commercial activity in the cities, where there were merchants by profession. There was, no doubt, in the commercial domain as in other departments of life, a certain retrogression due to the "barbarization" of manners, but there was no definite break with what had been the economic life of the Empire. The commercial activities of the Mediterranean continued with singular persistence. And the same may be said of agriculture, which, no doubt, was still the basis of economic life, but beside which commerce continued to play an essential part, both in daily life—by

[1] SIDONIUS APOLLINARIUS, *Epistulae*, VII, 7, ed. LUETJOHANN, M.G.H. SS. ANTIQ., vol. viii, p. 110.

[2] The Council of Orleans, 538, *loc. cit.*, p. 82, forbade clerics above the rank of deacon "*pecuniam commodere ad usuras.*" In 626–627, the Council of Clichy *ibid.*, p. 197, repeats the same prohibition in respect of the clergy and adds: "*Sexcuplum vel decoplum exigere prohibemus omnibus christianis.*"

the sale of spices, clothing, etc.—and in the life of the State—by virtue of the resources which the *tonlieu* procured for it—and in social life, owing to the presence of merchants and the existence of credit.[1]

[1] After the troubles of the 5th century there was undoubtedly a period of reconstruction, characterized by the very great number of new monuments which were then erected; and this would be inexplicable if we could not assume a very considerable degree of economic prosperity.

CHAPTER III

INTELLECTUAL LIFE AFTER THE INVASIONS

1. The Tradition of Antiquity[1]

It is needless to insist upon the increasing decadence of intellectual life and of the ancient culture after the 3rd century. This decadence was visible everywhere, in science, art, and letters. It was as though the very mind of man were suffering from degeneration. Pessimism and discouragement were universal. Julian's attempt at restoration was a failure, and after him the genius of antiquity no longer sought to escape from the grip of Christianity.

The new life of the Church long retained the vesture of the pagan life, which was never made for it. It still conformed to a literary tradition whose prestige it respected. It retained the poetry of Virgil and his school, and the prose of the orators. Although the content was different, the containing vessel was unchanged. The appearance of a Christian literature was much later in date than the birth of Christian sentiment.

The official and definitive triumph of Christianity under Constantine did not coincide with its actual victory, which was already won. It no longer encountered any opposition. Adhesion to the new faith was universal, but it was only upon a minority of ascetics and intellectuals that its hold was really complete. Many were drawn into the Church by interest: men of rank, like Sidonius Apollinarius, in order to retain their social influence, while the poor and needy sought shelter in it.

For many men of that time the life of the spirit was no longer the life of antiquity, but it had not yet become Christian, and it is easy to understand that for such people there was no literature

[1] This is naturally no more than a brief survey, which does not profess to do more than show that the ancient tradition was continued.

but the traditional literature.[1] The ancient schools of grammar and rhetoric still continued to determine the mental attitude of all these lukewarm believers.

The Germanic invasions in the West could not and did not in any way alter this state of affairs.[2] How should they have done so? Not only did the Germans bring no new ideas with them, but wherever they established themselves—with the exception of the Anglo-Saxons—they allowed the Latin tongue to remain as the sole means of expression. Here, as in all the other domains of life, they assimilated themselves to their new environment. Their attitude was the same in the intellectual as in the political or economic order. Hardly had their kings installed themselves when they surrounded themselves with rhetoricians, jurists and poets. These drafted their laws for them, wrote their correspondence, and worded the documents and records of their chancellery in accordance with the ancient models. In short, they kept intact the existing state of things. Among them too the decadence continued, with the only difference that its pace was accelerated, for it will be understood that barbarization was even more disastrous to intellectual than to material culture. Under the dynasties of the new States of the western basin of the Mediterranean the process that set in was the decadence of a decadence.

Consider in this respect the Ostrogothic kingdom. There everything continued as under the Empire. It is enough to recall the names of Theodoric's two ministers: Cassiodorus and Boëtius. And there were others. The poet Rusticus Elpidius, the author of a *Carmen de Christi Jesu Beneficii*, was Theodoric's physician and favourite.[3] We may also mention Ennodius, born, probably, at

---

[1] See for example EBERT, *Hist. de la litt. latine du Moyen Age*, translated by AYMERIC and CONDAMIN, vol. I, p. 445. He includes among the Christians those who had nothing of the Christian but the name: Claudius, Flavius Merobaudes, Sidonius Apollinarius. Another characteristic figure was Ennodius, probably born at Arles, whose education consisted entirely of rhetoric, *ibid.*, p. 461.

[2] R. BUCHNER, *op. cit.*, p. 85, says very truly: continuation of the *Spätantike*.

[3] EBERT, *op. cit.*, vol. I, p. 442.

Arles, in 473, who was so profane a writer, although he became bishop of Pavia in 511, as to celebrate the amours of Pasiphaë.[1] He was a rhetorician who became, so to speak, a professor of sacred eloquence. We learn through him that the schools of rhetoric in Rome were as busy as ever. He wrote his panegyric of Theodoric between 504 and 508, in the same inflated and pretentious style as that which marks his biography of Anthony,[2] the monk of Lérins. He also wrote of grammar, of rhetoric which "commands the universe," and of the bases of the Christian's education. He advised young men who wished to finish their education to seek out certain distinguished rhetoricians in Rome, and he also recommended the house of a lady "whose piety was equalled by her wit."[3] This literature, as we may judge, was largely a matter of phrases. But this very fact proves that there were still plenty of literati in the upper circles of Italian society of Theodoric's day.

Boëtius, born in Rome in 480, belonged to the distinguished family of the Anicii. Consul in 510, he became Theodoric's minister, and was entrusted with the duty of reforming the monetary system. He was executed in 525 for intriguing with Byzantium. He translated Aristotle, and his commentaries influenced the thought of the Middle Ages; he also translated the Isagogue of Porphyry, and the works of Greek musicians and mathematicians. Finally, in prison, he wrote *De consolatione philosophiae*, in which Christianity is blended with a stoico-Roman morality. He was a man of spiritual distinction, and a thinker.

Cassiodorus was a *grand seigneur*, born about 477. He was Theodoric's principal minister, who gained the sovereign's favour by a panegyric composed in his honour. At the age of twenty he was quaestor and Theodoric's secretary, and then consul. Even after Theodoric, even during the reign of Vitiges, he retained his position at Court; but his influence was no longer preponderant after the regency of Amalasuntha (535). In 540 he withdrew from the world in order to consecrate himself to the religious life in the

---

[1] ERBERT, *op. cit.*, vol. I, p. 464.   [2] *Ibid.*, vol. I, p. 467.
[3] *Ibid.*, vol. I, p. 468.

cloister of Vivarium, which he had founded in his territory of Bruttium, a possession which his great-grandfather had formerly defended against Genseric. It was his wish that the monks should collect in their cloisters all the literary works of classic antiquity. Perhaps this idea, that culture should take refuge in the monasteries, was inspired by the war of Justinian, which had prevented him from establishing the school of theology that he had dreamed of founding.

Here too we must mention Arator, who entered the service of the State under the reign of Athalaric, becoming *comes domesticorum* and *comes rerum privatarum*. He entered the Church, probably during the siege of Rome by Vitiges, for the sake of asylum. In 544 he publicly declaimed his poem *De actibus apostolorum* in the Church of San Pietro-in-Vinculi.

Venantius Fortunatus, born between 530 and 540, studied grammar, rhetoric and jurisprudence at Ravenna. In 560 he left for Gaul, where he won the favour of Sigebert of Austrasia and other great personages. At Poitiers he came into contact with Saint Radegunda, who had just founded there the monastery of the Holy Cross. There he became a priest, and he died Bishop of Poitiers.

His poems were mainly panegyrics; the more notable are those dedicated to Chilperic, whose talents he praises, and to Fredegond. He lauds the Roman eloquence of Caribert.[1] He praises Duke Lupus, a Roman who took pleasure in attracting to the court of his master those of his compatriots who, like Andarchius, were distinguished for their learning.[2] He celebrates the eloquence of Gogo; and on the occasion of the marriage of Sigebert and Brunhaut he composed an epithalamium in which Cupid and Venus figure. He is the author of an epitaph on a barbarian girl, Vilithuta, who died in childbed at the age of seventeen, and whose education had made her a Roman. He also wrote hymns.

Barthenius, who had studied in Rome, was Theodebert's *magister*

---

[1] EBERT, *op. cit.*, vol. I, p. 556.
[2] GREGORY OF TOURS, *Hist. Franc.*, IV, 46.

officiorum. Gregory of Tours[1] relates that he was stoned by the people, who held him responsible for the excessive burden of taxation. He was a connection of Arator's.[2]

The part played by the Roman rhetoricians was no less important among the Vandals. Dracontius addressed a poem entitled *Satis-factio* to King Gunthamund (484–496). He was a pupil of the grammarian Felicianus; and there is evidence in his works that the Vandals themselves attended the classes of the grammarians in company with the Romans. We find, also, that his family had retained possession of its estates. Having studied grammar and rhetoric, he devoted himself to the juridical career. He was afterwards persecuted by Gunthamund, who had him thrown into prison, and confiscated his property, on account of a poem in which he seems to have celebrated the Emperor to the king's disadvantage.[3]

Under Thrasamund (496–523) and Hilderic (523–530) flourished the poets of the Anthology: Florentinus, Flavius Felix, Luxorius, Mavortius, Coronatus and Calbulus, who, although Christians, wrote in the style of pagan antiquity.[4] Their poems celebrate the magnificent *termi* of Thrasamund and the monuments erected at Aliana;[5] and they mention the grammarian Faustus, the friend of Luxorius. Christianity, in these poems, is blended with obscenity.[6]

The Vandal count Sigisteus, the patron of the poet Parthenius, was himself a poet.[7] And we must not forget Fulgentius, a grammarian by profession, who wrote in Carthage during the last twenty years of the 5th century. An inflated and incorrect writer, he composed mythological allegories, the only means of preserving the faded splendours still cherished by the grammarians.

The same conditions existed among all the Germanic people. Sidonius was a great man in the country of the Burgundi.[8] Euric,

[1] GREGORY OF TOURS, *Hist. Franc.*, III, 36.
[2] HARTMANN, *op. cit.*, vol. I, p. 191.
[3] EBERT, *op. cit.*, vol. I, p. 409. [4] *Ibid.*, vol. I, p. 457.
[5] *Ibid.*, vol. I, p. 458. [6] *Ibid.*, vol. I, p. 460.
[7] MANITIUS, *Geschichte der Christlich-Lateinischen Poesie*, p. 402.
[8] A. COVILLE, *op. cit.*, p. 226.

the Visigothic king, was surrounded by rhetoricians. The Germanic kings, Wamba, Sisebert, Chindasvinth and Chintila were also writers. Such authors as Eugenius of Toledo, John of Biclaro and Isidore of Seville wrote in Latin, and in very good Latin too.[1]

Among the Franks, we must remember that King Chilperic himself was the author of Latin poems.[2]

Lastly, we must not overlook the influence of Constantinople, a centre of attraction to students and intellectuals. It seems above all to have been noted for its medical school, to which many passages in the works of Gregory of Tours make reference.

In short, the invasions did not modify the character of the intellectual life in the basin of the western Mediterranean. If we cannot say that literature continued to flourish, it did at least continue to vegetate, in Rome, Ravenna, Carthage, and Toledo, and in Gaul, although no new element made its appearance until the moment when the influence of the Anglo-Saxons began to make itself felt. The decadence of this literature was manifest, but the old tradition survived. Since there were still writers, there must still have been a public to read them, and even a comparatively scholarly public. The poets flattered the Germanic king as they formerly flattered the Emperor. Except that they were more insipid, they repeated the same themes.

This intellectual life, which preserved the traditions of antiquity, must have continued into the 7th century, since Pope Gregory the Great reproached Didier, Bishop of Vienne, with giving all his time to grammar, and in Spain there were historians of some merit up to the time of the Arab conquest.

But the contribution of the Germans to this life of the intellect was nil.[3]

[1] The Visigothic literature is superior to that of the other Germans, according to MANITIUS, Geschichte der Christlich-Lateinische Poesie, p. 402.

[2] Re the character of the Frankish culture, see H. PIRENNE, De l'état de l'instruction des laiques a l'époque merovingienne, REVUE BÉNÉDICTINE, April–July, 1934, p. 165.

[3] If, with EBERT, we are to find a reflection of the Germanic soul in the work of Fortunatus, we shall certainly have to see it a priori. See R. BUCHNER, op. cit., p. 84.

2. The Church

It is obvious that the Church continued to evolve along the same lines after the fall of the Emperors in the West as before. It constituted, indeed, the most striking example of the continuity of Romanism. Its faith in the Empire was all the greater inasmuch as it regarded the Empire as the providential scheme of human society. Its entire personnel was Roman, and was recruited from that aristocracy which incorporated such civilization as still survived.[1] It was not until a much later date that a few Barbarians entered the Church.

From the social point of view, its influence was immense. The principal personage in Rome was the Pope; in the city, the bishop. The man in search of a career, or a refuge from the turmoil of the age, took shelter in the Church, whether he was a great lord like Sidonius or Avitus, or a ruined man like Paulinus of Pella. Nearly all the writers who have just been mentioned ended in the bosom of the Church.

But there were also those who entered the Church out of conviction, whose motive was faith. And here, undoubtedly, we must attribute a very great influence to Oriental asceticism. This influence was felt in the West at an early date, and it constitutes one of the essential features of the epoch.[2]

Saint Martin, born in Hungary, who was Bishop of Tours (372–397) founded about 360 the monastery of Ligugé near Poitiers. Saint John Cassian, who had been a monk in Bethlehem, and then in Egypt and in Constantinople, founded Saint Victor of Marseilles about 413. And about 410 Honoratus, later Bishop

[1] See HÉLÈNE WIERUSZOWSKI, Die Zusammensetzung des gallischen und fränkischen Episkopats bis zum Vertrag von Verdun, in the BONNER JAHRBÜCHER, vol. 127, 1922, pp. 1–83. On p. 16 she gives statistics relating to the Bishops of Gaul in the 6th century, from which it appears that they were nearly all Roman.

[2] The influence of Egyptian monasticism made itself felt at Lérins. The British Saint Patrick, who converted Ireland in 432, lived at Lérins, and by him the religious and artistic influences of Egyptian monasticism were introduced into Ireland (BAUM, op. cit., cited by FORSCHUNGEN UND FORTSCHRITTE, vol. XI, 1935, c. 222 and 223).

of Arles, founded the monastery of Lérins in the diocese of Grasse; which was profoundly influenced by the Egyptian asceticism that we see spreading through Gaul about the same period,[1] simultaneously with Oriental monasticism.

The Barbarians made no attacks upon this monasticism. It may even be said that the confusion which they caused contributed largely to the development of monasticism, by driving many of the finer spirits of the time into the cloisters, out of a world which was becoming insufferable. Cassiodorus founded Vivarium on one of his own estates; Saint Benedict (480–543) laid the foundations of the celebrated abbey of Monte Cassino, imposing upon it the famous Benedictine Rule which was afterwards propagated by Gregory the Great.

The movement spread from South to North. Saint Radegunda went to Arles for instruction in the rule of Saint Caesarius, which she introduced in her own monastery at Poitiers.

This Caesarius was representative of his age.[2] The son of an influential family of Châlon-sur-Saône, he sought an asylum at Lérins at the age of twenty, in 490. His whole life revealed the Christian enthusiast. From 502 to 543 he was bishop of the ancient city of Arles, which Ausonius calls "the Gaulish Rome." The king of the Visigoths, Alaric II, banished him to Bordeaux. Later on we find that he came into contact with Theodoric. Looking toward the Papacy, he saw it, amidst all the political and social changes which he had witnessed, as the symbol of the vanished Empire. His ideal of the religious life was that of a monk; it should be a life consecrated to charity, preaching, singing hymns, and giving instruction. He held numerous synods with a view to reforming the Church. Thanks to him the Mediterranean city of Arles became the keystone of the Frankish church. Almost the whole of the canonical law of Merovingian France came from Arles in the

[1] GREGORY OF TOURS, *Hist. Franc.*, VIII, 15, mentions a Stylite at Eposium (Yvoy). For other excesses of asceticism, see DILL, *Roman Society in Gaul in the Merovingian Age*, p. 356.

[2] See his *Vita*, published in the SS. RER. MEROV., vol. III, p. 457.

6th century,[1] and the conciliary collections of Arles served as a model for all subsequent collections.[2] In 513 Pope Symmachus conferred upon him the right to wear the *pallium*, and made him his representative in Gaul. In the year 500 he had assumed the direction of a profligate monastery on an island in the Rhone near Arles, and had provided it with a rule.[3] Then, in 512, he founded at Arles a convent for women, which in 523 already contained 400 nuns. He gave it a rule, but was careful not to make it too severe, and he allowed for reading, dressmaking, the singing of hymns, and the writing of fair copies. He placed the convent under the protection of Rome.

His sermons, which were simple and popular, of which he despatched the manuscripts in all directions, had an enormous influence, in Gaul, Spain and Italy.

Like Saint Caesarius in Gaul, Saint Benedict was the great religious figure of the 6th century in Italy. Born, probably, near Spoleto, he was educated in Rome before he withdrew to the solitude of Subiaco. Ascetics gathered round him. In 529 he settled down with them at Monte Cassino. His rule owed much to the rules of Cassianus, Rufinus and Saint Augustine. It did not prescribe studies, although it mentions books to be read in Lent; it was practical in quality without excessive austerity. It was owing to the neighbourhood of Rome that it eventually became of world-wide importance.

The diffusion of monasticism at this period was extraordinary.[4]

---

[1] L. DUCHESNE, *Fastes épiscopaux de l'ancienne Gaule*, vol. I, 2nd ed., 1907, p. 145.

[2] *Ibid.*, pp. 142 et seq.

[3] SCHUBERT, *Geschichte der christlichen Kirche im Frühmittelalter*, p. 61.

[4] Saint Columban (d. 615) arrived in Gaul in 590. Cf. DE MOREAU, *Les missions médiévales*, 1932, p. 188. We read in HAUCK, *Kirchengeschichte Deutschlands*, vol. I, pp. 288 et seq., of the great number of monasteries which were founded in imitation of that of Luxeuil in the 7th century, especially in the North. One must take this influence into account, besides that of the Mediterranean. It seems that Luxeuil became more famous than Lérins; *ibid.*, vol. I, p. 296. However, the rule of Saint Columban, which was too ascetic, was not maintained, but was replaced by that of Saint Benedict.

Kings,[1] aristocrats and bishops[2] founded abbeys. The great propagators of monasticism were Saint Fructuosus, Bishop of Braga (d. 665), in Spain, and Gregory the Great in Rome.

Its influence was especially great on the shores of the Mediterranean. There it was apparently associated with the evangelization of the pagans, as we see from the biographies of those great Aquitanians, Saint Amand (d. 675–676) and Saint Remaclius (c. 650–670), who were both evangelists and monks.

The evangelists who went forth to convert the Anglo-Saxons were likewise monks. The mission which was led by Augustine, who took with him forty monks, landed in the kingdom of Kent about Easter 597.[3] By 627 Christianity had spread from Kent to Northumberland. The conversion of Britain was completed by 686.[4]

Thus it was from the Mediterranean that this northward extension of the Church proceeded, whose consequences were to be so important. It was the work of men who were entirely Romanized and highly cultivated, as were Augustine and his companions.

In 668 Pope Vitellius sent Theodore of Tarsus, who had studied in Athens, to be Archbishop of Canterbury. His friend Adrian, who accompanied him, was an African, a Greek and Latin scholar. It was he who, with the Irish, propagated the culture of the ancients among the Anglo-Saxons.[5]

Thus the Mediterranean was the home of a living Christianity. Nicetius, Bishop of Trèves, was a native of Limoges, and many other names could be cited. Thierry I sent some clerks from Clermont to Trèves.[6] The man of this period who exercised the greatest influence over the future was Gregory the Great. He was a patrician, like Cassiodorus. He began as a preacher; then, inspired

---

[1] For example, Sigebert III, who founded the Abbey of Stavelot-Malmédy, *Rec. des chartes de Stavelot-Malmédy*, ed. J. HALKIN and ROLLAND, vol. I, pp. 1 and 5.

[2] Concerning the monasteries of the 7th century, see HAUCK, *Kirchengeschichte Deutschlands*, vol. I, p. 138.

[3] DE MOREAU, *Les missions médiévales*, p. 138.

[4] DE MOREAU, *op. cit.*, p. 165.

[5] BEDE, *Historia Ecclesiastica*, IV, 1; MIGNE, *Patr. Lat.*, vol. 95, *circa* 171–172.

[6] HAUCK, *op. cit.*, vol. I, p. 122.

by the ascetic ideal, he sold his possessions, and with the product of the sale he founded seven convents. Although he was a monk, the Pope sent him as nuncio to Constantinople in 580. In 590 he himself became Pope. He died in 604. As a writer, he strove for simplicity. He disdained the ornaments of profane rhetoric, which he regarded as barren verbiage. Nevertheless, he was a cultivated man; but for him the matter was more important that the form, and his work constituted a complete rupture with the tradition of classic rhetoric. This rupture was bound to occur, not only because that rhetoric was manifestly sterile, but also because asceticism in recalling the Church to its mission, led it to the people.

Eugippius, in his life of Saint Severinus, had already refused to employ a style which the people would have difficulty in understanding.[1] And Saint Caesarius of Arles expressly stated that he took great pains to write in such a manner as to be understood by the unlettered.[2]

The Church was thus adapting itself. It was making literature an instrument of popular culture; that is to say, a means of edification.

Gregory the Great, according to Roger,[3] broke away from the literature of the ancients. He rebuked Didier, Bishop of Vienne, for devoting himself to the teaching of grammar, and singing the praises of Jupiter, although he was a Christian.[4]

Thus the Church, conscious of its mission, made use of the vulgar Latin, or rather, of a Latin devoid of rhetoric, accessible to the people.[5] It wished to write in the Latin of the people, which was a living tongue, the language of the age, which did not pay much attention to grammatical correctness. It wrote lives of the Saints for the people, which sought merely to edify them by the relation of miracles. This simplicity of language, which was adopted by Isidore of Seville (d. 646), did not exclude science. Isidore, by his compilations, tried to make the science of the ages accessible to

[1] EBERT, op. cit., vol. I, p. 482.   [2] Ibid., p. 503.

[3] ROGER, L'enseignement des lettres classiques d'Ausone a Alcuin, 1905, pp. 187 et seq.   [4] JAFFÉ-WATTENBACH, op. cit., No. 1824.

[5] GREGORY OF TOURS, Hist. Franc. Praefatio: philosophantem rhetorem intellegunt pauci, loquentem rusticum multi. Cf. SCHUBERT, op. cit., p. 67.

his contemporaries. Not a trace of the classic spirit survived in his writings. They related facts, and contained useful recipes. He was the Encyclopaedia of the Middle Ages. And he too was a Mediterranean.

Thus, it was in the "Romania" of the South that this new orientation of literature by the spirit of Christianity was effected. Barbarous, perhaps, in its form, it was none the less vital and influential. The Latin of this literature was the last kind of Latin to be written like the spoken language, like the language of the laity. For it was for the laity that all these clerics were writing, and they abandoned the classic tradition in order that the laity might understand them. The case was different in England, as there Latin had been imported as a learned tongue, for the needs of the Church, but no effort had been made to introduce it among the people, whose language remained purely Germanic.

A time was to come when the clergy would once more make use of a classic Latin. But by then this Latin would have become a learned tongue, written only for Churchmen.

3. Art

After the invasions there was no perceptible interruption in the artistic evolution of the Mediterranean region. Its art reveals the continuation of that process of orientalization which under the influence of Persia, Syria and Egypt was becoming increasingly manifest in the Empire.

There was an anti-Hellenistic reaction, which may be compared with the romantic reaction against classic art, and which revealed itself in the stylization of the figure, zoomorphy, and the love of design and ornament and colour.

The West was by no means immune to this progressive orientalization. It became still more perceptible as commercial relations with Syria, Egypt and Constantinople became more active. The Syrian merchants engaged in the luxury trade were responsible for disseminating Oriental goldsmiths' work and ivories, from the 3rd century onwards, even as far afield as Great Britain.

The influence of the Church, like that of monasticism, tended

in the same direction. The West, as always, followed the example
of the Church. In this respect the Germanic invasions did not
bring about any change.[1]

It might be said, on the contrary, that they collaborated in the
movement, for the Germans, and above all, the Goths, during
their sojourn in the Russian plains, were profoundly affected by
the Oriental influences that reached them by way of the Black
Sea. Their brooches, collars, rings, and articles of cloisonné work
in gold were influenced by this Sarmatian and Persian decorative
art, which was doubtless modified by an admixture of the intrinsic
features of the Bronze Age utensils. It was thus that they learned
to practise an art which the Romans called *ars barbarica*, and
which was diffused within the Empire even before the invasions,
since we find that it was practised at Lyons by an artisan who
was a native of Commagene in Asia Minor.[2] As early as the 4th
century cloisonné glass was in ordinary use in the Imperial armies.[3]

The local artisans practised an art with exotic motives. One
may ask, however, how far this art was practised by the Germans
themselves. We know from the Law of the Burgundi that they
had goldsmith slaves whose duty it was to provide ornaments for
the warriors and the women, and these slaves were doubtless
Greek at first, and afterwards Roman. It was they who diffused
this art within the Empire at the period of invasions; it flourished
among the Visigoths, as among the Vandals and the Burgundi.[4]

But in proportion as contact was established with the antique

---

[1] ROSTOVTZEFF, *Iranians and Greeks in South Russia*, Oxford, 1922, pp.
185–186, was able to show that what we call Merovingian art is merely the
European version of the Sarmatian art which originated in Central Asia.
See BREHIER, *L'art en France des invasions barbares a l'époque romane*, pp. 17
et seq., and especially pp. 23 and 26.

[2] BREHIER, *op. cit.*, p. 38.   [3] *Ibid.*, p. 28.

[4] Concerning the Visigoths, J. MARTINEZ SANTA-OLALLA, *Grundzüge einer
Westgotischen Archäologie*, 1934, cited by FORSCHUNGEN UND FORTSCHRITTE,
vol. XI, 1935, *circa* 123. This author distinguishes three periods in the art of
the Visigoths: Gothic before 500, Visigothic until 600, and then Byzantine.
During this last period Germanism was absorbed by the national and
Mediterranean environment.

tradition, this "barbaric" art was gradually restricted to the people. The kings and the magnates wanted something better. They could not conceive of any other art than that of the Empire. Chilperic showed Gregory of Tours the beautiful gold pieces which the Emperor had sent him, saying that he had had a golden dish made in Constantinople, and would have others made, "to honour the race of the Franks."[1] According to Zeiss,[2] *Tierornamentik* disappeared very early, and by the 6th century the genuinely Germanic vein of Visigothic art was exhausted.

The Germans, once installed in "Romania," did not evolve an original art, as did the Irish and the Anglo-Saxons. Among the latter, in the absence of Roman influence, art preserved its national character, just as the law and the institutions of the people had done. But its influence was not felt in Gaul until very much later: in the 7th century as regards Irish, and the 8th century as regards Anglo-Saxon art.[3]

Of this Barbarian art, which was greatly inferior to the masterpieces of Sarmatian art by which it was originally inspired, we have some very fine examples, such as the cuirass of Theodoric, the evangelistary of Theodelind in the cathedral of Monza, and the crowns of Guarrazar. It is difficult, however, to believe that these are Barbarian productions. Riegl and Zeiss admit that as far as the crowns are concerned the work is like that of the Roman artists. Saint Elio, who created various works of art,[4] was a Gallo-Roman. In such cases, then, we cannot speak of a genuinely Germanic art, but rather of Oriental art.

It should be possible to distinguish the influences due to the wholesale importation of goldsmiths' work and ivories from

[1] GREGORY OF TOURS, *Hist. Franc.*, VI, 2. Cf. FUSTEL DE COULANGES, *Les transformations de la royauté*, pp. 19 and 20.

[2] H. ZEISS, *Zur ethnischen Deutung frühmittelalterlicher Funde*, GERMANIA, vol. XIV, 1930, p. 12.

[3] In this connection, I believe that BREHIER, *op. cit.*, p. 59, was wrong to include, as a whole, the art of Merovingian Gaul, of Visigothic Spain, of Ostrogothic Italy, of the Lombards, and of the Anglo-Saxon and Scandinavian countries. [4] BREHIER, *op. cit.*, p. 56.

Byzantium, Syria and Egypt. According to Dawson,[1] the Irano-Gothic art which the Barbarians brought with them made way, in France, from the middle of the 6th century, and even earlier in the Midi, for the Syrian and Byzantine art which was spreading through the Mediterranean basin.[2] A Scandinavian writer has pointed to the importance of the Oriental motives in the Germanic art of the Anglo-Saxons.[3]

A Persian influence was introduced by the importation of Persian carpets, which reached even the centre of Gaul.[4]

The influence of the Coptic art of Egypt was introduced mainly by the ivories of Alexandria, and by textiles. We must remember, too, that when Saint Honoratus founded the monastery of Lérins in 410 a number of Egyptian monks came to settle there.

In short, the wholly Oriental art which came by way of the Mediterranean encountered the art of the Barbarians, which was also Oriental, so that there was a mutual interpenetration, the art coming from the South exercising a certain predominance, as its technique was more highly developed.[5]

This Oriental influence was perceptible everywhere in Gaul, Italy, Africa, and Spain. It imprinted a Byzantine stamp on the whole of the Occident.

The tomb of Chilperic, according to Babelon, was the work of Byzantine artists established in Gaul.[6] It was they who produced the more perfect works of art; the cruder examples were the work of unskilful Barbarian pupils. Schmidt concludes that the Barbarian art of this period was the work of Gallo-Roman slaves

---

[1] DAWSON, *The Making of Europe*, p. 97.

[2] MICHEL, *Histoire de l'art*, vol. I, 1905, p. 397, points to many monuments in Gaul—tombstones and sarcophagi, and notably the sarcophagus of Boëtius, Bishop of Carpentras—of which the art is purely Syrian.

[3] N. ABERG, *The Anglo-Saxons in England during the Early Centuries after the Invasions*, 1926, pp. 7–8.

[4] Sidonius Apollinarius speaks of the Turkish carpets which were in common use in Auvergne. MICHEL, *op. cit.*, vol. I, p. 399.

[5] MICHEL, *Histoire de l'art*, vol. I, p. 399.

[6] E. BABELON, *Le tombeau du roi Childéric*, MÉM. DE LA SOC. DES ANTIQ. DE FRANCE, 8th series, vol. VI, 1924, p. 112.

producing articles in the Germanic—that is to say, the Oriental—style.[1] The same orientalization is to be observed in all the other decorative arts, as well as the goldsmiths' work. The splendid fabrics which Dagobert offered to Saint Denis were Oriental tissues. Pope Adrian (772–795), during his pontificate, gave no fewer than 903 pieces of precious fabrics to the basilicas of Rome.[2] These were silken fabrics woven in Constantinople or elsewhere under the influence of Persian models.[3]

We see the same Orientalism in the decoration of the manuscripts. The sacramentarium of Gallone, a Visigothic production, is decorated with parrots with brilliant plumage, peacocks, griffins, lions, and serpents, which are sufficient indication of its origin. Armenian influences may also be detected in it.[4]

The manuscripts which were diffused in the 7th century by the Irish were, on the contrary, more national and more barbaric in character. We find in them a blending of indigenous motives of prehistoric origin with Oriental elements which were doubtless adopted from Gaulish art.[5]

The art of mosaic evolved in much the same way. The mythological and Christian subjects employed in the Gallo-Roman period disappeared, and were replaced by foliage, and the bestiary of which the Syrian and African mosaic of the 5th century affords so many examples.[6] In Saint Chrysogonus of Transtevere in Rome a mosaic pavement dating from the reconstitution of Gregory III in 731 shows eagles and dragons in alternate medallions in the midst of interlaced ornaments and rosettes.[7] Similarly, in the fragments of mosaic in the Church of St. Genesius at Thiers, built in 575 by Saint Avitus, Bishop of Clermont, we may recognize

---

[1] L. SCHMIDT, *Geschichte der Deutschen Stämme. Die Ostgermanen*, 2nd ed., 1934, p. 193. Cf. the *faber argentarius* which is cited by the *Lex Burgundionum*, X, 3, ed. VON SALIS, M.G.H. LEGES, vol. II[1], p. 50.

[2] BREHIER, *op. cit.*, p. 61.

[3] Various specimens may also be found in the treasuries of churches, for example at Sens. BREHIER, *op. cit.*, p. 63.

[4] BREHIER, *op. cit.*, p. 67.   [5] *Ibid.*, p. 69.

[6] *Ibid.*, p. 107.   [7] *Ibid.*, p. 107.

the imitation of a Persian fabric. "Nothing could prove better than this little monument, which is hardly one metre in length, the vogue of Oriental fabrics in Merovingian Gaul."[1]

It was in all probability the same with decorative painting. Gregory of Tours relates that Gondovald gave himself out as a *pictor*, whose speciality was the decoration of houses.[2] We gather from this text that private houses were decorated in bright colours, and doubtless also in the style of the Oriental fabrics.

The churches too were decorated in polychrome, and here, no doubt, the human figure must have played a great part, just as it did in the mosaics of San Vitale at Ravenna. Gregory the Great rebuked Bishop Serenus of Marseilles for destroying the paintings in his church, where, as the Pope explained, they served to instruct the people in religion.[3]

We must not imagine the 6th and 7th centuries as devoid of artistic activities. Building was going on everywhere.[4] We have only to recall such monuments of the first importance as the church of San Vitale at Ravenna. All the buildings of the period were marked by Byzantine luxury. At Clermont the bishop built a church with marble revetments, forty-two windows, and seventy columns.[5]

Fortunatus describes the church of Saint Germain, built in 537, with its marble columns and its stained glass windows, and the *Vita Droctovei* speaks of its mosaics and its paintings, and the gilt plaques of the roof.[6]

Leontinus of Bordeaux (about 550) built nine churches.[7] Sidonius, at the end of the 5th century, in the midst of the invasions, complained that hardly anything was done toward the maintenance of the ancient churches.[8] But when all was quiet again everyone

---

[1] BREHIER, *op cit.*, p. 109. [2] GREGORY OF TOURS, *Hist. Franc.*, VII, 36.

[3] SAINT GREGORY, *Registrum*, IX, 208, ed. HARTMANN, M.G.H. EPISTOLAE, vol. II, p. 195.

[4] The *Vita* of Saint Didier of Cahors tells us that this saint caused a number of churches to be built and decorated. Ed. R. POUPARDIN, p. 23.

[5] GREGORY OF TOURS, *Hist. Franc.*, II, 16.

[6] *Vita Droctovei*, M.G.H. SS. RER. MEROV., vol. III, p. 541.

[7] HAUCK, *op. cit.*, I, p. 220, speaks of the great number of churches built.

[8] *Ibid.*, p. 220.

made up for lost time. In all directions churches were built and restored, which obviously points to a certain degree of prosperity. Nicetius of Trèves, Vilicus of Metz, and Carentinus of Cologne restored and embellished churches.[1]

The Bishop of Mayence built the church of Saint George and a baptistery at Xanten. Didier of Cahors (630–655) built a number of churches in the city and the outskirts, as well as a monastery. To these we may add the churches built by Agricola at Châlons[2] and Dalmatius at Rodez.[3] Numbers of workmen (*artifices*) were summoned from Italy. We know that Bishop Nicetius sent for Italian *artifices* to come to Treves.[4] But there were also Barbarian architects.[5]

The baptistery of Poitiers will give us some idea of their work, and we see that they too were affected by the Oriental influence.[6]

In short, what we know concerning all the arts shows us, in every respect, as Brehier observes,[7] that the art of the period was a "Western art devoid of any classic influence." But he is mistaken in claiming that this art would have developed in the same direction as Arabic art had there been no Carolingian renaissance.

The obvious fact is that it was evolving in the direction of Byzantine art. The whole of the Mediterranean basin followed the example of Constantinople.

---

[1] Agericus of Verdun reports these words of Fortunatus (HAUCK, *op. cit.*, vol. I, p. 108): *Templa vetusta novas pretiosius et nova condis, cultor est Domini te famulante domus.* We shall find other examples in E. LESNE, *op. cit.*, p. 338.

[2] GREGORY OF TOURS, *Hist. Franc.*, V, 45.   [3] *Ibid.*, V, 46.

[4] It is probable that these builders were Milanese. HAUCK, *op. cit.*, vol. I, p. 220, n. 8.

[5] Mentioned by FORTUNATUS, *Carmina*, II, 8, M.G.H. SS. ANTIQ., vol. IV, p. 37. This text is perhaps in agreement with that of the *Vita* of Saint Didier of Cahors, ed. POUPARDIN, p. 38, where there is mention of a basilica constructed: *more antiquorum . . . quadris ac dedolatis lapidibus . . . non quidem nostro gallicano more.* The same *Vita* relates that Saint Didier built the walls of Cahors; *quadratorum lapidum compactione. Ibid.*, ed. POUPARDIN, p. 19.

[6] M. PUIG Y CADAFALCH refers to the cathedral of Egara (Tarrassa in Catalonia), built between 516 and 546, as betraying influences attributable to Asia Minor and Egypt. COMPTES RENDUS DE L'ACADEMIE DES INSCRIPTIONS ET BELLES-LETTRES, 1931, pp. 154 *et seq.*

[7] BREHIER, *op. cit.*, p. 111.

4. *The Secular Character of Society*

There is yet another fact which hitherto has hardly been noted, yet it constitutes a final proof that society, after the invasions, was precisely what it had been before them: namely, the secular character of that society. However great the respect which people might profess for the Church, and however great its influence, it did not constitute an integral part of the State. The political power of the kings, like that of the Emperors, was purely secular. No religious ceremony was celebrated on the accession of the kings, except in the case of the Visigothic kings from the end of the 7th century. There is no formula of devolution *gratia Dei* in their diplomas. None of their court functionaries were ecclesiastics. All their ministers and officials were laymen. They were heads of the church, appointing bishops and convoking Councils, and sometimes even taking part in them. In this respect there is a complete contrast between their governments and those subsequent to the 8th century.[1] The *scola* which they maintained at their court did not in any way resemble the palace school of Charlemagne. While they allowed the Church to undertake a number of voluntary public services, they did not delegate any such services to the Church. They recognized its jurisdiction only in matters of discipline. They taxed it. They protected it, but did not subordinate themselves to it. And it should be remarked that the Church, in return for their protection, was notably loyal to them. Even when the kings were Arian we do not find that the Church ever rebelled against them.[2]

This is explained by the fact that society itself was not yet dependent upon the Church in respect of its social life; it was still capable of providing the State with a lay personnel.

The senatorial aristocracy, trained in the schools of grammar and rhetoric, was the class from which the high officers of the government were drawn. We have only to recall the names of

[1] No one could enter the ranks of the clergy without the consent of the King or the Count. H. BRUNNER, *Deutsche Rechtsgeschichte*, vol. II, 2nd ed., 1928, p. 316.　　　　[2] BRUNNER, *op. cit.*, vol. II, 2nd ed., p. 418.

such men as Cassiodorus and Boëtius. And after their time, despite the decadence of culture, the same state of affairs continued. The palace, even under the Merovingians, never lacked for educated laymen. We know from Gregory of Tours that the children of the kings were carefully initiated into the literary culture of the age, and this applies with even greater force to the Ostrogoths and the Visigoths. The pompous style of the missives written by the Merovingian chancellery to the Emperors proves that even in the time of Brunehaut there were still scholarly clerks in the governmental offices.[1] And there is no doubt that these were laymen, since the chancellery, in conformity with the Imperial example, was composed exclusively of laymen.[2]

Many other examples may be cited. Asteriolus and Secundinus, favourites of Theodebert I, were each *rethoricis inbutus litteris;*[3] Parthenius, *magister officiorum et patricius*, under the same king, went to Rome to complete his literary education.[4] However, the education of these functionaries was not exclusively literary.[5]

Didier of Cahors, royal treasurer under Clotair II (613–629/630) studied the *gallicana eloquentia* and the *Leges Romanae*. In the 7th century many of the officials of the palace were certainly far more cultivated than has been supposed.

As far as the Visigoths are concerned, it is enough to read their laws, which are marked by verbosity and rhetorical turns of speech, but which, at the same time, are remarkable for their minute prescriptions in respect of social life, to realize that the literary culture of these officials was accompanied by a practical knowledge of affairs.

[1] HARTMANN, *op. cit.*, vol. II¹, p. 70.

[2] F. LOT, *A quelle epoque a-t-on cessé de parler latin?* BULLETIN DUCANGE, vol. VI , 1931, p. 100, believes that the only teaching then available was that of private masters.   [3] GREGORY OF TOURS, *Hist. Franc.*, III, 33.

[4] This is the Parthenius who was massacred at Trèves on account of the burdensome taxation which he imposed upon the people. GREGORY OF TOURS, *Hist. Franc.*, III, 36.

[5] Bonitus, the referendary of Sigebert III (634–656) is said to be *"grammaticorum inbutus iniciis necnon Theodosii edoctus decretis."* Vita S. Boniti, M.G.H. SS. RER. MEROV., vol. VI, p. 120.

Thus, the kings governed with the help of men who still preserved the literary and political traditions of Rome; but what is
perhaps more remarkable is the fact that they administered the
kingdom by means of a scholarly personnel. But it could not
have been otherwise. The administrative organization of the
Empire, which they were endeavouring to maintain, definitely
required the collaboration of educated agents. How otherwise
would it have been possible to draw up and to keep the registers
of the taxes, to undertake and record the surveys of land, and to
draft all the documents which emanated from the royal tribunal
and the chancellery of the palace? And even in the case of subordinate officials, how could they have kept their accounts of the
market tolls if they had not been able to read and write? The
fact that the *gesta municipalia* were recorded in the cities leads us
to the same conclusion.

Above all, the Roman law—or the Romanized law—with its
written procedure, and the recording of judgments, contracts,
and testaments, provided occupation for numbers of *notarii*
throughout the country. It was for these that Marculf wrote.
The enormous majority of these *notarii* were laymen, despite
the *diaconus* of whom we find mention in the formulae of
Bourges and Angers.[1]

It is evident that there were schools for all these functionaries,
as indeed I have shown in another volume.[2] Even among the
Lombards the schools had survived.[3]

Among the Visigoths the ability to write was so widely diffused
that the king fixed the price at which copies of the Law were to
be sold. Thus the ability to read and write was very general among
those who were in any way connected with the administration.

---

[1] M.G.H. FORMULAE, ed. ZEUMER, pp. 4 and 176. According to BRUNNER,
op. cit., vol. I, 2nd ed., p. 577, the formulae of Angers were written by a
scribe of the municipal curia. They probably date, in part, from the beginning
of the 7th century. The Bourges formulae were of the 8th century.

[2] H. PIRENNE, *De l'état de l'instruction des laiques a l'époque merovingienne*,
REVUE BENEDICTINE, vol. XLVI, 1934, p. 165.

[3] HARTMANN, *op. cit.*, vol. II², p. 27.

As an economic necessity, the same state of affairs existed among the merchants. A class of professional merchants engaged in long-distance trade could not have carried on their business without a minimum of education. We know, moreover, from Caesarius of Arles, that the merchants had literate clerks.

In the Merovingian epoch, then, writing was indispensable to the life of society. This explains why, in all the kingdoms constituted in the Occident, the Roman cursive was retained, in the form of the very small cursive which it assumed in the 5th century; it was a rapid script, a business hand, and not a calligraphy. It was from this that the Merovingian, Visigothic and Lombard scripts derived,[1] which were formerly called national scripts, but wrongly, for strictly speaking they were merely the continuation of the Roman cursive, perpetuated by the agents of the administration, the governmental offices, and the merchants.

This cursive writing thoroughly suited the living but decadent language of the period. In everyday life the Latin tongue was even more bastardized than in the literature; it had become a language full of inaccuracies and solecisms, ungrammatical, but none the less an authentic Latin. It was what the scholars called "rustic Latin." But they countenanced it and employed it, especially in Gaul, because it was the popular tongue, spoken by all. And the administration followed their example. It was doubtless this Latin that was taught in the little schools. There is not a single text that tells us, as certain texts of the 8th century will tell us, that in church the people could no longer understand the priest. Here again the language was, so to speak, barbarized, but there was nothing Germanic about this barbarization. The language survived, and it was this language that constituted, well into the 8th century, the unity of "Romania."[2]

---

[1] M. PROU, *Manuel de paléographie*, 4th ed., 1924, p. 65.

[2] LOT, *op. cit.*, in the BULLETIN DUCANGE, vol. VI, 1931, p. 102; MULLER, *On the use of the expression lingua Romana from the I to the IX Century*; ZEITSCHRIFT FÜR ROMANISCHE PHILOLOGIE, vol. XLIII, 1923, p. 9; F. VERCAUTEREN, *Le Romanus des sources franques*, REVUE BELGE DE PHILOLOGIE ET D'HISTOIRE, vol. XI, 1932, pp. 77–88.

CONCLUSION

From whatever standpoint we regard it, then, the period inaugurated by the establishment of the Barbarians within the Empire introduced no absolute historical innovation.[1] What the Germans destroyed was not the Empire, but the Imperial government *in partibus occidentis*. They themselves acknowledged as much by installing themselves as *foederati*. Far from seeking to replace the Empire by anything new, they established themselves within it, and although their settlement was accompanied by a process of serious degradation, they did not introduce a new scheme of government; the ancient *palazzo*, so to speak, was divided up into apartments, but it still survived as a building. In short, the essential character of "Romania" still remained Mediterranean. The frontier territories, which remained Germanic, and England, played on part in it as yet; it is a mistake to regard them at this period as a point of departure. Considering matters as they actually were, we see that the great novelty of the epoch was a political fact: in the Occident a plurality of States had replaced the unity of the Roman State. And this, of course, was a very considerable novelty. The aspect of Europe was changing, but the fundamental character of its life remained the same. These States, which have been described as national States, were not really national at all, but were merely fragments of the great unity which they had replaced. There was no profound transformation except in Britain.

There the Emperor and the civilization of the Empire had disappeared. Nothing remained of the old tradition. A new world had made its appearance. The old law and language and institutions were replaced by those of the Germans. A civilization of a new type was manifesting itself, which we may call the Nordic or

---

[1] These things were retained: the language, the currency, writing (papyrus), weights and measures, the kinds of foodstuffs in common use, the social classes, the religion—the role of Arianism has been exaggerated—art, the law, the administration, the taxes, the economic organization.

Germanic civilization. It was completely opposed to the Mediterranean civilization syncretized in the Late Empire, that last form of antiquity. Here was no trace of the Roman State with its legislative ideal, its civil population, and its Christian religion, but a society which had preserved the blood tie between its members; the family community, with all the consequences which it entailed in law and morality and economy; a paganism like that of the heroic poems; such were the things that constituted the originality of these Barbarians, who had thrust back the ancient world in order to take its place. In Britain a new age was beginning, which did not gravitate towards the South. The man of the North had conquered and taken for his own this extreme corner of that "Romania" of which he had no memories, whose majesty he repudiated, and to which he owed nothing. In every sense of the word he replaced it, and in replacing it he destroyed it.

The Anglo-Saxon invaders came into the Empire fresh from their Germanic environment, and had never been subjected to the influences of Rome. Further, the province of Britain, in which they had established themselves, was the least Romanized of all the provinces. In Britain, therefore, they remained themselves: the Germanic, Nordic, Barbarian soul of peoples whose culture might almost be called Homeric has been the essential factor in the history of this country.

But the spectacle presented by this Anglo-Saxon Britain was unique. We should seek in vain for anything like it on the Continent. There "Romania" still existed, except on the frontier, or along the Rhine, in the decumate lands, and along the Danube —that is to say, in the provinces of Germania, Raetia, Noricum and Pannonia, all close to that Germania whose inhabitants had overflowed into the Empire and driven it before them. But these border regions played no part of their own, since they were attached to States which had been established, like that of the Franks or the Ostrogoths, in the heart of "Romania." And there it is plain that the old state of affairs still existed. The invaders, too few in number, and also too long in contact with the Empire were inevitably absorbed, and they asked nothing better. What may well surprise us is that there was so little Germanism in the new States, all of which were ruled by Germanic dynasties. Language, religion, institutions and art were entirely, or almost entirely, devoid of Germanism. We find some Germanic influences in the law of those countries situated to the north of the Seine and the Alps, but until the Lombards arrived in Italy these did not amount to very much. If some have held a contrary belief, it is because they have followed the Germanic school and have wrongly applied to Gaul, Italy, and Spain what they find in the *Leges Barbarorum* of the Salians, the Ripuarians and the Bavarians. They have also extended to the period which preceded the Carolingians what is true only of the latter. Moreover, they have exaggerated the role of Merovingian Gaul by allowing themselves to be governed by the thought of what it later became, but as yet was not.

What was Clovis as compared with Theodoric? And let it be noted that after Clovis the Frankish kings, despite all their efforts, could neither establish themselves in Italy, nor even recapture the Narbonnaise from the Visigoths. It is evident that they were tending towards the Mediterranean. The object of their conquest beyond the Rhine was to defend their kingdom against the Barbarians, and was far from having the effect of Germanizing it. But to admit that under the conditions of their establishment in the Empire, and with the small forces which they brought with them, the Visigoths, Burgundi, Ostrogoths, Vandals and Franks could have intended to Germanize the Empire is simply to admit the impossible. *Stat mole sua.*

Moreover, we must not forget the part played by the Church, within which Rome had taken refuge, and which, in imposing itself upon the Barbarians, was at the same time imposing Rome upon them. In the Occident, in the Roman world which had become so disordered as a State, the Germanic kings were, so to speak, points of political crystallization. But the old, or shall we say, the classic social equilibrium still existed in the world about them, though it had suffered inevitable losses.

In other words, the Mediterranean unity which was the essential feature of this ancient world was maintained in all its various manifestations. The increasing Hellenization of the Orient did not prevent it from continuing to influence the Occident by its commerce, its art, and the vicissitudes of its religious life. To a certain extent, as we have seen, the Occident was becoming Byzantinized.

And this explains Justinian's impulse of reconquest, which almost restored the Mediterranean to the status of a Roman lake. And regarding it from our point of view, it is, of course, plainly apparent that this Empire could not last. But this was not the view of its contemporaries. The Lombard invasion was certainly less important than has been supposed. The striking thing about it is its tardiness.

Justinian's Mediterranean policy—and it really was a Mediterranean policy, since he sacrificed to this policy his conflicts with the Persians and the Slavs—was in tune with the Mediterranean spirit of European civilization as a whole from the 5th to the 7th century. It is on the shores of this *mare nostrum* that we find all the specific manifestations of the life of the epoch. Commerce gravitated toward the sea, as under the Empire; there the last representatives of the ancient literature—Boëtius, Cassiodorus— wrote their works; there, with Caesarius of Arles, and Gregory the Great, the new literature of the Church was born and began to develop; there writers like Isidore of Seville made the inventory of civilization from which the Middle Ages obtained their knowledge of antiquity; there, at Lérins, or at Monte Cassino, monasticism, coming from the Orient, was acclimatized to its Occidental environment; from the shores of the Mediterranean came the missionaries who converted England, and it was there that arose the characteristic monuments of that Hellenistico-Oriental art which seemed destined to become the art of the Occident, as it had remained that of the Orient.

There was as yet nothing, in the 7th century, that seemed to announce the end of the community of civilization established by the Roman Empire from the Pillars of Hercules to the Aegean Sea and from the shores of Egypt and Africa to those of Italy,

Gaul, and Spain. The new world had not lost the Mediterranean character of the ancient world. All its activities were concentrated and nourished on the shores of the Mediterranean.

There was nothing to indicate that the millenary evolution of society was to be suddenly interrupted. No one was anticipating a catastrophe. Although the immediate successors of Justinian were unable to continue his work, they did not repudiate it. They refused to make any concession to the Lombards; they feverishly fortified Africa; they established their themes there as in Italy; their policies took account of the Franks and the Visigoths alike; their fleet controlled the sea; and the Pope of Rome regarded them as his Sovereigns.

The greatest intellect of the Occident, Gregory the Great, Pope from 590 to 604, saluted the Emperor Phocas, in 603, as reigning only over free men, while the kings of the Occident reigned only over slaves: *Hoc namque inter reges gentium et reipublicae imperatores distat, quod reges gentium domini servorum sunt, imperatores vero reipublicae domini liberorum.*[1]

[1] JAFFÉ-WATTENBACH, *Regesta*, No. 1899.

Part Two

ISLAM AND THE CAROLINGIANS

CHAPTER I

THE EXPANSION OF ISLAM IN THE MEDITERRANEAN BASIN

1. *The Islamic Invasion*

Nothing could be more suggestive, nothing could better enable us to comprehend the expansion of Islam in the 7th century, than to compare its effect upon the Roman Empire with that of the Germanic invasions. These latter invasions were the climax of a situation which was as old as the Empire, and indeed even older, and which had weighed upon it more or less heavily throughout its history. When the Empire, its frontiers penetrated, abandoned the struggle, the invaders promptly allowed themselves to become absorbed in it, and as far as possible they maintained its civilization, and entered into the community upon which this civilization was based.

On the other hand, before the Mohammedan epoch the Empire had had practically no dealings with the Arabian peninsula.[1] It contented itself with building a wall to protect Syria against the nomadic bands of the desert, much as it had built a wall in the north of Britain in order to check the invasions of the Picts; but this Syrian *limes*, some remains of which may still be seen on crossing the desert, was in no way comparable to that of the Rhine or the Danube.[2]

The Empire had never regarded this as one of its vulnerable points, nor had it ever massed there any large proportion of its military forces. It was a frontier of inspection, which was crossed by the caravans that brought perfumes and spices. The Persian

[1] I need not speak here of the kingdom of Palmyra, which was destroyed in the 3rd century, and which lay to the north of the Peninsula. VASILIEV, *Histoire de l'Empire byzantin*, French translation, vol. I, 1932, p. 265.

[2] VASILIEV, *op. cit.*, vol. I, p. 265, citing DUSSAUD, *Les Arabes en Syrie avant l'Islam*, Paris, 1907.

Empire, another of Arabia's neighbours, had taken the same precaution. After all, there was nothing to fear from the nomadic Bedouins of the Peninsula, whose civilization was still in the tribal stage, whose religious beliefs were hardly better than fetichism, and who spent their time in making war upon one another, or pillaging the caravans that travelled from south to north, from Yemen to Palestine, Syria and the Peninsula of Sinai, passing through Mecca and Yathreb (the future Medina).

Preoccupied by their secular conflict, neither the Roman nor the Persian Empire seems to have had any suspicion of the propaganda by which Mohammed, amidst the confused conflicts of the tribes, was on the point of giving his own people a religion which it would presently cast upon the world, while imposing its own dominion. The Empire was already in deadly danger when John of Damascus was still regarding Islam as a sort of schism, of much the same character as previous heresies.[1]

When Mohammed died, in 632, there was as yet no sign of the peril which was to manifest itself in so overwhelming a fashion a couple of years later. No measures had been taken to defend the frontier. It is evident that whereas the Germanic menace had always attracted the attention of the Emperors, the Arab onslaught took them by surprise. In a certain sense, the expansion of Islam was due to chance, if we can give this name to the unpredictable consequence of a combination of causes. The success of the attack is explained by the exhaustion of the two Empires which marched with Arabia, the Roman and the Persian, at the end of the long struggle between them, which had at last culminated in the victory of Heraclius over Chosroes (d. 627).[2]

Byzantium had just reconquered its prestige, and its future seemed assured by the fall of the secular enemy and the restoration to the Empire of Syria, Palestine and Egypt. The Holy Cross, which had long ago been carried off, was now triumphantly restored to Constantinople by the conqueror. The sovereign of India sent his felicitations, and the king of the Franks, Dagobert,

[1] VASILIEV, *op. cit.*, vol. I, p. 274.   [2] *Ibid.*, p. 263.

concluded a perpetual peace with him. After this it was natural to expect that Heraclius would continue the Occidental policy of Justinian. It was true that the Lombards had occupied a portion of Italy, and the Visigoths, in 624, recaptured from Byzantium its last outposts in Spain; but what was that compared with the tremendous recovery which had just been accomplished in the Orient?

However, the effort, which was doubtless excessive, had exhausted the Empire. The provinces which Persia had just surrendered were suddenly wrested from the Empire by Islam. Heraclius (610–641) was doomed to be a helpless spectator of the first onslaught of this new force which was about to disconcert and bewilder the Western world.[1]

The Arab conquest, which brought confusion upon both Europe and Asia, was without precedent. The swiftness of its victory is comparable only with that by which the Mongol Empires of Attila, Jenghiz Khan and Tamerlane were established. But these Empires were as ephemeral as the conquest of Islam was lasting. This religion still has its faithful today in almost every country where it was imposed by the first Caliphs. The lightning-like rapidity of its diffusion was a veritable miracle as compared with the slow progress of Christianity.

By the side of this irruption, what were the conquests, so long delayed, of the Germans, who, after centuries of effort, had succeeded only in nibbling at the edge of "Romania"?

The Arabs, on the other hand, took possession of whole sections of the crumbling Empire. In 634 they seized the Byzantine fortress of Bothra (Bosra) in Transjordania; in 635 Damascus fell before them; in 636 the battle of Yarmok gave them the whole of Syria; in 637 or 638 Jerusalem opened its gates to them, while at the same time their Asiatic conquests included Mesopotamia and Persia. Then it was the turn of Egypt to be attacked; and shortly after the death of Heraclius (641) Alexandria was taken, and before long the whole country was occupied. Next the invasion, still continuing, submerged the Byzantine possessions in North Africa.

[1] VASILIEV, *op. cit.*, vol. I, p. 280.

All this may doubtless be explained by the fact that the invasion was unexpected, by the disorder of the Byzantine armies, disorganized and surprised by a new method of fighting, by the religious and national discontent of the Monophysites and Nestorians of Syria, to whom the Empire had refused to make any concessions, and of the Coptic Church of Egypt, and by the weakness of the Persians.[1] But all these reasons are insufficient to explain so complete a triumph. The intensity of the results were out of all proportion to the numerical strength of the conquerors.[2]

Here the great problem is to determine why the Arabs, who were certainly not more numerous than the Germans, were not, like the latter, absorbed by the populations of the regions which they had conquered, whose civilization was superior to their own. There is only one reply to this question, and it is of the moral order. While the Germans had nothing with which to oppose the Christianity of the Empire, the Arabs were exalted by a new faith. It was this, and this alone, that prevented their assimilation. For in other respects they were not more prejudiced than the Germans against the civilization of those whom they had conquered. On the contrary, they assimilated themselves to this civilization with astonishing rapidity; they learnt science from the Greeks, and art from the Greeks and the Persians. In the beginning, at all events, they were not even fanatical, and they did not expect to make converts of their subjects. But they required them to be obedient to the one God, Allah, and His prophet Mahommed, and, since Mahommed was an Arab, to Arabia. Their universal religion was at the same time a national religion. They were the servants of God.

"Islam" signifies resignation or submission to God, and "Musulman" means "subject." Allah is the One God, and it is therefore

[1] L. HALPHEN, *Les Barbares. Des grandes invasions aux conquêtes turques du XIe siècle*, Paris, 1926, p. 132: "That the Arabs were victorious was due to the fact that the world which they attacked was ready to fall into ruins."

[2] DAWSON, *Les Origines de l'Europe*, French translation, p. 153, regards religious enthusiasm as the essential cause of the conquests.

logical that all His servants should regard it as their duty to enforce obedience to Allah upon the unbelievers. What they proposed was not, as many have thought, their conversion, but their subjection.[1] And this subjection they enforced wherever they went. After the conquest they asked nothing better than to appropriate the science and art of the infidels as part of their booty; they would cultivate them to the glory of Allah. They would even adopt the institutions of the unbelievers in so far as these were useful to them. For that matter, they were forced to do so by their own conquest. In governing the Empire which they had founded they could no longer rely on their tribal institutions; just as the Germans were unable to impose theirs upon the Roman Empire. But they differed from the Germans in this: wherever they went, they ruled. The conquered were their subjects; they alone were taxed; they were excluded from the community of the faithful. The barrier was insuperable. No fusion was possible between the conquered populations and the Musulmans. What a contrast between them and Theodoric, who placed himself at the service of those he had conquered, and sought to assimilate himself to them!

In the case of the Germans, the conqueror spontaneously approached the conquered. With the Arabs it was the other way about; the conquered had to approach the conquerors, and they could do so only by serving Allah, as the conquerors served Him, and by reading the Koran, like the conquerors; and therefore by learning the language, the sacred and consummate language of the conquerors.

There was no propaganda, nor was any such pressure applied as was exerted by the Christians after the triumph of the Church. "If God had so desired" says the Koran "He would have made all humanity a single people," and it expressly condemns the use of violence in dealing with error.[2] It requires only obedience to Allah, the outward obedience of inferior, degraded and despicable

[1] VASILIEV, op. cit., vol. I, p. 279, citing GOLDZIHER, Vorlesungen über den Islam, 1910.

[2] Ibid., vol. I, p. 275.

beings, who are tolerated, but who live in abjection. It was this that the infidel found so intolerable and demoralizing. His faith was not attacked; it was simply ignored; and this was the most effective means of detaching him from it and leading him to Allah, who would not only restore his human dignity, but would open to him the gates of the Musulman State. It was because his religion compelled the conscientious Musulman to treat the infidel as a subject that the infidel came to him, and in coming to him broke with his country and his people.[1]

The German became Romanized as soon as he entered "Romania." The Roman, on the contrary, became Arabized as soon as he was conquered by Islam.[2] It is true that well into the Middle Ages certain small communities of Copts, Nestorians and, above all, Jews, survived in the midst of the Musulman world. Nevertheless, the whole environment was profoundly transformed. There was a clean cut: a complete break with the past. Wherever his power was effective, it was intolerable to the new master that any influence should escape the control of Allah. His law, derived from the Koran, was substituted for Roman law, and his language for Greek and Latin.

When it was converted to Christianity the Empire, so to speak, underwent a change of soul; when it was converted to Islam both its soul and its body were transformed. The change was as great in civil as in religious society.

With Islam a new world was established on those Mediterranean shores which had formerly known the syncretism of the Roman civilization. A complete break was made, which was to continue even to our own day. Henceforth two different and hostile civilizations existed on the shores of *Mare Nostrum*. And although in our own days the European has subjected the Asiatic, he has not assimilated him. The sea which had hitherto been the centre of

[1] For that matter, many were converted to Islam by interest. In Africa, according to Ibn Khaldoun, the Berbers apostatized twelve times in seventy years.

[2] In Spain, the 9th century, even the Christians no longer knew Latin, and the texts of the Councils were translated into Arabic.

Christianity became its frontier. The Mediterranean unity was ✓ shattered.

The first expansion slowed down a little under the Caliph Othman, and his assassination in 656 gave rise to a political and religious crisis which continued until the accession of Moawiya in 660.

It was quite in the natural order of things that a power endowed with an expansive force like that of Islam should impose itself upon the entire basin of the great inland sea. And it did indeed endeavour to do so. From the second half of the 7th century it aimed at becoming a maritime power in regions where Byzantium, under Constans II (641–668), was supreme. The Arabian ships of the Caliph Moawiya (660) began to invade Byzantine waters. They occupied the island of Cyprus, and off the coast of Asia Minor they won a naval victory over the Emperor Constans II himself. They seized the island of Rhodes, and advanced upon Crete and Sicily.[1] Converting the port of Cyzicus into a naval base, they again and again besieged Constantinople, which successfully opposed them, making use of Greek fire, until in 677 they abandoned the attempt.[2]

The advance towards Africa, begun by the Emir of Egypt, Ibn Saud, in 647, ended in a victory over the Exarch Gregory. However, the fortresses built in the reign of Justinian had not succumbed, and the Berbers, forgetting their ancient hostility to the Romans, co-operated with the latter in opposing the invaders. Once more the importance of Africa was revealed, whose conquest by the Vandals had formerly provoked the defensive decline of the Empire in the West. On Africa depended the security of Sicily and Italy, and the sea passage to the West. It was doubtless in order that he might defend Africa that Constans II, after the last visit to Rome ever paid by a Byzantine Emperor, established himself in Syracuse.

---

[1] VASILIEV, op. cit., vol. I, p. 282.

[2] They attacked Constantinople in 668 and 669; in 673 they inaugurated a blockade which lasted nearly five years. HALPHEN, op. cit., p. 139.

At this moment the disorders of the Caliphate brought about a respite. But with the accession of Moawiya in 660 the struggle was resumed. In 664 another great *razzia* inflicted a fresh defeat upon the Byzantines. The army which they had sent to Hadrumut was defeated and the fortress of Djelula captured, after which the invaders withdrew.[1] But in order to counter any further offensives of the Byzantines, who held the cities on the coast, and also to contain the Berbers of the Aures range, Okba-ben-Nafi, in 670, founded Kairouan, to be the stronghold of Islam until the end of time.[2] It was from Kairouan that raids, attended by massacres, were made against the Berbers, who still held out in their mountains. In 681 Okba, by a formidable thrust, reached the Atlantic. But a counter-offensive of the Berbers and the Romans swept the Arabs back; the Berber prince Kossayla entered Kairouan as a conqueror, and the Berbers who had embraced Islam hastened to abjure it.[3] It was now the turn of the Byzantines to take the offensive. Defeated at Kairouan, Kossayla's Musulmans fell back upon Barka, where they were surprised and massacred by a body of Byzantine troops which had landed there (689). Their leader was killed in the battle.[4]

This victory, which restored the coast of Africa to the Byzantines, threatened the whole Arab invasion of the Mediterranean. The Arabs, in desperation, returned to the charge, and Carthage was taken by assault (695). The Emperor Leontius realized the peril, and equipped a fleet, which, under the command of the patrician John, succeeded in retaking the city.

In the meantime the Berbers, gathering round the mysterious queen known as the Kahina, defeated the Arab army near Tebessa and drove it back into Tripolitana.[5]

But in the following year Hassan returned to the attack and captured Carthage (698), whose conquest was on this occasion

[1] JULIAN, *op. cit.*, p. 318.　　　　　　　　　　　　[2] *Ibid.*, p. 319.
[3] *Ibid.*, p. 320. It seems to me that this author has altogether minimized the part played by the Byzantines and has exaggerated the achievement of the Berbers.
[4] *Ibid.*, p. 321.　　　　　　　　　　　　[5] *Ibid.*, pp. 322-323.

final. The inhabitants had fled. The ancient city was immediately replaced by a new capital, at the head of the gulf: Tunis, whose harbour—Goletta—was to become the great base of Islam in the Mediterranean. The Arabs, who at last had a fleet, dispersed the Byzantine vessels. Henceforth they had the control of the sea. Before long the Greeks retained only the fortress of Septem (Ceuta) with a few fragments of *Mauretania Secunda* and Tingitana, Majorca, and a few cities in Spain. It seems that they erected these scattered possessions into an exarchate, which survived ten years longer.[1]

This was the end of the Berber resistance under the Queen Kahina. Captured in the Aures mountains, she was massacred, and her head was sent to the Caliph.

In the following years the Arabs set their stamp upon Africa. Musa Ibn Nosair subdued Morocco and imposed Islam on the Berber tribes.[2]

It was these new converts who were shortly to conquer Spain. As a matter of fact, Spain had already been harried, simultaneously with Sardinia and Sicily. This was the necessary consequence of the occupation of Africa. In 675 the Arabs had attacked Spain by sea, but had been repulsed by the Visigothic fleet.[3] The Straits of Gibraltar could not hold the conquerors in check, and the Visigoths were aware of the fact. In 694 King Egica accused the Jews of conspiring with the Musulmans, and it is possible, indeed, that the persecutions to which they had been subjected had led them to hope that the Musulmans would conquer the country. In 710 the King of Toledo, Achila, dispossessed by Rodrigo, Duke of Baetica, fled to Morocco, where he doubtless solicited the aid of the Musulmans. The latter, at all events, took advantage of the situation, for in 711 a Berber army, whose strength is estimated at 7,000, crossed the Straits under the command of Tarik. Rodrigo being defeated at the first encounter, all the cities opened their gates to the conqueror, who, reinforced in 712 by a second army, finally took possession of the country. In 713 Musa, the governor of

[1] JULIAN, *op. cit.*, p. 323.   [2] *Ibid.*, p. 327.
[3] LOT, PFISTER and GANSHOF, *Histoire du Moyen Age*, vol. I, p. 240.

North Africa, proclaimed the sovereignty of the Caliph of Damascus in the capital of Toledo.[1]

But why stop at Spain? After all, the country merged into the Narbonnaise. No sooner was the Peninsula completely subdued than in 720 the Musulmans captured Narbonne, and then laid siege to Toulouse, thus encroaching on the Frankish kingdom. The king, who was powerless, did nothing. Duke Eudes of Aquitaine drove them back in 721, but Narbonne still remained in their hands. And from Narbonne, in 725, a new and formidable attack was launched. Carcassonne was taken, and the knights of the Crescent advanced as far as Autun, which was sacked on August 22nd, 725.

In 732 another *razzia* was launched by the Emir of Spain, Abd-er-Rhaman, who, setting out from Pampeluna, crossed the Pyrenees and marched on Bordeaux. Eudes, defeated, took refuge with Charles Martel. Owing to the manifest impotence of the Midi, it was from the North that the final reaction against the Musulmans came. Charles marched with Eudes to meet the invader and encountered him in the same gap near Poitiers where Clovis had formerly overcome the Visigoths. The battle took place in October 732. Abd-er-Rhaman was defeated and slain,[2] but the danger was not averted. The threat was now to Provence; that is to say, to the coast. In 735 the Arab governor of Narbonne, Jussef Ibn Abd-er-Rhaman, seized the city of Arles, with the help of accomplices whom he found in the surrounding country.[3]

Then, in 737, the Arabs captured Avignon, with the help of Maucontus, and ravaged the country, as far as Lyons, and also in Aquitaine. Charles once more marched against them. He recaptured Avignon, and proceeded to attack Narbonne, before which

---

[1] HALPHEN, *op. cit.*, pp. 142–143.

[2] This battle has not the importance which has been attributed to it. It cannot be compared with the victory over Attila. It marked the end of a raid, but its effect was not really decisive. If Charles had been defeated all that would have happened would have been that the Musulmans would have pillaged the country more extensively.

[3] BREYSIG, *Jahrbücher des Fränkischen Reiches. Die Zeit Karl Martels*, pp. 77–78.

he defeated an Arab army which had come by sea in aid of their co-religionists, but he failed to take the city. He returned to Austrasia with an immense booty, for he had taken, destroyed and burned Maguelonne, Agda, Béziers and Nimes.[1]

These victories did not prevent the Arabs from making a fresh incursion into Provence in 739. This time they threatened the Lombards also; but Charles, with the aid of the latter, once more repulsed them.[2]

What followed is obscure; but it seems that the Arabs once more subdued the Provençal coast, and maintained their hold upon it for some years. Pippin expelled them in 752, but attacked Narbonne in vain.[3] He did not finally take the city until 759. This victory marks, if not the end of the expeditions against Provence, at least the end of the Musulman expansion in the West of Europe.[4] Just as Constantinople resisted the great attack of 718, and thereby protected the Orient, so here the intact forces of Austrasia, the vassals of the Carolingians, preserved the Occident.

However, while in the Orient the Byzantine fleet succeeded in driving Islam from the waters of the Aegean, in the Occident it obtained control of the Tyrrhenean Sea.

There was a succession of expeditions against Sicily, in 720, 727,

---

[1] BREYSIG, *Jahrbücher des Fränkischen Reiches. Die Zeit Karl Martels*, p. 84.

[2] *Ibid.*, p. 86.

[3] H. HAHN, *Jahrbücher des Fränkischen Reichs*, 741–752, p. 141.

[4] Provence was still fated to suffer much devastation. In 799 the Saracens pillaged the coast of Aquitaine, doubtless coming from the Atlantic side, *Miracula S. Filiberti*, M.G.H. SS., vol. XV, p. 303. Cf. W. VOGEL, *Die Normannen und das Fränkische Reich*, Heidelberg, 1907, p. 51, No. 4. In 768 the Moors were already causing alarm in the neighbourhood of Marseilles, *Chronique du pseudo-Frédégaire, Continuatio*, M.G.H. SS. RER. MEROV., vol. II, p. 191. In 778 they threatened Italy, JAFFÉ-WATTENBACH, *Regesta*, No. 2424. In 793 they attacked Septimania, BÖHMER-MUHLBACHER, *Regesten*, p. 138; in 813 Nice and Civita Vecchia, and in 838 Marseilles. In 848 Marseilles was captured. In 857 and 850 Provence was ravaged. In 889 the Arabs established themselves at Sant Tropez and La Garde Freynet. On the Atlantic coast there were Saracens, who had come from Spain in the 8th century, on the island of Noirmoutier: POUPARDIN, *Monuments de l'histoire des abbayes de Saint-Philibert*, 1905, p. 66.

728, 730, 732, 752, 753; interrupted for a time by civil disturbances in Africa,[1] they were resumed in 827 under the Aghlabite Emir Siadet Allah I, who profited by a revolt against the Emperor to attempt a sudden attack upon Syracuse. An Arab fleet left Susa in 827, but the Byzantines continued the war with energy, and a Byzantine fleet raised the siege of Syracuse.

The Musulmans received reinforcements from Spain, and then from Africa. In August–September 831 they took Palermo after a year's siege, thus acquiring a defensive base in Sicily. Despite this check, the Byzantines continued a vigorous resistance both on sea and on land. They could not, however, prevent the Musulmans, assisted by the Neapolitans, from capturing Messina in 843. In 850 the seat of the Byzantine resistance was carried, and Syracuse, after a heroic defence, succumbed on May 21st, 878.

While the Byzantine Empire was endeavouring to save Sicily, Charlemagne was at grips with the Musulmans on the frontiers of Spain. In 778 he despatched an army which was defeated defore Saragossa, and whose rearguard was massacred at Roncesvalles. He then adopted a defensive attitude, until the Saracens invaded Septimania (793), when he established the Spanish March (795)[2], which his son Louis, king of Aquitaine, employed as his base when seizing Barcelona in 801. After various fruitless expeditions, and in particular one which was led by the *missus* Ingobert in 810, Tortosa also fell into Louis' hands in 1811. On the other hand, he failed to take Huesca, and he advanceed no farther.[3]

The truth is that Charlemagne enountered an extremely vigorous resistance in Spain; and Eginhard exaggerates when he declares that Charlemagne occupied the whole country as far as the Ebro. In reality he reached the river only at two points—in the upper valley, to the south of Navarre; and in the lower valley, at Tortosa, if we can believe that this city was really occupied.[4]

[1] HARTMANN, *op. cit.*, vol. III, pp. 170–171.

[2] RICHTER and KOOHL, *Annalen des Fränkischen Reichs im Zeitalter der Karolinger*, p.132.

[3] KLEINCLAUSZ, *Charlemagne*, Paris, 1934, pp. 326 *et seq.*

[4] *Ibid.*, p. 330.

That Charlemagne was able to derive so little advantage from the taking of Barcelona was due to the fact that he had no fleet. He could do nothing against the Saracens, who were in possession of Tunis, dominated the Spanish coast, and held the islands. He attempted to defend the Balearics, and won some ephemeral victories there. In 798 these islands were ravaged by the Musulmans.[1] In the following year, in response to the appeals of the inhabitants, Charlemagne sent them some troops, which were doubtless transported on the islanders' vessels. This military demonstration appears to have been efficacious, for the Arab ensigns were sent to the king as trophies.[2] We do not find, however, that the Franks continued in occupation of these islands.

Charlemagne, in fact, was almost constantly at war in the region of the Pyrenees. The upheavals which were disturbing the Musulman world favoured his operations. The establishment of the Omayyad Caliphate of Cordova in 765 in opposition to the Caliphate of the Abbasids of Baghdad was advantageous to the Franks, since it was in the interest of each of these powers to treat them with consideration.

Charlemagne had but little success in other parts of the Mediterranean. In 806 the Saracens seized the little island of Pantellaria and sold the monks whom they found there into slavery in Spain. They were ransomed by Charles.[3] That same year Pippin, his son, King of Italy, attempted to drive the Saracens out of Corsica, where they had established themselves. He equipped a fleet, and according to the Carolingian annalists he made himself master of the island. But in the following year it had once more fallen into the hands of the enemy.[4]

Charles immediately sent the constable Burchard against them, who forced them to withdraw after a battle in which they lost thirteen ships. But once more the victory was ephemeral, for in

[1] RICHTER and KOHL, *op. cit.*, p. 141.
[2] *Annales regni Francorum*, a° 799, ed. KURZE, M.G.H. SS. *in us. schol.*, p. 108.
[3] KLEINCLAUSZ, *op. cit.*, p. 332, No. 2.
[4] *Annales regni Francorum*, a[is] 806 and 807, ed. KURZE, pp. 122 and 124.

808 Pope Leo III, speaking to Charles of the measures which he was taking for the defence of the Italian coast, begged him to make himself responsible for Corsica.[1] As a matter of fact, we find that in 809 and 810 the Saracens occupied Corsica and Sardinia.

The situation was aggravated when Africa, the victim of endemic disturbances, was organized under the dynasty of the Aghlabites, who acknowledged the Caliph of Baghdad, Haroun-al-Raschid.

In 812 the Saracens of Africa, despite the arrival of a Greek fleet, commanded by a patrician and reinforced by vessels from Gaeta and Amalfi, pillaged the islands of Lampedusa, Ponza and Ischia. Leo II put the coasts of Italy in a state of defence,[2] and the Emperor sent him his cousin Wala to assist him. Charles also entered into negotiations with the patrician George, but the latter concluded a ten years' truce with the enemy. However, the truce was disregarded, and the naval war continued; even the destruction by a tempest of a Saracen fleet of a hundred ships in 813 only checked for a time the *razzias* of the Spanish Arabs, who continued to pillage Civita Vecchia, Nice, Sardinia, and Corsica, from which they returned with five hundred captives.

In the midst of these wars, however, some diplomatic approaches were attempted. As early as 765 Pippin had sent an embassy to Baghdad. In 768 he received, in Aquitaine, envoys from the Saracens of Spain, who came through Marseilles. In 810 Haroun-al-Raschid despatched an embassy to Charlemagne, and he, in 812, signed a treaty with the Spanish El-Hakem.

These various endeavours, however, led to nothing. And Charlemagne, incapable of resisting the Musulman fleets, was compelled more and more to resign himself to the defensive, parrying with difficulty the blows which he received.

After his death the situation became still worse. It is true that in 828 Bonifacio of Tuscany, with a small fleet, whose function was to protect Corsica and Sardinia, made an attack upon the African

---

[1] JAFFÉ-WATTENBACH, *Regesta*, No. 2515; KLEINCLAUSZ, *op. cit.*, p. 331.
[2] *Ibid.*, p. 33.

coast between Carthage and Utica.[1] We may suppose that he took advantage of the fact that the Musulmans were just then fully occupied in Sicily. But a few years later Italy, to the north of the Byzantine cities, was completely at the mercy of the Musulmans. Brindisi and Tarento were ravaged (838), Bari conquered (840), and the Byzantine and Venetian fleets were defeated. In 841 the Musulmans ravaged Ancona and the Dalmatian coast as far as Cattaro. And Lothair, in 846, made no secret of the fact that he feared the annexation of Italy.[2]

In 846 seventy vessels attacked Ostia and Porto, when the Musulmans advanced, ravaging the country, to the very walls of Rome, profaning the church of San Pietro. The garrison of Gregoriopolis was unable to check them. They were finally repulsed by Guido di Spoleto. Lothair's expedition in the following year did not succeed in recovering Bari.

In 849, at the instigation of the Pope, Amalfi, Gaeta and Naples formed a league against the Saracens, and assembled a fleet at Ostia; the Pope, Leo IV, going thither to bless it.[3] It won a great naval victory over the Saracens. At the same time, the Pope surrounded the Vatican city with a wall, the enclosed area being known as the *Civitas Leonina* (848–852).[4]

In 852 the Pope settled some Corsican refugees in Porto, which he fortified, but the new town did not prosper. He also created Leopoli, to take the place of Civita Vecchia, now emptied by the terror which the Saracens inspired.[5] At the same time he restored Orta and Ameria in Tuscany, to provide a refuge for the inhabitants at the time of the Musulman raids.[6] But this did not prevent

---

[1] HARTMANN, *op. cit.*, vol. III, p. 179, observes that this was the only overseas expedition which the Franks attempted. Cf. RICHTER and KOHL, *op. cit.*, p. 260.

[2] M.G.H. CAPIT., vol. II, p. 67. Provence was again pillaged in 849. HARTMANN, *op. cit.*, vol. III, p. 224. And again in 890. M.G.H. CAPIT., vol. II, p. 377.

[3] JAFFÉ-WATTENBACH, *Regesta*, p. 330.

[4] M.G.H. CAPIT., vol. II, p. 66. In 846 Lothair ordered a subscription throughout the Empire in aid of the erection of this wall.

[5] HARTMANN, *op. cit.*, vol. III, p. 213.

[6] JAFFÉ-WATTENBACH, *Regèsta*, No. 2959. The Italian coasts were ravaged in 872.

the Musulmans, in 876 and 877, from ravaging the Roman Campagna, and the Pope's appeals to the Emperor of Byzantium were fruitless. The disasters which Byzantium was suffering at this moment in Sicily, where Syracuse succumbed to the enemy (878), doubtless prevented her from intervening, and finally the Pope was compelled to buy off the attacks of the Moors by an annual payment of 25,000 *mancusi* of silver. Yet so far he had had to deal only with mere bands of pirates whose sole object was pillage. In 883 the Abbey of Monte Cassino was burned and destroyed.[1] In 890 the Abbey of Farfa was besieged; it held out for seven years. Subiaco was destroyed, and the valley of the Anio and Tivoli were pillaged. The Saracens made themselves a stronghold not far from Rome, at Saracinesco, and another in the Sabine hills at Ciciliano. The Roman Campagna became a desert: *reducta est terra in solitudinem*. Peace was restored only in 916, when John X, the Emperor, the princes of Southern Italy, and the Emperor of Constantinople, who sent some galleys to Naples, forced that city and its neighbours to abandon their alliance with the Saracens, and then, with their assistance, finally defeated the terrible invaders on the Garigliano.

We may therefore say that after the conquest of Spain, and above all of Africa, the Western Mediterranean became a Musulman lake. The Frankish Empire, having no fleet, was powerless. Naples, Gaeta and Amalfi still possessed a fleet. But their commercial interests impelled them to abandon Byzantium, as being too remote, and to enter into relations with the Musulmans.

It was thanks to their defection that the Saracens finally succeeded in taking Sicily. The Byzantine fleet, it is true, was powerful, even more powerful than the fleets of the maritime cities of Italy, thanks to the Greek fire, which made it a terrible instrument of war; but once Sicily was taken it was almost completely cut off from the Occident, where its further appearances were rare and ineffectual. Nevertheless, it enabled the Emperors to safeguard

[1] GAY, *L'Italie méridionale et l'Empire byzantin*, 1904, p. 130.

their Empire, which lay mainly on the coast;[1] and it was thanks to the fleet that the Grecian waters retained their freedom, and that Italy finally escaped from the grip of Islam. Thirty years after its conquest by the Musulmans in 840, Bari was retaken by the fleet of the Emperor Basil, which consisted of 400 vessels.[2] This was the essential fact which prevented the Musulmans from obtaining a foothold in Italy, maintained the Byzantine sovereignty there, and assured the safety of Venice.

Again, it was by means of its fleet that Byzantium was able to maintain some sort of supremacy over Naples, Amalfi, and Gaeta, whose policy consisted in siding now with the Emperor, now with the Duke of Benevento, and even at times with the Musulmans, in order to preserve the autonomy which was necessary to their commerce.

The expansion of Islam was thus unable to absorb the whole of the Mediterranean. It encircled the Mediterranean on the East, the South, and the West, but it was unable to obtain a hold upon the North. The ancient Roman sea had become the frontier between Islam and Christianity. All the old Mediterranean provinces conquered by the Musulmans gravitated henceforth toward Baghdad.[3]

At the same time the Orient was cut off from the Occident. The bond which the Germanic invasion had left intact was severed. Byzantium was henceforth merely the centre of a Greek Empire

[1] The fleet defended Byzantium not only against the Musulmans, but also against the Franks; in 806 the despatch of a fleet against which Charlemagne was powerless sufficed to persuade him to renounce Venice. At sea, the Franks depended absolutely upon the Italian fleets; in 846 Lothair, having no fleet of his own, requested the Venetians to attack the Saracens of Benevento *navali expeditione*. M.G.H. CAPIT, vol. II, p. 67.

[2] SCHAUBE, *Handelsgeschichte der Romanischen Völker des Mittelmeergebiets*, Munich, 1906, p. 26. Louis II's Italian campaign of 866 to 873 was unsuccessful owing to the disputes which arose between him and the Italians, who at one moment even took him prisoner. HARTMANN, *op. cit.*, vol. III, pp. 265, 288, 296.

[3] In speaking of Africa, M. Marcais says: "The bridges are cut between Africa and Christian Europe. She lives with her eyes fixed upon Baghdad or Cairo."

which could no longer pursue Justinian's policy. It was reduced to defending its last possessions. Its farthest Western outposts were Naples, Venice, Gaeta and Amalfi. The fleet still enabled it to remain in touch with them, and thus prevented the Eastern Mediterranean from becoming a Musulman lake. But the Western Mediterranean was precisely that. Once the great means of communication, it was now an insuperable barrier.

Islam had shattered the Mediterranean unity which the Germanic invasions had left intact.

This was the most essential event of European history which had occurred since the Punic Wars. It was the end of the classic tradition. It was the beginning of the Middle Ages, and it happened at the very moment when Europe was on the way to becoming Byzantinized.

2. *The Closing of the Western Mediterranean*

So long as the Mediterranean remained Christian, it was the Oriental navigation that maintained commercial intercourse with the Occident. Syria and Egypt were its two principal centres; and these two wealthy provinces were the very first to fall under the domination of Islam. It would obviously be an error to believe that this domination put an end to all economic activity. Although there was great confusion and disorder, and although many Syrians migrated to the Occident, we must not suppose that the economic machinery collapsed. Damascus had become the first capital of the Caliphate. Spices were still imported, papyrus was still manufactured, the seaports were still active. Once they paid taxes to the conquerors, the Christians were not molested. Commerce, therefore, continued, but its direction was changed.[1]

It goes without saying that when an actual war was in progress

[1] Concerning the closing of the Occidental Mediterranean by Islam (but this does not refer to the Orient), see the text of the Christian Arab Yahya-Ibn-Said of Antioch, who, in the 11th century, stated that he had not a reliable list of the "patriarchs of Rome" since Pope Agathon (678–681). BEDIER, *Charlemagne et la Palestine*, REVUE HISTORIQUE, vol. CLVII, 1928, p. 281.

the conqueror did not allow his subjects to trade with the conquered. And when peace had restored the commercial activity of the conquered provinces, Islam directed it into new trade routes, which were opened up by the immensity of its conquests.

These new trade routes connected the Caspian Sea with the Baltic, by way of the Volga, and the Scandinavians, whose merchants frequented the shores of the Black Sea, were suddenly compelled to follow the new route. Of this we need no further proof than the many Oriental coins found in Gothland.

We may be certain that the disturbances inseparable from the conquest of Syria (634–636) and then of Egypt (640–642) must have hindered navigation.[1]

The ships must have been requisitioned for the fleet which Islam suddenly organized in the Aegean Sea. Moreover, one can hardly imagine that merchants would have sailed through the midst of the hostile fleet, unless to take advantage of the situation, as many of them must have done, by turning pirate.

We may certainly conclude that from the middle of the 7th century navigation between the Musulman ports of the Aegean Sea and those ports which had remained Christian had become impossible; or if there was any, it must have been almost negligible.

It may have been possible to maintain navigation, under the protection of the fleet, between Byzantium and the adjacent coast, still defended by the capital, and the other Greek regions of Greece, the Adriatic, Southern Italy, and Sicily, but we can hardly suppose that the Byzantine vessels could have sailed any farther, since Islam was attacking Sicily as early as 650.

As for the commercial activities of Africa, the continual ravaging of the country from 643 to 708 undoubtedly put an end to them. The few rare vestiges of commerce that may have survived disappeared after the taking of Carthage and the foundation of Tunis in 698.

---

[1] It is not by chance that the series of pseudo-Imperial coins in Gaul stops at Heraclius (610–641). Cf. PROU, *Catalogue des monnaies mérovingiennes*, pp. xxvii–xxviii.

The conquest of Spain in 711, and the conditions of insecurity obtaining on the coast of Provence immediately after this conquest, absolutely put an end to any possibility of sea-borne trade in the Western Mediterranean. The remaining Christian ports could not have maintained communications by sea, since they had no fleet, or practically none.

Thus, it may be asserted that navigation with the Orient ceased about 650 as regards the regions situated eastward of Sicily, while in the second half of the 7th century it came to an end in the whole of the Western Mediterranean.

By the beginning of the 8th century it had completely disappeared. There was no longer any traffic in the Mediterranean, except along the Byzantine coast. As Ibn-Khaldoun says (with the necessary reservation as regards Byzantium): "the Christians could no longer float a plank upon the sea." The Mediterranean was henceforth at the mercy of the Saracen pirates. In the 9th century they seized the islands, destroyed the ports, and made their *razzias* everywhere. The great port of Marseilles, which had formerly been the principal emporium of Western trade with the Levant, was empty. The old economic unity of the Mediterranean was shattered, and so it remained until the epoch of the Crusades. It had resisted the Germanic invasions; but it gave way before the irresistible advance of Islam.

How could the Occident have resisted? The Franks had no fleet. The Visigothic fleet was destroyed, while the enemy was well prepared. The port of Tunis, and its arsenal, were impregnable. On all the coasts *Ribat* were established: semi-religious, semi-military posts, which were in touch with one another, and maintained a perpetual state of war. The Christians could do nothing against this maritime power; the most striking proof of this being the fact that they made only one petty raid on the African coast.

It is necessary to insist upon this point, since some excellent scholars do not admit that the Musulman conquest can have produced so complete a break. They even believe that the Syrian merchants continued, as of old, to frequent Italy and Gaul in the course of the 7th and 8th centuries. It is true that Rome, in particular, extended a welcome to a number of Syrians during the first few decades that followed the conquest of their country by the Arabs. Their influence and their numbers must have been considerable, for several of them—like Sergius I (687–701) and Constantine I (708–715)—were elevated to the Papacy. From Rome a certain number of these refugees, whose prestige was assured by their knowledge of the Greek language, presently migrated northwards, taking with them the manuscripts, ivories, and jewellery with which they had provided themselves on leaving their country. The Carolingian sovereigns did not fail to employ them in the movement of literary and artistic revival which they were fostering. Charlemagne instructed some of them to revise the text of the Gospel. It was probably one of their compatriots who left at Metz a Greek text of the *Laudes*, which is mentioned as having been there in the 9th century.

We may see another proof of the Syrian penetration into the Occident after the 7th century in the influence of the art of Asia Minor on the development of decorative motives in the Carolingian epoch. We know, moreover, that many of the ecclesiastics of "Francia" journeyed to the East in order to worship at the Holy Places of Palestine, and that they returned bringing not only relics, but doubtless also manuscripts and church ornaments.

It is a well-known fact that Haroun-al-Raschid, anxious to obtain the assistance of Charlemagne in his conflict with the Omayyads, granted him the sepulchre of Christ,[1] and also a vague protectorate over the Holy Places.

But all these details, however interesting they may be to the historian of civilization, tells us nothing of the economic history of the age. The immigration of scholars and artists does not in any

---

[1] According to KLEINCLAUSZ, *La légende du protectorat de Charlemagne sur la Terre Sainte*, SYRIA, 1926, pp. 211–233, Haroun granted the Emperor only the sepulchre of Christ. BÉDIER, dealing with the same question, *op. cit.*, REVUE HISTORIQUE, vol. CLVII, 1928, pp. 277–291, considers that although no protectorate was granted, Haroun did concede to Charles a "moral authority" over the Christians of Palestine.

way prove the existence of commercial relations between the countries from which they came and those in which they sought refuge. Was not the 15th century, when so many learned Byzantines fled into Italy to escape the Turks, the very period when Constantinople ceased to be a great port? We must not confuse the circulation of merchandise with the movements of pilgrims, scholars and artists. The former traffic presupposed the organization of transport and the permanent exchange of imports and exports, but the latter followed the hazard of circumstances. Before we should be justified in affirming the persistence of Syrian and Oriental navigation in the Tyrrhenean Sea and the Gulf of Lyons after the 7th century, we should have to prove that Marseilles and the ports of Provence remained in communication with the Levant after this date. But the last text which we can produce in this connection is a document relating to Corbie, dated 716.[1]

According to this text the magazine of the fisc at Marseilles, or at Fos, must still have been full of spices and oil at this period: that is, of products imported from Asia and Africa. I believe, however, that this is merely an archaism. We have here a document confirming certain ancient privileges of the Abbey of Corbie; it probably reproduced earlier texts verbatim. It is, indeed, impossible that African oil can still have been imported at this time. We may assume, of course, that the *cellarium fisci* was drawing upon its stocks, but in that case we have no proof of the existence of active commercial relations in 716. At all events, this is the latest mention that we have of Oriental products warehoused in the ports of Provence. For that matter, four years later the Musulmans were landing on this coast and pillaging the countryside. Marseilles was then dead. It is idle to object, in proof of its activity, that pilgrims were still passing through it on their way to the East. It is a

[1] R. BUCHNER, *op. cit.*, p. 48, considers that there were still commercial relations at this date, but not later; more particularly because the Abbey of St. Denis did not again have its privileges confirmed. In 695 it obtained a *villa* in exchange for a revenue in kind levied on the public treasury. PH. LAUER, *Les diplomes originaux des Mérovingicns*, pl. 24. Cf. LEVILLAIN, *Études sur l'abbaye de Saint-Denis*, BIBL. ÉCOLE DES CHARTES, vol. XCI, 1930, pp. 288 *et seq.*

fact that such pilgrims, since they could not traverse the valley of the Danube, which was occupied by the Avars, and then by the Hungarians, must have crossed the sea. But we find, whenever it is possible to trace the itineraries followed, that the pious travellers embarked in the ports of Byzantine Italy. Saint Willibald, the future Bishop of Eichstädt, embarked in 726 at Gaeta, after crossing the Alps. Madalveus, Bishop of Verdun, going to Jerusalem about 776, embarked upon a ship sailing from Apulia to Constantinople.[1]

The letters of Saint Boniface tell us that the Anglo-Saxons travelled to Rome overland instead of by way of Marseilles, which necessitated the crossing of the Alps. And in the 9th century the monk Bernard, proceeding to Alexandria, sailed from Tarento.[2]

Not only is it impossible to find a single text which mentions the continued presence of Syrian or Oriental merchants, but we shall discover that from the 8th century onwards all the products which they used to import were no longer to be found in Gaul; and this argument is unanswerable.[3]

Papyrus was the first to disappear. All the works written in the West on papyrus of which we have knowledge are of the 6th or

---

[1] There was still a certain amount of navigation in the 8th century. For example, the Popes often sent their ambassadors to Pippin *marino itinere* on account of the Lombards. But the very fact that this is specially mentioned shows that it was exceptional. Similarly, the ambassadors sent by the Caliphs to Pippin and Charles came by way of Marseilles, Porto, Venice and Pisa.

[2] BUCHNER, *op. cit.*, p. 49, gives other examples, which show that there was no longer navigation between Marseilles and Rome. KLEINCLAUSZ is mistaken in declaring that the legates sent by Charlemagne to Byzantium embarked at Marseilles.

[3] I admit that this does not hold good if the *Cappi* mentioned in 877 by the capitulary of Kiersy (M.G.H. CAPIT., vol. II, p. 361, §31) were, as is supposed by M. THOMPSON, *Economic and Social History of the Middle Ages*, 1928, p. 269, Syrian merchants. But if we are to accept this we must assume with him that *Cappi* is merely the Latinized form of the Greek κάπηλος, which becomes *Kapila* in Syrian, meaning a merchant.

But apart from the fact that this is a linguistic impossibility, it should be noted that the expression *Cappi* is applied only to the Jews. And lastly, this famous *apax legomenon* is undoubtedly due to a mistaken reading on the part of Sirmond, who, in 1623, edited this text from a manuscript which has since disappeared.

the 7th century. Until 659–677 nothing but papyrus was used in the royal Merovingian chancellery. Then parchment made its appearance.[1] A few private documents were still written on papyrus, doubtless obtained from old stocks of this material, until nearly the end of the 8th century. There is no sign of it after that. And the explanation cannot be that it was no longer manufactured, for this supposition is disproved by the beautiful papyrus documents of the 7th century in the Arab Museum of Cairo. The disappearance of papyrus in Gaul can only have been due to the fact that commerce first declined and then ceased. Parchment does not seem to have been widely used at first. Gregory of Tours, who calls it *membrana*, mentions it only once,[2] and seems to indicate that it was manufactured by the monks for their own use. Now, we know that the habits of a chancellery are extremely tenacious. If at the close of the 7th century the royal offices had ceased to make use of papyrus it was because it was becoming very difficult to obtain any.

Papyrus was still used to some extent in Italy. The Popes employed it for the last time in 1057. Are we to suppose, with Breslau, that they were using up old stocks? Did it come from Sicily, where the Arabs introduced its manufacture in the 10th century? As a matter of fact, it has been disputed that it came from Sicily. It seems to me that it was probably obtained through the trade of the Byzantine ports: Naples, Amalfi, Gaeta, Venice.

But as regards Gaul, it was no longer procurable.

Mention of spices, like that of papyrus, disappears from the texts after 716.[3]

---

[1] The first royal instrument on parchment is dated September 12th, 677.

[2] *Liber Vitae Patrum*, M.G.H. SS. RER. MEROV., vol. I, p. 742.

[3] This has been denied on the strength of a text which follows the famous statutes of the Abbot Adalhard of Corbie in a manuscript which M. Levillain believes was written shortly after 986. LEVILLAIN, *Les statuts d'Adalhard*, LE MOYEN AGE, 1900, p. 335. Now, as these statutes were drawn up in 822, it has been generally agreed that this text was written between 822 and 986.

If this was so, it would show that it must have been possible still to obtain papyrus at this period, or at all events after 822, from the market of Cambrai, and therefore, throughout Gaul. It is, however, very extraordinary to find

The statutes of Adalhard of Corbie mention only *pulmentaria*, which was a kind of vegetable soup.[1]

Actually spices must have disappeared at the same time as papyrus, since they came in the same vessels.

Let us glance through the capitularies. Actually only those spices and exotic products are mentioned which could be cultivated in the *villae*,[2] such as madder, cummin and almonds.[3] But there is not a single reference to pepper, cloves (*cariofilo*), nard (*spico*), cinnamon, dates or pistachios.

The Carolingian *tractoriae* mention, among the foodstuffs which were served to functionaries on their travels, bread, pork, fowls, eggs, salt, herbs, vegetables, fish, and cheese, but not a single kind of spice.[4]

Similarly, the *tractoria* "*de conjecta missis dando*"[5] of 829 enumerates as provisions to be furnished to the *missi*, 40 loaves, pork or lamb, 4 fowls, 20 eggs, 8 setiers of wine, 2 measures of beer, 2 measures of wheat. It is a rustic menu.

The *Capitula episcoporum*[6] of 843–850 allow for the bishops, when they travel from place to place, 100 loaves, pork, 50 setiers of wine, 10 fowls, 50 eggs, 1 lamb, 1 porker, 6 measures of oats for the horses, 3 cartloads of hay, honey, oil and wax. But in all this list there is no mention of condiments.

---

that there is nothing which confirms this text. And yet the matter is easily explained. The text in question is not related to the statutes; it is a subsequent addition, and it dates, without the slightest doubt, from the Merovingian epoch.

The essential content of the text is a long list of the spices which the monks of Corbie were able to buy in the market of Cambrai. Now if we run through this list we shall find, with a few additions, all the products mentioned in the Corbie charter of 716. At first sight, of course, nothing could be simpler than to find the explanation of this concordance in the fact that these products were still being exported. And this explanation has been adopted; it is, unfortunately, impossible. *Polyptyque de l'abbé Irminon*, ed. B. GUERARD, vol. II, p. 336.

[1] DUCANGE, *Glossarium*, v° *pulmentum*.

[2] M.G.H. CAPIT., vol. I, p. 90. Capitulary "*de villis*," circa 70.

[3] *Ibid.*, vol. I, p. 91, *ibid.*   [4] *Formulae*, ed. K. ZEUMER, p. 292.

[5] M.G.H. CAPIT., vol. II, p. 10.   [6] *Ibid.*, p. 83.

We see from the letters of Saint Boniface how rare and expensive spices had become. He received or sent presents which consisted of small quantities of incense.[1] In 742–743 a cardinal sent him *aliquantum cotzumbri quod incensus, Domino offeratis*.[2] In 748 an archdeacon of Rome also sent him a small consignment of spices and perfume.[3] These gifts prove the rarity of spices to the north of the Alps, since they constituted valuable presents. We should note, however, that they all came from Italy. They were no longer reaching the port of Marseilles. The *cellarium fisci* was empty, or even—which is very probable—had been burned by the Saracens. And spices were no longer an article of normal commerce. If small quantities still found their way into the country, it was by means of pedlars.

In all the literature of the period, although this is very abundant, there is hardly any mention of spices.

It may be asserted, in view of this scarcity, that by the end of the 7th century and the beginning of the 8th spices had disappeared from the normal diet. They did not reappear until after the 12th century, when the Mediterranean was reopened to commerce.

The same thing applies, of course, to the wine of Gaza, which also disappeared. Oil was no longer exported from Africa. Such oil as was still used came from Provence. Henceforth the churches were lit with wax candles.

Similarly, the use of silk seems to have been almost entirely unknown at this period. I find only one mention of it in the capitularies.[4]

We know how simply Charlemagne was accustomed to dress. The court would certainly have imitated him. But no doubt this

---

[1] M.G.H. EPIST. SELECTAE, in 8vo, vol. I, 1916, ed. TANGL, p. 156.

[2] *Ibid.*, p. 97.   [3] *Ibid.*, pp. 189 and 191.

[4] M.G.H. CAPIT., vol. I, p. 251, in the *Brevium Exampla* composed about 810, in which there is mention, in the treasury of a church, of a *dalmatica sirica*, of *fanones lineos serico paratos*, of *linteamina serico parata*, of *manicas sericeas auro et margaritis paratas et alias sericeas*, of *plumatium serico indutum*. These were all church ornaments, but no doubt a certain number of them dated from an earlier period.

simplicity, which contrasts so strongly with the Merovingian luxury, was a matter of necessity.

We must conclude, from all this, that imports from the Orient had ceased in consequence of the Islamic expansion.

We note another very striking fact: the increasing rarity of gold. We see it in the Merovingian gold coins of the 8th century, which were alloyed with a constantly increasing proportion of silver. Evidently gold had ceased to arrive from the Orient. While it continued to circulate in Italy, it became so rare in Gaul that it was no longer employed as currency. From the time of Pippin and Charlemagne only silver *denarii* were struck, with very rare exceptions. Gold resumed its place in the monetary system only when spices resumed theirs in the normal diet.

This is an essential fact more eloquent than all the texts. It must be admitted that the circulation of gold was a consequence of commerce, since where commerce survived—that is, in southern Italy, gold continued to be in common use.

One consequence of the suppression of the Oriental trade and maritime traffic was the disappearance of professional merchants in the interior of the country. Henceforth merchants are hardly ever mentioned in the documents of the period; any references that do occur may be understood as applying to occasional merchants. I can find no mention at this period of a single *negotiator* of the Merovingian type: that is, a merchant who lent money at interest, was buried in a sarcophagus, and gave of his goods to the churches and the poor. There is no evidence whatever of the continued existence in the cities of colonies of merchants, or of a *domus negotiantum*. There can be no doubt that as a class the merchants had disappeared. Commerce itself had not disappeared, for we cannot imagine a period without any sort of exchange, but it had assumed a different character. As we shall presently see, the spirit of the age was hostile to it, except in the Byzantine countries. Moreover, the fact that very few laymen were able to read and write rendered impossible the continued existence of a class living normally by sale and purchase. The disappearance of loans at interest affords further evidence of the economic regression produced by the closing of the sea.

Let no one imagine that the Musulmans of Africa and Spain, or even of Syria, could have taken the place of the former merchants of the Byzantine Levant. At first the Musulmans and the Christians were permanently at war. They had no notion of trading, but only of pillaging. The documents do not mention a single Musulman as established in Gaul or Italy. It is a proven fact that the Musulman traders did not instal themselves beyond the frontiers of Islam. If they did trade, they did so among themselves. We do not find a single indication, after the conquest, of any traffic between Africa and the Christians, with the already mentioned exception of the Christians of Southern Italy. But there is no sign of any traffic with the Christians of the Provençal coast.

Under these circumstances the only persons who were still engaged in commerce were the Jews. They were numerous everywhere. The Arabs neither drove them out nor massacred them, and the Christians had not changed their attitude to them. They therefore constituted the only class to make its living by trading. At the same time, thanks to the contacts which they maintained among themselves, they constituted the only economic link which survived between Islam and Christendom, or, one may say, between East and West.

3. *Venice and Byzantium*

It may be said that the Islamic invasion was as decisive for the East as for the West of Europe. Before this invasion the Emperor of Constantinople was still the Roman Emperor. The policy of Justinian in this respect is characteristic: he claimed that the entire Mediterranean was subject to the Imperial authority. After the invasion, on the contrary, the Emperor was reduced to the defensive in Greek waters, until in the 11th century he appealed to the West for assistance. Islam immobilized and engrossed him. Here we have the whole explanation of his policy. Henceforth the Occident was closed to him.

Once Africa and Carthage were lost, after an obstinate defence under disastrous conditions, the sphere of action of Byzantine policy was confined to Italy; but even here only the coastal regions were retained. In the interior of the country Byzantium could no longer resist the Lombards. Her impotence led to the revolt of the Italians and the defection of the Pope. Henceforth the Empire strove to retain only Sicily, the Adriatic, and the cities of the South, but these outposts of Byzantium were becoming more and more autonomous.

The expansion of Islam came to a halt on the Byzantine frontier. Islam had robbed the Empire of its Syrian, Egyptian and African provinces, to some extent by exploiting national differences. But the Greek nucleus resisted, and by resisting it saved Europe, and doubtless, in saving Europe, it saved Christianity.

But the encounter was tremendous. Byzantium, twice attacked while Islam was at the height of its vigour, owed her victory to her fleet. She remained, in spite of all, a great naval power.

Of all the westward prolongations of the Byzantine Empire, the most important and the most original was the extraordinary city of Venice, the story of which, if we except the United Provinces, constitutes the most curious chapter in the economic history of the ages. The first inhabitants of the sandy and desolate islands of the lagoon were wretched fugitives, escaping from the hordes of Attila in the 5th century, at the time of the attack upon Aquileia. Other fugitives came to join them at the time of the Frankish occupation of Istria in the time of Narses,[1] and still more on the occasion of the Lombard invasion. The islands were thus populated by an exodus which was at first only temporary, but then became permanent. Grado received the greater number of the fugitives from Aquileia, whose bishop assumed the title of patriarch, and became the spiritual head of the new Venetia. Caorle, in the estuary of the Livenza, was peopled by emigrants from Concordia, who were accompanied by their bishop. Next Heracliana was founded, and Aquileia by the Piave. The people of Altinum took

[1] HARTMANN, *op. cit.*, vol. II², pp. 102 *et seq.*

refuge on Torcello, Murano, and Mazzorbo. The refugees from Padua settled at Malamocco and Chioggia. In the beginning the group of islands from which Venice was afterwards to rise were the most sparsely populated: Rialto, Olivolo, Spinalunga, Dorso-duro were occupied only by a few fishers.[1]

In the primitive Venetia of the 6th or 7th century the religious centre was Grado, the political centre Heracliana, and the com-mercial centre Torcello. Escaping from the conquerors on terra firma, the Byzantine administration still survived, represented by a few functionaries and *tribuni*.

Here dwelt a population which was essentially maritime; the words in which Cassiodorus describes it make us think of the inhabitants of the primitive Holland. "It looks from a distance as though the boats were gliding over the meadows, for one does not see their hulls."[2] It will be readily understood that such a life was favourable to the development of energy and ingenuity. In the beginning the people lived by fishing and the manufacture of salt, which their boats carried to the mainland, exchanging it for corn. The only commercial centre of the region was Comacchio at the mouth of the Po, which was frequented by Byzantine ships bringing oil and spices. Comacchio, the seaport for the Po Valley, doubtless profited by the cessation of the Oriental trade with the Gulf of Lyons. A commercial treaty which was made about 715 between the city and Luitprand, in which there is mention of pepper, shows that the port was in communication with the Levant.[3]

Doubtless the Venetians were quick to imitate their neighbours. At all events, Venetian commerce developed in the course of the 8th century. In 787–791 their merchants were excluded from Ravenna at the request of Charlemagne—which proves that they were not willing to acknowledge him as king of the Lombards;[4] and this necessarily meant a closer alliance with Byzantium. Their relations with the Emperor could only be advantageous to them;

---

[1] CH. DIEHL, *Une république patricienne. Venise*, p. 5.
[2] DIEHL, *op. cit.*, p. 7.   [3] R. BUCHNER, *op. cit.*, p. 58.
[4] JAFFÉ-WATTENBACH, *Regesta*, No. 2480.

he was too remote for them to be otherwise. Their ideal was autonomy under one or two Doges, elected by them, and ratified by Byzantium.

From time to time causes of difference arose, when Venice turned toward the Frankish Emperor. In 805, for example, she sent an embassy to Charles in order to place herself under his protectorate. But this step is rather to be referred to party conflicts in the cities, and to disputes with Grado, whose patriarch had already applied to Charles for protection in 803.[1] At this time Venice had just been extending her rule to the small cities of the Dalmatian coast, and was doubtless fearing a reaction on the part of Byzantium. Little note has been taken of this incident, but it was none the less of the greatest importance. Charles, in reply to the embassy of the Venetians, immediately annexed their city to the kingdom of Italy; and this offered his Empire an opportunity of becoming a maritime power and obtaining a foothold in Dalmatia. But it did not avail itself of the opportunity. Byzantium, on the contrary, was quick to see the danger. In the following year Nicephorus despatched a fleet which obtained the immediate submission of Venice. There was no reaction from Charles; he confined himself to offering the patriarch of Grado a refuge in his States.[2]

In 807 the King of Italy, Pippin, concluded a truce with the commander of the fleet, Nicetas, and the Venetians surrendered the culprits to the βασιλεύς, who exiled them. He rewarded his partisans by the titles of spatharius and ὕπατος.[3]

The affair was too tempting to be dropped. In 810 Pippin, having borrowed the shipping of Comacchio, recaptured Venice and the Dalmatian coast.[4] But a Byzantine fleet, under the command of Paul, a prefect of Cephalonia, compelled him immediately to abandon his conquests. He died the same year (July 8th). Charles hastened to invite the Byzantine legates to Aix, where he

---

[1] RICHTER and KOHL, *op. cit.*, vol. II, p. 166.

[2] *Ibid.*, p. 172; HARTMANN, *op. cit.*, vol. III, p. 60.

[3] *Ibid.*, vol. II, p. 178.   [4] HARTMANN, *op. cit.*, vol. III, p. 62.

concluded peace with them, surrendering Venice and the cities of Istria, Liburnia and Dalmatia. This peace became a definite treaty on January 13th, 812: the Carolingian Empire surrendered the sea on which it had just given such striking evidence of its impotence.[1] Venice was definitely beginning to enter the Byzantine orbit, and to mark, on the frontier of the Occident, the commencement of a different world. Her *piazza* proves this more eloquently than all the documents.

The peace of 812 left Venice in an exceptionally favourable situation. It was the condition of her future greatness.[2] On the one hand, her union with the Empire enabled her to expand in the Orient, and this without threatening her autonomy, since the Empire had need of her support in its struggle against Islam. On the other hand, it opened the Occident to her enterprise, for when he renounced the possession of the city Charles acknowledged its right to trade within the Frankish Empire. Secure against attack from the West, Venice had nothing to fear, apart from Comacchio, which held the mouth of the Po. In 875, therefore, she destroyed her rival, who disappeared for good. Henceforth the markets and the ports of Upper Italy—Pavia, Cremona, Milan, and the rest— were dependent upon the commerce of Venice.[3]

There remained the Saracen peril. Here the interest of Venice was the same as that of the Emperor. In 828 he asked for the assistance of her warships. In 840 Venice came to the help of the Empire by sending sixty of her ships; upon which the Musulmans burned Ancona and captured the Venetian vessels.[4] In 867–871 Venice made war upon Bari from the sea, in concert with the Byzantines and Louis II, who attacked the city from the land. But in 872 the Musulmans attacked Dalmatia; and in 875 they besieged Grado. Nevertheless, Venice retained the mastery of the

[1] RICHTER and KOHL, *op. cit.*, vol. II, p. 188; HARTMANN, *op. cit.*, vol. III, p. 64.

[2] HARTMANN, *op. cit.*, vol. III, p. 66.

[3] HARTMANN, *Die Wirtschaftlichen Anfänge Venedigs*, VIERTELJAHRSCHRIFT FÜR SOZIAL UND WIRTSCHAFTSGESCHICHTE, vol. II, 1904, pp. 434–442.

[4] SCHAUBE, *op. cit.*, p. 3.

Adriatic, and by so doing assured navigation to the Levant. This, however, did not by any means prevent Venice from trafficking with Islam. It is true that the Emperor, as early as 814–820, had prohibited trading with the Saracens of Syria and Egypt, but the Venetians traded with the infidel, even while they fought him. It was from Alexandria that a fleet of ten ships brought the relics of Saint Mark to Venice in 827, the Venetians having stolen them unknown to the Christians, as to the Musulmans, of the city.[1]

The most important branch of Venetian trade was the traffic in the Slav slaves of the Dalmatian coast. In 876 the Doge prohibited this trade, but in vain. In the middle of the 9th century the merchants were even selling Christian slaves to the Musulmans.[2]

The commercial treaty concluded between Venice and Lothair in 840,[3] which shows that the city was essentially mercantile, forbade the sale of Christian slaves and of eunuchs. Venice was above all a port and a market. She played the part which had formerly been played by Marseilles. From Venice passengers embarked for the Levant, and from Venice timber for building purposes was exported to Egypt.

From the Orient came spices and silk, which were immediately re-exported to the mainland, to Pavia and Rome.[4] There must also have been some traffic across the Alps,[5] although the amount of this trade would have been insignificant at the period of which we are speaking.

Venice also had as her market the whole of the Dalmatian coast. It was probably with this coast that the busiest trade was carried on.

Compared with the Occident, Venice was another world. The Venetians had the mercantile spirit, and were not embarrassed by

[1] HARTMANN, op. cit., vol. III, p. 68.

[2] SCHAUBE, op. cit., p. 3, No. 3 and p. 22; A. DIPSCH, Die Wirtschaftsentwicklung der Karolingerzeit, vol. II, 2nd ed., 1922, p. 143.

[3] M.G.H. CAPIT., vol. II, p. 130.

[4] THOMPSON, Economic and Social History of the Middle Ages, 1928, p. 267.

[5] R. BUCHNER, op. cit., p. 59.

interdicts relating to *turpe lucrum*.[1] This mentality was merely the mentality which had disappeared in the Western world and in Italy since the Arab conquests, but which still survived in Venice, and in the other Byzantine centres in Southern Italy.

Bari, for example, was still entirely Greek, and retained its Byzantine municipal institutions until the reign of Bohemond.[2] Although Bari was occupied by the Musulmans until 871, their "Soudan" granted permits for navigation to monks going to Jerusalem, and recommended them to the Caliph of Baghdad.[3]

It was the same with Salerno, Naples, Gaeta, and Amalfi on the west coast. These were essentially active seaports, and, like Venice, they maintained only a very loose connection with Byzantium; they also fought for their autonomy against the Duke of Benevento. Their hinterland was far wealthier than that of Venice, for Benevento had retained its gold currency, and they were not far from Rome, which remained, owing to its churches, and the afflux of pilgrims, a great consumer of spices, perfumes, precious fabrics, and even of papyrus. Moreover, in the duchy of Benevento there was still a comparatively refined civilization. Paulus Diaconus taught Greek there to the princess Adelperga; and there Duke Arachis, at the close of the 8th century, built a church of Santa Sofia which he embellished with ornaments brought from Constantinople; he plumed himself upon importing from the Orient silken fabrics, purple, and vases of chiselled gold and silver, as well as products from India, Arabia and Ethiopia.[4]

Emphasis must be laid upon the fact that the dukes of Benevento had retained the gold currency,[5] and even the Byzantine monetary

---

[1] See in this connection the curious history of Saint Géraud of Aurillac. F. L. GANSHOF, *Note sur un passage de la vie de S. Géraud d'Aurillac*, MELANGES JORGA, 1933, pp. 295–307.

[2] BREHIER, *Bulletin historique. Histoire byzantine*, REVUE HISTORIQUE, vol. CLIII, 1926, p. 205.

[3] GAY, *L'Italie meridionale et l'Empire byzantin*, p. 66.

[4] *Ibid.*, pp. 46–48.

[5] They paid their fines in gold *solidi* to the Frankish kings.

system.[1] The continuation of the Mediterranean unity was still visible here, though it disappeared later.

These maritime cities of the South retained a fleet. In 820 there is mention of eight merchant vessels returning from Sardinia to Italy[2] which were captured by Saracen pirates. One must conclude that it was with their ships that the African expedition of Boniface of Tuscany was undertaken in 828, for we know that there was an understanding to this effect between the two Emperors.

The Pope spoke to Charlemagne of the Greek ships (*naves Graecorum gentis*) which he had caused to be burned at Civita Vecchia. Sometimes these ships may have sailed as far as the coast of Provence, and they may have made their appearance in the 9th century at Marseilles and Arles. But the navigation of these cities gravitated toward the Levant, and its orbit was Byzantine. Yet this did not prevent them, any more than the Venetians, from maintaining relations with the Arab ports of Spain and Africa, and even, like the Neapolitans, of coming to the help of the latter in the attack upon Sicily. Such behaviour was due to a mentality like that of the obliging allies who furnished munitions to Germany during the Great War.

In 879 the Greek admiral sent to defend Sicily held up numbers of merchant vessels which, despite the War, were trading between Italy and Sicily. He took such quantities of oil from them—a proof that they were coming from Africa—that the price of this commodity in Constantinople fell to a derisory figure.[3]

This trade between the ports of Southern Italy and the Musulmans was also a trade in slaves. The Pope rebuked them for it.[4] Already, in 836, the treaty between Naples and the Duke of Benevento granted the merchants of the city the widest commercial liberty within the duchy, to which they were probably indispensable. But it forbade them to buy Lombard slaves for the purpose

---

[1] ENGEL and SERRURE, *Traité de numismatique*, p. 288.
[2] *Annales regni Francorum*, a° 820, ed. KURZE, M.G.H. SS. *in us. schol.*, p. 153: *In Italico mari octo naves negotiatorum de Sardinia ad Italium revertentium.*
[3] GAY, *op. cit.*, p. 112.   [4] *Ibid.*, p. 33.

of selling them again.[1] From this we learn that these slaves came from Lombardy; that is to say, from the Frankish Empire.

Yet these same vendors of human flesh and blood won, in 849, a great naval victory off Ostia for the Pope. And Saint Januarius was as greatly venerated in Naples as was Saint Mark in Venice.

Of these cities, Amalfi was the most purely mercantile. It possessed only a small mountainous territory, whose forests provided it with the timber which its vessels carried as far afield as Syria.[2]

In other respects there was no understanding between these mercantile centres and the Duke of Benevento. There was no understanding even between the different cities. About 830 Naples, the better to resist the Duke, obtained support from the Saracens. She allied herself with them again, about 870, against her rival Amalfi, and then, in 880, against the Byzantine influence, which since the reign of Basil I had once more become effective.[3] At this moment Gaeta also effected a rapprochement with the Saracens, but then reverted to the Pope, who made concessions to its *hypatos*.[4] In 875 some ships recruited from all the Southern cities, in co-operation with a Saracen fleet, pillaged the Roman coast, and Louis II declared that Naples had become another Africa.[5] In 877 Pope John VIII sought in vain, by means of money and excommunication, to detach Amalfi from the Saracens. However, that same year this city undertook to protect the coast of Southern Italy from Saracen attack.[6]

At first sight, nothing could appear more confused than the policy of these commercial cities. It is explained, however, by their constant and exclusive anxiety to protect their commerce. Their alliances with the Musulmans did not prevent them from resisting to the utmost any attempt at conquest on the part of the latter.

In 856 the Saracens, with the object of obtaining possession of Southern Italy, which they attacked simultaneously through Bari

[1] GAY, *op.cit*, pp. 41–42.   [2] *Ibid.*, p. 49.
[3] *Ibid.*, pp. 98 and 127.   [4] *Ibid.*, p. 128.
[5] *Ibid.*, p. 98.   [6] HARTMANN, *op. cit.*, vol. III², p. 35.

182

and from the West, made an attempt upon Naples, and destroyed Misenum.[1] Although the cities were perfectly willing to trade with the Saracens, they had no intention of falling under their yoke, nor of allowing them to obtain control over their home waters. Their policy in this respect was precisely like that of the Venetians. They distrusted everybody but themselves, and had no intention of obeying anyone. But they were implacable rivals, and had no hesitation in allying themselves with the Musulmans in order to destroy one another. Thus, in 843, Naples helped the Musulmans to wrest Messina from the Byzantine Empire to which Naples itself belonged. But the subjection of these cities to Byzantium was purely nominal. They took action only when their prosperity was directly threatened. For this reason they did not support the efforts of Lothair against the Musulmans in 846, nor those of Louis II at a later date.[2] Gay very truly says: "By an invincible force, the maritime States, Gaeta, Naples, Amalfi, were constantly led to ally themselves with the Saracens. . . . For them the essential thing was to protect the coast and safeguard their commercial interests. By negotiating with the Saracens they obtained their share of the booty and continued to enrich themselves. The policy of Naples and Amalfi was above all the policy of merchants who lived by pillage as much as by regular trade."[3] This was why they did not help the Emperor to defend Sicily. Their policy was that of the Dutch in Japan in the 17th century. For that matter, with whom could they have traded if they had neglected the Musulman coasts? The Orient was monopolized by Venice.

To summarize the situation: The Christian Mediterranean was divided into two basins, the East and the West, surrounded by Islamic countries. These latter, the war of conquest having come to an end by the close of the 9th century, constituted a world apart, self-sufficing, and gravitating toward Baghdad. It was toward this central point that the caravans of Asia made their

---

[1] HARTMANN, op. cit., vol. III¹, p. 249.   [2] M.G.H. CAPIT., vol. II, p. 67.
[3] GAY, op. cit., p. 129.

way, and here ended the great trade route which led to the Baltic, by way of the Volga. It was from Baghdad that produce was exported to Africa and Spain. The Musulmans themselves did not trade with the Christians, but they did not close their ports to the latter. They allowed them to frequent their harbours, to bring them slaves and timber, and to carry away whatever they chose to buy.

Christian navigation, however, continued active only in the Orient, and the furthermost point of Southern Italy remained in communication with the Orient. Byzantium succeeded in preventing Islam from obtaining the mastery of the sea. Ships continued to sail from Venice along the Adriatic coast and the coast of Greece to the great city on the Bosphorus. And further, they did not cease to frequent the Musulman ports of Asia Minor, Egypt, Africa, Sicily and Spain. The ever-increasing prosperity of the Musulman countries, once the period of expansion was over, benefited the maritime cities of Italy. Thanks to this prosperity, in Southern Italy and in the Byzantine Empire an advanced civilization survived, with cities, a gold currency, and professional merchants: in short, a civilization which had retained its ancient foundations.

In the Occident, on the contrary, the coast from the Gulf of Lyons and the Riviera to the mouth of the Tiber, ravaged by war and the pirates, whom the Christians, having no fleet, were powerless to resist, was now merely a solitude and a prey to piracy. The ports and the cities were deserted. The link with the Orient was severed, and there was no communication with the Saracen coasts. There was nothing but death. The Carolingian Empire presented the most striking contrast with the Byzantine. It was purely an inland power, for it had no outlets. The Mediterranean territories, formerly the most active portions of the Empire, which supported the life of the whole, were now the poorest, the most desolate, the most constantly menaced. For the first time in history the axis of Occidental civilization was displaced towards the North, and for many centuries it remained between the Seine and the

Rhine. And the Germanic peoples, which had hitherto played only the negative part of destroyers, were now called upon to play a positive part in the reconstruction of European civilization.

The classic tradition was shattered, because Islam had destroyed the ancient unity of the Mediterranean.

CHAPTER II

THE CAROLINGIAN COUP D'ÉTAT
AND THE VOLTE-FACE OF THE PAPACY

1. *The Merovingian Decadence*

Of all the States which the Germans founded in the Occident at the close of the 5th century in the basin of the Mediterranean, the two which had the most brilliant beginnings, the Vandal and Ostrogothic kingdoms, had fallen under the attacks of Justinian. In 629 the Visigoths reconquered from the Empire the scrap of territory which it still retained in the Peninsula.[1] The Franks had remained intact. As for the Lombards, it seemed for a moment that they were about to reconstitute the kingdom of Italy for their own benefit. The fact that the Empire was compelled to defend itself against the Persians had favoured their enterprise; and it had been necessary, in order to cope with them, to have recourse to a Frankish alliance, which was not without its dangers. However, just as the victory of Heraclius seemed to portend a resumption of the Byzantine offensive, Islam suddenly made its irruption into the Empire.

Before this irruption the Empire finally retreated. It had lost Africa, and its Italian possessions were menaced by the Musulmans established in Sicily. The Visigoths had been annihilated. The Franks, though Islam had broken through in the South, had made a recovery at Poitiers; notwithstanding which they were cut off from the sea. The Lombards alone had not yet encountered the attacks of Islam, which, on the contrary, had actually been advantageous to them, for they had loosened the grip of Byzantium, now obliged to turn to the Eastern front; and, on the other hand, they had protected them against the Frankish peril.

It was, however, reserved for France, having checked the conti-

[1] LOT, PFISTER and GANSHOF, *Histoire du Moyen Age*, vol. I, p. 237.

nental expansion of Islam in the West, to reconstitute Europe upon new foundations.

It was on France that the future depended. But France, as she appeared at this moment, was very different from the France of the Merovingians. Her centre of gravity was no longer inside "Romania." It had shifted towards the Germanic North, and with this new France there appeared, for the first time, a political force which ceased to gravitate toward the Mediterranean, where Islam was predominant. With the Carolingians Europe finally assumed a new orientation. Until their advent Europe had continued to live the life of antiquity. But all the traditional conditions were overthrown by Islam. The Carolingians were to find themselves in a situation which was not of their making, but having found it they exploited it in such away as to open up a new epoch. The part which they played is only to be explained by the change of equilibrium imposed on the world by Islam. The *coup d'état* by which they replaced the Merovingian dynasty, the only dynasty which had subsisted since the invasions, was itself very largely explained by the closing of the Mediterranean by the Saracens. This will become obvious if we study the Merovingian decadence without prejudice. If it has not been sufficiently realized, this is because the Frankish period has always been regarded as a whole, in which the Carolingians appeared, so to speak, as the continuation of the Merovingians; and it has been held that this continuity was manifest in the laws and the institutions of the age as well as in its economy and social organization. As a matter of fact, there was an essential difference between the Merovingian epoch and the Carolingian period. To begin with, the European situations with which they were respectively confronted offer a complete contrast. Fustel de Coulanges has very truly said: "If we consider the one hundred and fifty years that follow the death of Clovis . . . we shall realize that the people did not greatly differ from what they had been in the last century of the Empire. But if, on the other hand, we transport ourselves to the 8th and the 9th centuries, we shall see that society, under externals which were perhaps more Roman, was absolutely different from what it had been under Roman authority."[1] Waitz was perfectly right to divide these two epochs, just as Brunner was wrong to unite them.

The break between the two worlds was made final with Pippin's *coup d'état*. But it had long been coming. The Merovingian State, after the death of Dagobert I in 639, had been passing through a prolonged period of decadence. And this decadence was essentially the decadence of the monarchy. We have already seen that the royal power was absolute, a feature which it had adopted from the Roman Empire. If the State was to be governed at all the king had to retain the power of asserting his will; and, for that matter, neither he nor this mode of government encountered opposition of any kind, whether national or political.[2] The very partitions by which populations and territories were so frequently divided were essentially the affair of kings dividing up their inheritance. The peoples were indifferent to such changes. The prestige of the dynasty was very great, and the only explanation of this prestige is to be found in the Church, for it cannot be explained by any kind of Germanic sentiment.

It was in Germania itself that Grimoald, the son of Pippin I, attempted in 656 to usurp the place of the lawful king, which excited the indignation of the Franks and led to the arrest and execution of the culprit.[3]

The king relied upon the support of the Church, which he protected and actually dominated. In 644, when the monarchy was beginning to decline, Sigebert III was still forbidding the convocation of synods without his authorization.[4]

The Merovingian decadence is generally dated back to Clotair II's edict of 614. But it seems to me that this edict was a means of

---

[1] FUSTEL DE COULANGES, *L'invasion germanique et la fin de l'Empire*, p. 559.

[2] FUSTEL DE COULANGES, *Les transformations de la royauté pendant l'époque carolingienne*, p. 85.

[3] RICHTER, *Annalen des Fränk. Reichs im Zeitalter der Merowinger*, p. 168.

[4] RICHTER, *op. cit.*, p. 167.

securing the support of the Church by strengthening its position; above all, by granting privileges of jurisdiction.[1]

In any case, Dagobert I was still a great king, who made war upon the Germans, and enjoyed a position in Europe such as none of his predecessors had enjoyed since the reign of Theodebert.

Under the Merovingians the Frankish kingdom was a power which filled an international rôle, and was guided by an unvarying policy; which was, to install itself securely on the shores of the Mediterranean. Ever since their settlement in Gaul the Merovingians had endeavoured to reach Provence. Theodoric had warded them off, whereupon they turned their attention to Spain, and engaged in a conflict with the Visigoths.[2]

Justinian's war against the Ostrogoths was presently to give them access to the sea. The Emperor having solicited their help in 535, Vitiges, in order to prevent an alliance between the Emperor and the Franks, ceded Provence to them, which Theodoric had formerly prevented them from conquering from the Visigoths.[3] Installed upon the coast, and seeking to obtain a foothold in Italy, Theodebert allied himself for the moment with the Ostrogoths, to whom he sent an army 10,000 strong.[4] But before long, turning at once against the Goths and the Byzantines, he conquered in 539 the greater part of Venetia and Liguria.[5]

At this time the monarchy was so vigorous that almost as soon as the Italian campaign ended, Childebert and Clotair resumed the war against the Visigoths (542), seized Pampeluna, and ravaged the valley of the Ebro; but they were defeated before Saragossa and were finally repulsed by Theudes.[6]

The check suffered in Spain once more threw the Frankish kings against Italy. In 552 a Frankish army, reinforced by Alamans,

---

[1] FUSTEL DE COULANGES, Les transformations de la royauté pendant l'époque carolingienne, p. 9, can see absolutely nothing in the Edict of 614 to indicate a decline of the monarchy. For the contrary opinion, see LOT in LOT, PFISTER and GANSHOF, Histoire du Moyen Age, vol. I, pp. 321–322.

[2] RICHTER, op. cit., pp. 49 and 53.

[3] HARTMANN, op. cit., vol. I, p. 267.   [4] Ibid., pp. 282–283.

[5] Ibid., p. 284. Cf. RICHTER, op. cit., p. 57.   [6] RICHTER, op. cit., p. 58.

once more marched into the Peninsula, making war upon the Imperial troops and pillaging the country, until its remnants, decimated by sickness and crushed by Narses, were compelled to retreat into Gaul.

Vanquished in the field, the Franks succeeded in obtaining an important province by political means. In 567 the Visigothic territory between the Garonne and the Pyrenees became Frankish on the marriage of Chilperic and Galswintha.[1]

For the Merovingians, the arrival of the Lombards in Italy was a fresh cause of war in that country.

The Lombards had attacked Provence in 568. Being repulsed, they invaded it afresh in 575.[2] In 583, at the request of Pope Pelagius II, who implored his intervention against the Lombards, Childebert II formed an alliance against them with the Emperor Maurice (who paid for this alliance with 50,000 gold *solidi*), and despatched a Frankish army which fought in Italy, though without success, until the year 585.[3]

The same year, however (585), Gontran attacked Septimania. His forces were repulsed with great loss by Reccared, the son of Leovigild. But the state of hostility continued. In 589 Gontran renewed his attack, but this time he suffered a final defeat near Carcassonne.[4]

This defeat of the Frankish arms appeared all the more serious inasmuch as in 568 Childebert's army had been defeated by the Lombards in Italy,[5] which in 589 led the king to conclude peace with them.

But Childebert had not renounced his Italian policy. In the following year (590) he despatched a fresh expedition against the Lombards. It was unsuccessful, and this time he had to resign himself to concluding peace.[6]

Dagobert, the last great king of the Merovingian dynasty, continued this policy of intervention in Italy and Spain. In 605 he

[1] RICHTER, *op. cit.*, p. 69.　　　　[2] *Ibid.*, pp. 70 and 72.
[3] *Ibid.*, p. 81.　　　　[4] *Ibid.*, pp. 87 and 93.
[5] *Ibid.*, p. 92.　　　　[6] *Ibid.*, p. 94.

allied himself with the Emperor Heraclius, and in 630 he supported the Visigothic pretender Sisenand against King Svinthila.[1] Dagobert was the last representative of the traditional policy of his dynasty. After him there was no further political intervention in Italy or in Spain, apart from one expedition—which was unsuccessful—in 662–663.[2]

The monarchy was also growing weaker in the North; in Germania, Thuringia became independent, and Bavaria almost so, and the Saxons assumed a threatening attitude. Thus from 630–632 the Merovingian State, retreating within itself, fell into a condition of decadence. To this, no doubt, the incessant civil conflicts between the kings contributed, as well as the conflict between Fredegond and Brunehaut; and then the intrigues of Brunehaut, until her hideous death in 613. But it must be remembered that until 613 these civil conflicts had been the general rule. What rendered them more serious thenceforth was the continued minority of the kings. When Chilperic II ascended the throne in 715 it was twenty-five years since any Frankish king had lived to reach his majority. The explanation may be found in the debauchery and the sexual excesses of these princes, to whom everything was permitted. Most of them were doubtless degenerates. Clovis II died insane. It was this that gave the Merovingian decadence its dismal aspect, which contrasted so greatly with the decadence of the Roman Emperors of the West, and later, with that of the Carolingians. None of these kings had any influence whatever; they were puppets in the hands of the mayors of the palace, against whom they did not even attempt to react. Not one of them attempted to have his mayor of the palace assassinated, as the Emperors had formerly done at Ravenna; on the contrary, it was often they who were assassinated. They lived under the tutelage of their mothers, and sometimes of their aunts. But since the days of Brunehaut, who was, however, a Visigoth, the queens were chosen for their beauty. Queen Nautechild was a servant (*puella de*

[1] RICHTER, *op. cit.*, pp. 159 and 161.
[2] HARTMANN, *op. cit.*, vol. II, p. 247.

191

ministerio), with whom Dagobert had an intrigue. The result of all this was that the mayor of the palace became omnipotent. His position was like that of the Japanese Shogun.

The shrinking of the resources at the disposal of the Merovingian kings in the 7th century subjected them more and more to the influence of the territorial aristocracy, whose power continually increased. Naturally, as the aristocracy has always done, it sought to obtain control of the monarchy, and therefore to render it elective.

So long as the king was powerful he was able to hold the aristocracy in check. He made such appointments as he chose in the counties, and also, in actual fact, in the bishoprics. He condemned whomsoever he thought fit on a charge of *lèse-majesté*, which, thanks to the subsequent confiscation, enriched his treasury. So long as the treasury provided him with sufficient resources he had in his hands an admirable *instrumentum regni*. It should be noted that since the *tonlieux* belonged to the king the treasury was abundantly supplied so long as commerce continued to flourish.

This treasury enabled the king to maintain a royal *trustis* or bodyguard, which might really be called his permanent army.[1]

Now, if the "antrustions" were to remain loyal to their oath, when the kings themselves were continually setting the example of perjury, they had to be paid. But the treasury, which was the actual basis of the royal power, began to dwindle in the course of the 7th century. In the first place, it could no longer count on the booty of foreign war. There were no longer any foreign wars, and there were no more Byzantine subsidies. The king was by no means a "landed proprietor" entirely dependent on his estates.[2] For proof of this we need only read Gregory of Tours. He did of course possess numbers of estates and of *villae*, which constituted his fisc. He was able to give them generously and even

[1] GUILHIERMOZ, *Essai sur les origines de la noblesse*, p. 70.
[2] LOT, PFISTER and GANSHOF, *op. cit.*, pp. 318–320.

squander them for the benefit of his friends, and of the churches, which he overwhelmed with favours.[1]

But I find no mention, in Gregory of Tours, of the political influence exercised by means of this property. So long as the king was powerful in other respects, he could take back what he had given. And I can hardly see how, with all this continual distribution, he could base his power upon the territorial fisc, the apportionment of which was constantly varying. Everything indicates that it was the impost that constituted the bulk of his revenue. Fustel de Coulanges considers that this alone was enough to enrich the monarchy and satisfy all the needs of its government.[2]

But how was it that this impost, a legacy inherited from Rome, which had never been suppressed, was beginning to yield less and less? According to Fustel de Coulanges, we must look for the explanation in the obduracy of the bishops, and the immunities granted to magnates and dignitaries, both secular and ecclesiastical. In this case it was the king himself who sapped the basis of his power.[3] In the same way the yield of the *tonlieux* seem to have been continually reduced by the exemptions which he granted.

But we still have to find some explanation for this policy of the kings, which ended by destroying the very basis of their power. Why did they not grant the impost itself, as was sometimes done later? They undoubtedly granted exemptions, but they did not surrender the rights of the crown. Moreover, the exemptions from taxation—that is to say, from the *tonlieux*—affected only the monasteries, and the main circulation of merchandise was certainly not due to them. It was due, of course, to commerce. And we

---

[1] The very immensity of the donations in land made by the kings, which, according to LOT, PFISTER and GANSHOF, *op. cit.*, p. 340, made the clergy wealthier than at any other period, indicates that the kings cannot have attributed any very great importance to these lands, or to their products, or even to the impost which they yielded. It must therefore be accepted that the *teloneum* constituted by far the greater part of their resources.

[2] FUSTEL, *Les transformations*, pp. 29 et seq.

[3] See all the examples given by FUSTEL DE COULANGES, *Les transformations*, pp. 32 *et seq.*, of the remission or abolition of the land tax. Concerning exemptions, see LOT, PFISTER and GANSHOF, *op. cit.*, pp. 316–317.

must agree that as commerce diminished the indirect taxes—that is, the tolls or dues—must have diminished in proportion. Now, as we have already seen, the decline of commerce must have begun about the year 650, a date which exactly corresponds with the progress of anarchy in the kingdom. The pecuniary resources of the king had certainly diminished enormously by the end of the 7th century. We have a curious proof of this in the fact that in 695 the king gave the *villa* of Massigny to the Abbot of Saint Denis in return for the surrender by the latter of a perpetual pension of 300 *solidi* which he was drawing from the treasury. Thus the king preferred his monetary resources to his land.[1]

We cannot doubt that these resources depended principally upon tolls imposed on the circulation of merchandise. The collection of such tolls was infinitely easier than the collection of the land tax, and met with hardly any resistance. There is no evidence that the bishops intervened in this connection. However, the land tax was certainly retained, as well as the *tonlieu*, but it yielded less and less. No doubt the magnates, taking advantage of the increasing weakness of the king, wrested from him an increasing number of privileges of immunity. But it would be a mistake to regard these immunities as the cause of the king's weakness; they were in reality a consequence of it.

It seems evident, then, that the impairment of the treasury, which had the effect of weakening the monarchy and the State, was due above all to the increasing anaemia of commerce.[2] Now this was due to the disappearance of maritime commerce resulting from the expansion of Islam along the coasts of the Mediterranean. And the decadence of commerce must have been felt especially in Neustria, where the commercial cities were situated. This explains

---

[1] H. PIRENNE, *Le Cellarium fisci*, BULLETIN DE LA CLASSE DES LETTRES DE L'ACADÉMIE ROYALE DE BELGIQUE, 1930, p. 202.

[2] The reader must not imagine that I am exaggerating the importance of commerce. Regarded from the absolute point of view it was doubtless small enough; but the commerce of the Middle Ages was not very extensive, yet consider what resulted from the prohibitions effecting English wools, for example, in the 13th and 14th centuries!

why this part of the kingdom, which had been the foundation of the royal power, was destined gradually to surrender its commerce to Austrasia, whose life was evidently less dependent on a monetary economy. As for the impost, it was not collected from the Bavarians or the Thuringians; as regards the Saxons, we know that they paid 500 cows as tribute.[1] It is certain, therefore, that the regions of the North which were essentially agricultural were much less affected by the decadence of commerce. Thus it is easily understood that after the collapse of the urban and commercial economy the movement of restoration was bound to come from them. The decline of commerce, by concentrating the whole life of the country on the soil, gave the aristocracy a power that could not be thwarted. In Neustria the aristocracy immediately endeavoured to take advantage of the king's increasing weakness. The monarchy, of course, attempted to resist. The policy of Brunehaut was revived, as far as we can judge from our scanty information, by the mayor of the palace, Ebroin. The despotism of which he was accused in 664 was undoubtedly explained by his attempt to maintain the royal administration—that is to say, administration in the Roman manner—with its royal personnel, which attempted to impose its will upon all, even upon the magnates.

One may regard the assassination of Ebroin in 680 or 683 as marking the final defeat of the kings in their struggle against the magnates. Now at this moment, which coincided approximately with the taking of Carthage, the maritime commerce was reduced almost to nonentity.

Henceforth the king was in the hands of the aristocracy. He may have attempted, in order to continue his resistance, to find support in the Church. But the Church itself was lapsing into anarchy. To realize this we have only to read the episcopal lists drawn up by Mgr. Duchesne.[2] The yshow that the disorder of the churches was infinitely greater in the South of Gaul than in

---

[1] F. LOT, *La conquête du pays d'entre Seine-et-Loire par les Francs*, REVUE HISTORIQUE, vol. CLXV, 1930, pp. 249–251.

[2] *Fastes épiscopaux de l'ancienne Gaule*, 3 vols.

the North. Generally speaking, the bishops of the South, whose influence had been preponderant in the Church of Gaul, disappeared about 680, and did not reappear until the close of the 8th century. We must, of course, allow for the fact that names may have been lost by accident, but the disappearance was so general that we are bound to attribute it to a deep-seated cause.

At Perigueux, after Ermenomaris (673–675) there were no further bishops until the 10th century.[1] It was the same at Agen.[2] At Bordeaux there were none between 673–675 and 814,[3] and at Mende none between 627 and the reign of Louis the Pious.[4] At Limoges there was an interruption of a century in the series of bishops after Emenus,[5] and at Cahors after Beto (673–675);[6] at Auch the bishops did not make their appearance again until 836.[7] There is no mention of any bishop at Lectoure,[8] Saint Bertrand de Comminges, Saint Lizier, Aire, or Autun between 696 and 762,[9] at Châlons between 675 and 779,[10] at Geneva between 650 and 833,[11] at Die between 614 and 788,[12] at Arles between 683 and 794.[13] There were similar interruptions at Orange, Avignon, Carpentras, Marseilles, Toulon (697–879), Aix (596–794), Antibes (660–788), Embrun (677–828, Béziers (693–788), Nîmes (680–788), Lodève (683–817), Uzès (675–788), Agde (683–788), Maguelonne (683–788), Carcassonne (683–788), and Elne (683–788).[14] According to Lot, the last Council held in Gaul was 695, and there was not another until 742.[15]

We note also the disappearance of the synods in the last third of the 7th century. There were none in the 8th century under Pippin and Carloman. Leblanc also notes the increasing rarity of inscriptions.

[1] DUCHESNE, op. cit., vol. II, p. 88.
[2] Ibid., vol. II, p. 64.
[3] Ibid., vol. II, p. 62.
[4] Ibid., vol. II, p. 55.
[5] Ibid., vol. II, p. 52.
[6] Ibid., vol. II, pl. 46.
[7] Ibid., vol. II, p. 97.
[8] Ibid., vol. II, p. 98.
[9] Ibid., vol. II, p. 181.
[10] Ibid., vol. II, p. 194.
[11] Ibid., vol. I, p. 229.
[12] Ibid., vol. I, p. 235.
[13] Ibid., vol. I, p. 261.
[14] Ibid., vol. I, passim.
[15] LOT, PFISTER and GANSHOF, op. cit., p. 332.

In view of the considerable influence which the bishops had exercised in the cities since the 7th century, we are obliged to conclude that the urban institutions had lapsed into a state of decadence; and doubtless whatever they had been able to preserve of their *curiae* disappeared in the midst of this anarchy.

The urban life which had been maintained by the influence of commerce was obliterated. The Mediterranean sources of commerce, which the invasions of the 5th century had not seriously affected, were dried up now that the sea was closed.

It is characteristic of the times that the great senatorial families which had furnished the ecclesiastical personnel of the dioceses and the great lay officers of the administration became increasingly rare in this profoundly changed environment.[1] It is evident that from the middle of the 7th century society was becoming rapidly de-Romanized, and the process was complete, or nearly so, by the beginning of the 8th century. It was the same population, but it was no longer the same civilization.

There is evidence to this effect. According to the *Vita* of Saint Didier of Cahors (§ 655), the city, which was flourishing under his episcopacy, fell into a condition of atrophy after his death.[2] Similarly, Lyons, where there was still one great merchant in 601, fell into a frightful state of decadence, which had reached its maximum when, about 800, Leidrad wrote his report to Charlemagne.[3]

The anarchy which descended upon Gaul in consequence of the decadence of the royal power led to the dismemberment of the country. From 675–680 Aquitaine became a separate duchy, with a life of its own.

On the other hand, Austrasia—which had not been affected by the disappearance of commerce and of the cities, where the royal administration was less highly developed, and where society gravi-

---

[1] The last mention of a person of senatorial rank in Gaul dates from the beginning of the 8th century. LOT, PFISTER and GANSHOF, *op. cit.*, p. 311, No. 69.
[2] Ed. POUPARDIN, p. 56.
[3] COVILLE, *Recherches sur l'histoire de Lyon*, 1928, p. 283.

tated entirely about the great domains—assumed an increasingly marked preponderance. At the head of its aristocracy the family of the Pippins made its appearance, which had already played an important part in the events that led to the fall of Brunehaut. It was a family of great Belgian landowners.[1] About 640 Itte, the wife of Pippin I (of Landen) founded the monastery of Nivelles, and her generosity enabled the Irish apostle Saint Phelan to found the *monasterium Scottorum* at Fosses. Lierneux—a family estate— was presented by Pippin II, between 687 and 714, to the monastery of Stavelot-Malmedy.[2]

In 691 Begge, the wife of Ansegise and the mother of Pippin II, founded at Andenne a monastery to which she withdrew, and where she ended her days in 693. Pippin II gave to Saint Ursmar, abbot of Loddes between 697 and 713, the *villae* of Leernes and Trazegnies.[3] They had a strong fortress at Chèvremont, which constituted part of their domain of Jupille. Not far away, at Herstal, on the Meuse, was a residence which was to become one of their favourite dwellings, and which is often referred to, as a *palatium*, after 752. It was in this region, on the edge of the forest of Ardennes, that they felt themselves to be really at home. True countryfolk as they were, they seem to have felt nothing but dislike for the residence of Metz, which was the capital of Austrasia. It was at Liège that Grimoald, the son of Pippin II, was killed in 714 by a Frisian. In 741 Carloman and Pippin the Short imprisoned their brother Grifon at Chèvremont, after the death of Charles Martel.

Besides their Walloon estates they had many others in Germany, but the region of Liège was their native country, the country in which the name of Pippin was so frequently met with even in the Middle Ages, and where it survives to this day in Pepinster.

For the first time, here was a family of the North, at least semi-

---

[1] F. ROUSSEAU, *La Meuse et le pays mosan en Belgique*, Namur, 1930, pp. 45 and 221 (ANNALES DE LA SOCIÉTÉ D'ARCHÉOLOGIE DE NAMUR, vol. XLI).

[2] *Recueil des chartes de Stavelot-Malmedy*, ed. ROLAND and J. HALKIN, vol. I, p. 39.   [3] F. ROUSSEAU, *op. cit.*, p. 226.

Germanic, by law a family of the Ripuarian Franks, without senatorial connections, and in any case without any Roman alliances, which was about to play the leading part in the State. The Carolingians were not well adapted to the Neustrian environment, which was hostile to them. This explains why, whereas the first Pippin was incontestably able to impose his influence upon the king while the latter remained in Austrasia, he had no influence over him when he settled in Neustria.[1] This undoubtedly gave rise to discontent among the magnates of Austrasia, in consequence of which Dagobert I, in 632, appointed his son, the future Sigebert III, his viceroy.

Thus, in this "Francia," where there was not the slightest trace of national hostility so long as there was a strong monarchy, division began to appear, directly the monarchy became decadent, in the visible opposition which manifested itself between Romanism and Germanism.[2]

In these regions of the North, the domains of the Salic Law and the Ripuarian Law, manners were far less civilized than in the South; indeed, there were still pagans here. And in proportion as the power of the monarch declined, the influence of the regional aristocracies became more and more preponderant, manifesting itself very perceptibly in the recruitment of the regional authorities and the clergy.[3]

Now, the Pippins were the heads of this Austrasian aristocracy, which was attempting to shake off the tutelage of the palace and secure for itself certain hereditary functions, and which manifested a marked antipathy for the Romans of Neustria. When they imposed themselves upon the monarchy as mayors of the palace it was felt

---

[1] RICHTER, op. cit., p. 159.

[2] One may perhaps already detect some signs of this in the Vita S. Eligii, II, 20, M.G.H. SS. RER. MEROV., col. IV, p. 712, where during his apostolate in the north of Gaul the saint is addressed in the following words: *Nunquam tu, Romane, quamvis haec frequenter taxes, consuetudines nostras evellere poteris.*

[3] H. WIERUSZOWSKI, op. cit., BONNER JAHRBÜCHER, 1921, states that under the Pippins the clergy became Germanized, but this process certainly began in Austrasia.

at once that their action was definitely hostile to the absolutism of the sovereign; it was anti-Roman and, one might say, "anti-antique."

In Neustria Ebroin represented a tendency which was the exact opposite of that of the Pippins. The king being a minor, he was appointed by the magnate to exercise the sovereign power.[1]

He at once attempted to dominate the aristocracy, to which he himself did not belong, and to make an end of the hereditary rights of the palatine families, and he seems to have given employment to men of humble birth, who owed him everything (656). This policy was naturally resisted by the great families, at the head of which we find Saint Leger, since 659 Bishop of Autun.

There was a visible conflict between the defenders of the royal power and the aristocracy. It is a characteristic fact that the kings themselves played no part in this conflict.

On the death of Clotair III (573), Ebroin, fearing the intervention of the magnates, immediately placed Thierry III on the throne. But the magnates, who now claimed the right of intervening in the appointment of the king, refused to acknowledge Thierry, choosing as king his brother Childeric II.[2]

This time it was a representative of the aristocracy, Saint Leger, who actually exercised the supreme power. He forced the king to make large concessions to the magnates: henceforth the high officials could not be sent from one country to another. This still further increased the influence of the magnates, whose authority began to assume a kind of hereditary character; yet this measure, imposed by the aristocracy, was not to the advantage of the Pippinides. Here we may note that opposition between the South and the North, of which we have already spoken, and no doubt one of the motives of this opposition was to prevent the new king, who had been set upon the throne with the help of the Austrasian aristocracy, from imposing upon Neustria magnates of Austrasian origin.[3]

[1] See the texts in FUSTEL DE COULANGES, *Les transformations*, p. 80.
[2] FUSTEL DE COULANGES, *op. cit.*, p. 100.   [3] *Ibid.*, p. 101.

The office of mayor of the palace was suppressed in Neustria and in Burgundy, but Vulfoald remained the mayor of the palace in Austrasia. It seems that some attempt was made to establish a rotation of magnates in the palace. But the magnates could not agree together, and Childeric II took this opportunity of getting rid of Leger, whom he banished to Luxeuil (675). The reaction of the magnates was prompt: that same year Childeric II was assassinated. Thierry III succeeded to the throne. But in the revulsion of feeling which followed this murder Ebroin was restored to power, being elevated to the dignity of mayor of the palace. The result of this, says Fustel de Coulanges,[1] was "enormous changes in respect of functions and dignities." The entire personnel of the palace was changed. Leger was sentenced to death, having first been blinded, in accordance with the Byzantine custom.[2] The whole aristocratic party formed a solid opposition against Ebroin, and it now set all its hopes upon Pippin, who in Austrasia had assumed the dignity of mayor of the palace on the death of Vulfoald. By what right? Doubtless as the descendant of Pippin I and Grimoald;[3] that is to say, by virtue of that very principle of heredity which Ebroin was opposing in Neustria. Pippin, in Austrasia, exercised a *de facto* power; the chroniclers have laid stress upon this, saying of him: "*dominabatur in Austria.*"[4] The difference between the power which he claimed and that which Ebroin exercised was flagrant. Unlike Ebroin, he was not a functionary. He owed his power to the marriages of his family, and to the fact that he was the recognized leader of the aristocracy which was beginning to group itself about him. If we are to believe the *Annales Mettenses*, "many of the *grandi* of Neustria, cruelly treated by Ebroin, passed from Neustria into Austrasia and took refuge with Pippin." (681). Thus Austrasia, Frankish by race, was becoming the protagonist of the aristocracy.[5]

Since the death of Dagobert II—that is to say, since his assas-

---

[1] FUSTEL DE COULANGES, *op. cit.*, p. 106.   [2] RICHTER, *op. cit.*, p. 173.

[3] Ansegisus, the father of Pippin, was not mayor of the palace.

[4] FUSTEL DE COULANGES, *op. cit.*, p. 168.   [5] *Ibid.*, p. 178.

sination, perhaps at the instigation of Ebroin, in 679—there was no longer a king in Austrasia. Pippin, who had succeeded, as mayor, to Vulfoald, who was doubtless overthrown on this occasion, marched against Ebroin, but was defeated near Laon.[1] Ebroin was assassinated shortly afterwards, in 680 or 683, by Ermenfridus, who sought refuge in Austrasia with Pippin. It is very difficult to feel assured that Pippin was not involved in this affair.

Ebroin having been assassinated, Waratton succeeded him as mayor of the palace in Neustria; he immediately made peace with Pippin. But he was overthrown by his son Gislemar, who marched against Pippin, and defeated him at Namur. Gislemar, it seems, was assassinated. Waratton, once more mayor of the palace, confirmed the peace which he had signed with Pippin in 683. He died in 686, and his son-in-law Berchier succeeded to him.[2]

He immediately encountered the opposition of the magnates; of these the majority, and among them the Bishop of Reims, rallied to Pippin. The latter marched against Berchier and Thierry III, defeating them at Tertry, near Saint Quentin, in 687. Berchier was assassinated in 688, and Pippin was acknowledged by the king as mayor of the palace. Henceforward he was the only mayor of the palace in the whole kingdom. But he was so far from regarding himself as the servant of the king that he did not even establish himself at the court. He sent the king one of his confidential supporters: *Nordebertum quondam de suis*,[3] and he himself returned to Austrasia.

2. *The Carolingian Mayors of the Palace*

In 688, then, the mayor of the palace of Austrasia imposed his tutelage on the kingdom. But he did not remain beside the king. It was enough for him that he had conquered his rival, the mayor

[1] RICHTER, *op. cit.*, 174.

[2] RICHTER, *op. cit.*, p. 175. According to the *Liber Historiae Francorum* M.G.H. SS. RER. MEROV., vol. II, p. 322, *circa* 48, he was *statura pusillum, sapientia ignobilem, consilio inutilem.*

[3] *Liber Historiae Francorum, loc. cit.*, p. 323.

of the palace of Neustria, and had taken his place. The affairs of the kingdom interested him only in so far as they served to strengthen his position in the North. This, for him, was the essential thing. It was threatened by the proximity of Frisia, in which paganism still prevailed, and whose prince, Ratbod, had perhaps already been encouraged to oppose Pippin by his enemies the Neustrians. At all events, the war which broke out in 689 went against him. He was defeated at Wyk-lez-Duurstete and had to surrender West Frisia to the conqueror.[1] It will be understood that this victory must have increased Pippin's prestige in every respect. It was in this country that the Anglo-Saxon Willibrord made his appearance in the following year (690), when he set to work upon the conversion of the Frisians. He was the first intermediary between the Carolingians and the Anglo-Saxon Church. The relations between these two powers were afterwards to have important consequences. A little later we find Pippin protecting another Anglo-Saxon missionary, Suitbert, to whom his wife Plectruda gave a domain, on one of the islands of the Rhine, on which he built the monastery of Kaiserswerth.[2]

Having conquered the Frisians, Pippin, between 709 and 712, turned upon the Alamans, who had constituted themselves as an independent duchy. He does not seem to have derived much profit from this campaign.[3] He never again saw Neustria, but until his death (in December 714) he continued to retain his hold upon it by means of a representative. As a matter of fact, in 695, on the death of Norbert, he sent his own son Grimoald to Childebert II as mayor of the palace. The Carolingian family thus had entire control of the monarchy. They had it so well in hand that when Grimoald was assassinated, a few weeks before his own death, Pippin appointed, as his successor in Neustria, Theodebald, the bastard son of Grimoald, aged six.[4] Thus the position of mayor of the palace was regarded by Pippin as a family possession, a kind of monarchy, parallel with the actual monarchy.

---

[1] RICHTER, *op. cit.*, p. 177.   [2] *Ibid.*, p. 182.
[3] *Ibid.*, p. 181.   [4] *Ibid.*, p. 182.

But he had carried matters too far. The Neustrian aristocrats found that they were being unduly sacrificed to the Carolingians; nevertheless, the Carolingians took some steps which were in their favour, as, for example, deciding that the Courts should be chosen by the bishops and the magnates—a step which King Dagobert III did nothing to oppose.

In 715, a few weeks after the death of Pippin II, the *grandi* of Neustria rebelled against Plectruda, the wife of Pippin, who, like a Merovingian queen, was acting as regent for Theodebald. This is not to be regarded as a national movement. It was merely the reaction of an aristocracy which was anxious to shake off the tutelage of the mayors and resume the direction of the palace. It is very evident that there was a reaction against the supporters of Pippin, whom the latter had placed in positions of power.[1]

The magnates appointed Raginfred to be mayor of the palace; but a bastard of Pippin's, Charles, the first to bear this Germanic name (*vocavit nomen ejus lingua propria carlum*),[2] who was twenty-five years of age, and had escaped from the prison in which Plectruda had held him captive, put himself at the head of his Austrasian supporters. In order to oppose him, Raginfred allied himself with Rathbod. At the same time the Saxons crossed the frontier. It was then that young Dagobert died, probably assassinated. His son, the infant Thierry, was sent to the monastery of Chelles, and the magnates chose as their king Chilperic II—son of Childeric I, assassinated in 673—who was relegated to a cloister. This was the first Merovingian for twenty-five years to ascend the throne in his majority; and he was the last. Royalty was merely an instrument upon which the aristocracy played.[3]

Charles, attacked simultaneously by Ratbod, who ascended the Rhine in boats, accompanied by the Frisians, as far as Cologne, and by the Neustrians, led by the king and Raginfred, fled into the Eifel.[4] But he attacked and defeated the Neustrians at Amblève during their withdrawal in 716. He would willingly have made

---

[1] RICHTER, *op. cit.*, p. 183: *fuit illo tempore valida persecutio.*
[2] *Ibid.*, p. 176.   [3] *Ibid.*, p. 184.   [4] *Ibid.*, p. 185.

peace with them, on condition, of course, that he recovered the position of mayor of the palace.

But the refusal of his adversaries compelled him to fight them. He defeated them at Vincy, near Cambrai, on March 21st, 717. Then, having laid waste the environs of Paris, he returned to Austrasia, and chose for his king Clotair IV, of whom we know nothing except that he was related to the Merovingians.[1] On returning to his domains he deposed the Bishop of Reims, Rigobert, who had not supported him, and gave his bishopric to Milon, Bishop of Trèves *sola tonsura clericus*, who was thus bishop of two dioceses, in defiance of canon law.[2] But for Charles the Church was merely a means of obtaining partisans.[3] A magnificent capital was thus placed at his disposal.[4]

As mayor of the palace, Charles bore himself like a sovereign. In 718 he undertook a punitive expedition against the Saxons, whose territory he ravaged as far as the Weser.

In 719 Chilperic and Raginfred, abandoning their northern allies, entered into negotiation with Eudes, who had created a duchy for himself in Aquitaine, and who came to join them in Paris in order to march against Charles. Thus a Romanic coalition had actually been formed against the latter. However, the con-

---

[1] RICHTER, *op. cit.*, p. 185.

[2] FUSTEL DE COULANGES, *Les transformations*, p. 189, despite the evidence, is unwilling to believe that there was a Germanic reaction. It is true that it was unconscious. [3] RICHTER, *op. cit.*, p. 185.

[4] We can obtain some idea from the history of the Abbey of Saint-Pierre de Gand of what was then happening. The enemies of the Abbot Celestin sent to the *princeps* Charles, and accused Celestin of having written to Raginfred. Charles, in consequence, *privavit eum a coenobiali monachorum caterva ac de eadem qua morabatur expulit provincia. Villas quoque que subjacebant dominio monasterii Blandiniensis, suos divisit per vasallos absque reverentia Dei.* This situation continued, says the annalist, until the reign of Louis the Pious. Thus the possessions of the Church, which included those of the monasteries, were the booty that rewarded the loyal vassals. It is a positive fact that Charles owed his fortune to their support (*Liber traditionum S. Petri*, ed. A. FAYEN, 1906, p. 5). Charles even had ecclesiastics put to death without having any regard for the synods: for example, in 739, the Abbot Wido of Saint-Vaast of Arras, the head of a conspiracy (BREYSIG, *op. cit.*, pp. 87–88).

federates did not dare to abide the onset of Charles, who was advancing against them. Eudes escorted Chilperic, with his treasure, which he carried with him, into Aquitaine. But Clotair IV died, and Charles, concluding peace with Eudes, acknowledged Chilperic II as the sovereign of the entire monarchy.[1]

Chilperic died in 720, and the Franks chose as his successor Thierry IV, the son of Dagobert III, and a minor. As for Rahinfred, did he retain the dignity of mayor? He had taken refuge in Angers, whence, in 724, he led a revolt against Charles. This was to be the last reaction of the Neustrians. Charles, who had concluded peace with Eudes of Aquitaine, was able to turn his attention to fighting in the North. In 720 he resumed the war against the Saxons, and he seems to have continued it in 722. At the same time he supported Willibrord's activities among the Frisians, and doubtless also the efforts of Saint Boniface, whom Gregory II (715–731) had created bishop of the pagan peoples of Germany.

In 725 he attempted for the first time to subdue Bavaria. Favoured by the dissensions in the ducal family, he advanced as far as the Danube, having first, it seems, prepared for his campaign by concluding an agreement with the Lombards. In 728 he undertook a second expedition, which did not, however, make him the master of Bavaria, which preserved its autonomy under Duke Hubert. In 730 we find him in Alemania, which he seems to have reunited to "Francia." In 734 he subdued Frisia, finally conquering it for Christianity. At last, in 738, he made another expedition against the Saxons. The result of all these wars in the North was the annexation of Frisia and Alemania.

But Charles was presently obliged to turn against Islam. In 720 the Arabs of Spain, having crossed the Pyrenees, had taken possession of Narbonne and laid siege to Toulouse. In the spring of 721 Eudes marched against them, defeated them under the walls of Toulouse, and drove them out of Aquitaine, but failed to recover Narbonne.[2] In 725 the Saracens made a great *razzia*, taking Carcassonne, and occupying, apparently by agreement, the whole

[1] RICHTER, *op. cit.*, p. 186.   [2] *Ibid.*, p. 187.

country as far as Nîmes, and then ascending the valley of the Rhone. In August they came to Autun, which they pillaged, and then returned to Spain, laden with booty.

Eudes, conscious that he was threatened in Aquitaine, safe-guarded himself by giving his daughter in marriage to Othman, the Arab chief of the frontier.

But at this time the Arabs were as greatly disturbed by civil commotions as the Christians. In 732 the Governor of Spain, Abd-er-Rhaman, who had just killed Othman, crossed the Pyrenees, besieged Bordeaux, defeated Eudes at the passage of the Garonne, and ravaging the countryside, moved northwards toward the Loire. Eudes appealed to Charles for assistance, and he, in October 732, at the head of an army which was doubtless composed mainly of Austrasians, defeated and repulsed the invader, and then turned back without advancing farther.

But in the following year, 733, he arrived in Burgundy, and occupied the city of Lyons; he certainly made an attempt to take possession of the Midi; for *leudes probatissimi* were instructed to hold the country in check.[1] As far as Aquitaine was concerned he was doubtless counting on Eudes. But it does not appear that in doing these things he was taking any sort of measures against Islam.

In 735 Eudes died, and Charles immediately fell upon Aquitaine. He occupied the cities, and for better security left them in the hands of his vassals. He undertook nothing against the Arabs, who had just advanced from Narbonne to Arles, doubtless in virtue of the previously signed agreement, and it does not appear that he offered them the least resistance. Thus the entire shore of the Gulf of Lyons was occupied by Islam. According to the chronicle of Moissac, the Saracens remained four years in the country, subjecting it to pillage.[2]

Charles, failing to subdue Aquitaine, left Chunold the son of Eudes there as duke, in consideration of an oath of vassalage.[3] He then proceeded to the Rhone valley, which he subdued as far

[1] RICHTER, *op. cit.*, p. 195.   [2] *Ibid.*, p. 196.   [3] *Ibid.*, p. 196.

as Marseilles and Arles. This time the men of the North actually took possession of the country. But their invasion provoked a reaction, at the head of which a certain "duke" Maurontus made his appearance. The sources do not enable us to understand exactly what happened, but it seems that Maurontus was acting in concert with the Saracens. In 737 the latter seized Avignon. After besieging the city, Charles captured it, and descending the Rhone, proceeded to attack Narbonne, which the Arabs surrendered. Charles then turned back, burning Nîmes, Agde, and Béziers on the way.[1]

He evidently wished to terrorise this southern population, for it is absurd to suppose that he can have destroyed these cities in order to prevent another Arab invasion. But while he was once more fighting in Saxony the Musulmans again advanced into Provence, and captured Arles. Charles appealed to the Lombards for assistance. Luitprand, whose frontiers they were threatening, crossed the Alps and drove them back. All this time Maurontus was still holding out. In 739, Charles, with his brother Childebrand, marched against him and reconquered the country down to the sea.

After these achievements, Charles died on October 21st, 741. Since the death of Thierry IV in 727 he had governed without a king. Before dying he divided the State—or perhaps one should rather say the government of the State—between his two sons: Carloman, the elder, to whom he gave Austrasia, and Pippin. Bavaria and Aquitaine were not included in this partition; they remained autonomou sduchies. Although it was made *consilio optimatum suorum*, this arrangement immediately gave rise to difficulties: Grifon, a bastard son of Charles, rebelled; his brothers imprisoned him at Chevremont. Then there was a rising in Burgundy; the Alamans and the Aquitainians took up arms, while the Saxons resumed the conflict. The two brothers began by

---

[1] RICHTER, *op. cit.*, p. 197. There had already been a rebellion in Provence against Pippin of Herstal, led by the patrician Antenor. PROU, *Catal. des monnaies mérovingiennes*, p. cx. It is impossible to suppose that there was no national hostility at work in all this. The *Formulae Arvernenses* attribute the disappearance of charters, which had to be restored, to the *hostilitas Francorum*. BRUNNER, *Deutsche Rechtsgeschichte*, vol. I, 2nd ed., p. 581, n. 31.

marching against the Aquitainians of Duke Chunold, whom the chronicler who continued Fredigarius calls *Romanos*. They pursued them as far as Bourges, and destroyed the castle of Loches; they then fell upon the Alamans, marching across their country as far as the Danube, and subduing it.[1] Then, in 743, they defeated the Duke of Bavaria and made him a vassal.

That same year, 743, doubtless on account of these rebellions, they decided to raise to the throne, which their father had left vacant, the last of the Merovingians, Childeric III (743–757), whose precise relationship to the preceding kings is uncertain.

In 747 Carloman resigned the government and became a monk in the monastery of Monte Cassino. Pippin continued to govern alone at the side of his phantom king. He had still some trouble with Grifon, whom he had restored to liberty, and who incited the Saxons and Bavarians to rise. But this was a passing incident, without further consequences.

In 749–750 there was at last a quiet year.[2] Pippin might consider that his position was assured. Born in 714, he was then, at thirty-six years of age, in the prime of life. Was he to continue to bear this subordinate title of mayor of the palace? How could he do so? He had now vassals of his own everywhere. All, except in Aquitaine, were bound to him by oath, and the position of these followers of his was dependent upon his personal power. He therefore felt that this power was assured, and it was further legitimized by its *de facto* heredity.

He was even reconciled with the Church, which his father had treated so ill, and whose spoils were in the possession of his supporters. In 742 Carloman, at the instigation of Boniface, convoked a synod in Austrasia, the first for decades, to restore order in the Church, whose personnel had become terribly degraded.[3] In 744 a second synod assembled at Soissons, and before long a third Austrasian synod was convoked.

In 745, after these efforts at reform, which, as we see, proceeded mainly from the North, whereas until the beginning of the 8th

[1] RICHTER, *op. cit.*, p. 202.   [2] *Ibid.*, p. 214.   [3] *Ibid.*, pp. 203–204.

century all ecclesiastical progress came from the Midi, the first general assembly of the Frankish Church was held under the presidency of Saint Boniface. And this time we see the intervention of Papal influence, for it was the Pope who convoked the assembly.

Pippin and Carloman were thus brought into touch with the Pope by Boniface. And the whole Church, which was organizing itself in Germany, still regarded them, thanks to Boniface, as its protectors. How could they do other than appeal to the head of this Church to ratify and sanction the power which they exercised and possessed? An alliance with the Papacy seemed indicated. It was all the more readily effected inasmuch as it was to the interest of the Papacy, as Pippin very well knew, since the Pope had already appealed to Charles Martel for support.

3. *Italy, the Pope and Byzantium. The Volte-face of the Papacy*

The Church, on the fall of the Imperial government in the West, had loyally cherished its memories of and its reverence for that Roman Empire whose organization was reflected in its own, with its dioceses (*civitates*) and its provinces. It not only venerated but in a certain sense it continued the Empire, since the upper ranks of its personnel were composed entirely of descendants of old senatorial families who remembered the Empire with respect and regret. The whole Church was subject to Roman law. It regarded the events of 476 as having no real importance. It had acknowledged the Emperor of Ravenna; it now acknowledged the Emperor of Constantinople. What is more, it acknowledged him as its head. The Pope, in Rome, was his subject, corresponded with him, and maintained an apocrisiary in Constantinople. He loyally attended the synods and other Imperial convocations.

The Emperor himself, when things were normal, regarded and venerated the Pope as the first patriarch of the Empire, having primacy over the patriarchs of Constantinople, Jerusalem, Antioch, and Alexandria.[1]

[1] The Pope was acknowledged by Phocas as "the head of all the Churches," in opposition to the patriarch of Constantinople, who had assumed the title of Oecumenicus. VASILIEV, *op. cit.*, vol. I, p. 228.

This unrestricted adhesion of the Western Church to the Empire is all the more comprehensible inasmuch as until the pontificate of Gregory the Great the limits of the ancient Roman Empire were those of the Church, or approximately so. It was true that the formation of the Germanic kingdoms, established on the ruins of the Empire, had divided the Church among several States, ruled by different kings; towards whom, however, it had from the very first manifested an absolute loyalty. Although in reality the Empire no longer existed, there was still an Empire for the Pope of Rome.[1]

Even under Theodoric, whom he had never consented to regard as anything more than a functionary of the Empire, the Pope had not ceased to acknowledge the authority of the Empire. The triumphant return of the Roman armies under Justinian had still further confirmed his subordination. Elected by the clergy and the Roman people, the Pope, after the entry of Belisarius into Rome, had applied to the Emperor for the ratification of his election. And from the pontificate of Vigilius (537–555), from the year 550, the Pope dated his documents in the name of the Emperor.

Vigilius, moreover, owed his tiara to the Emperor. In 537, while Vitiges was besieging Rome, Pope Silverius, on the pretext that he had an understanding with the Goths, was deposed by Belisarius, and deported to the island of Palmataria. Appointed by the Emperor Theodosius, Vigilius replaced Silverius on the Papal throne.[2] Justinian was not slow to profit by his appointment: claiming the right to impose upon the Pope the religious absolutism of the Emperor, in respect of the affair of the three chapters—that is to say, the affair of the Imperial Edict of 543, which anathematized three theologians of the 5th century, alleged to be Nestorians, with the object of giving satisfaction to the Monophysites and of effecting a reconciliation between them and the State and the Orthodox.

But the Occidentals, and above all the Africans, protested. Pope

[1] He dated his documents from the accession of the Emperor.
[2] HARTMANN, *op. cit.*, vol. I, p. 384.

Vigilius, invited to approve the Edict, refused to do so, and excommunicated the patriarch of Constantinople, but finally gave way in 548. However, being confronted with the opposition of the Occidental bishops, Vigilius withdrew his acquiescence. An Oecumenical Council was then convoked in Constantinople, but Vigilius, although he was detained in that city, refused to attend it, together with the great majority of the Occidental bishops, so that the Oecumenical Council was in reality nothing but a Greek Council, under the presidency of the patriarch of Constantinople. By this Council the three chapters were condemned, and Vigilius, refusing to submit, was exiled by Justinian to an island in the Sea of Marmora.[1] He finally gave way, and was authorized to return to Rome, but died in the course of the journey, at Syracuse, in 555.[2]

Like Vigilius himself, his successor Pelagius I, consecrated in 555, was appointed by Justinian. He did his best to preserve the peace of the Church, which remained divided upon the question of the three chapters, despite the tragic crisis to which the wars were subjecting Italy.

The Lombards, whom the Imperial armies, detained in Asia and on the Danube,[3] were powerless to check, overran the country. The Empire was now passing through one of the most troublous and critical periods of its history. Justin II, unable to send troops, advised the Pope to fight the Lombards with gold, and to form an alliance against them with the Franks.

However, the Lombards, in the reign of the Emperor Tiberius II (578–582), invaded the country as far as Spoleto and Benevento. Pope Pelagius II seconded the efforts of the Emperor to obtain an alliance with the Franks, but in vain. Italy became a prey to the most terrible disorder.

Yet Rome, the seat of the Pope, and Ravenna, the Imperial city, held out against the enemy. The Emperor Maurice (582–602)

---

[1] VASILIEV, op. cit., pp. 201–202.
[2] HARTMANN, op. cit., vol. I, pp. 392–394.
[3] VASILIEV, op. cit., vol. I, p. 225.

sent an exarch to Ravenna, armed with plenary powers, but with insufficient troops at his disposal.

At the moment when Gregory the Great (590–604) ascended the pontifical throne the peril was greater than ever. In 592, communications being cut between Rome and Ravenna, Arnulf, Duke of Spoleto, appeared under the walls of Rome; and in 593 the city was once more threatened, this time by King Agilulf. Gregory had to defend the city unaided. He applied himself vigorously to the task of defence; doubtless for his own sake, but also for the Emperor.

At this moment the Patriarch of Constantinople, taking advantage of the almost desperate situation of Rome, assumed the title of Oecumenicus. Gregory protested immediately. The Emperor Phocas gave him the satisfaction he required, acknowledging the Pope of Rome as "the head of all the Churches."[1]

And then, surrounded on all hands by the invaders, who attacked the very walls of the city, and abandoned by the Emperor, the Pope, in affirmation of his power as the supreme head of Christendom, erected a column in the Forum.[2]

But the fact that the Pope was abandoned in Rome increased his power and prestige. It was in 596 that he sent his first missions to England, under the leadership of Augustine. His object in so doing was to win souls, and he never doubted that he was thereby laying fresh foundations for the majesty of the Roman Church and its independence of Byzantium. He guided and inspired his missionaries from afar. But it was not granted to him to witness the birth of that Anglo-Saxon Church which was to determine the destinies of Rome.

The following years were to be decisive for the Papacy.

Heraclius had just averted the Persian peril from Constantinople. The Empire had once more become a great power. It would have succeeded in recovering the whole of Italy from the Lombards, when suddenly Islam burst into the Mediterranean (634). Attacked

---

[1] HARTMANN, *op. cit.*, vol. II¹, p. 180.
[2] VASILIEV, *op. cit.*, p. 228.

on all sides, Byzantium had to abandon the war against the Lombards. Rome was left to defend herself.

For the Church, the conquest of the Asiatic and the African shores of the Mediterranean by the Musulmans was the most terrible of catastrophes. Apart from the fact that it reduced the territory of Christendom to Europe alone, it was presently the cause of the great schism which finally divided the West from the East—Rome, where the Pope was enthroned, from Byzantium, the seat of the last Patriarch of the East to survive the Islamic inundation.

Heraclius, having reconquered Syria, Palestine and Egypt, where the Monophysites were predominant, from the Persians, aspired, as Justinian had done, to restore the unity of the Church by concessions in the domain of dogma. The Monophysites, who recognized in Christ only one substance, the divine, were insuperably opposed to the Orthodox, who regarded Him both as man and God. However, it seemed as though it should not have been impossible to reconcile these two opposite points of view, for while the Orthodox affirmed that there were two substances in Christ they nevertheless recognized only one life in Him. It might therefore be possible to reconcile Orthodoxy and Monophysism in the single doctrine of Monothelism.

To reinforce the unity of religious and Imperial sentiment against the Musulman invaders, the Emperor believed that the moment had come to reconcile Monophysites and Orthodox by proclaiming the doctrine of Monothelism, and imposing it on all Christendom by the publication of the "Ecthesis" (638).[1]

This manifestation came too late to save the Empire, for by this time Syria was already conquered by Islam. On the other hand, it had the effect of causing Rome to rebel against Byzantium. Pope Honorius declared the Monothelist doctrine to be heretical.

Presently Egypt succumbed in its term, conquered by Islam. The two principal centres of Monophysism were irremediably lost. Nevertheless, Constantinople did not abandon Monothelism. Constant II, in 648, published the "Type"—the type of faith—

---

[1] VASILIEV, op. cit., vol. I, p. 294.

prohibiting any disputes upon questions of dogma, and confirming the doctrine of Monothelism.

Rome did not surrender, and in the Synod of Lateran Pope Martin I condemned both the Ecthesis and the Type, declaring them to be tainted with heresy.

The Emperor Constant II responded to the resistance of the Pope by ordering the Exarch of Ravenna to arrest Martin, who was sent to Constantinople. He was there convicted of having attempted to provoke a rebellion against the Emperor in the Western provinces, was imprisoned, after suffering terrible humiliations, and was finally exiled to the Crimea, where he died in September 655.

The victory of Constantine IV over the Arabs, by liberating Constantinople, was doubtless the origin of the Emperor's abandonment of Monothelism in favour of a return to Rome. The *rapprochement* was effected under Vitalianus; in 680 Constantine IV (668–685) convoked the Sixth Oecumenical Council in Constantinople, which condemned Monothelism and acknowledged the Pope as "head of the principal seat of the Universal Church." Thus the pressure of Islam drew the Emperor back to the West.

The Sixth Council made it clear to Monophysite Syria, Palestine and Egypt that Constantinople had abandoned all hope of reconciliation with the provinces torn from the Empire. The Emperor's peace with Rome was therefore purchased at the price of the total abandonment of the Monophysite and Monothelist populations of the Eastern provinces.

Constant II, however, had already given indications of the same orientation towards the West when, despite the doctrinal differences which then divided him from the Pope, he repaired to Rome, where he was received with veneration by Vivalianus on July 5th, 663. He may perhaps have dreamed of re-installing himself in the ancient capital of the Empire; but he must have recognized that his presence there was impossible, since he had no army to repel the Lombard threat, and twelve days later he left for Sicily, establishing himself at Syracuse, where he could at least count on his fleet. He died there, assassinated, in 668.

Not long afterwards, in 677, Constantine IV, with the help of Greek fire, drove the Arab fleet from Constantinople, and compelled the Caliph Moawiya to pay him tribute, and, on the other hand, assured the Empire's Italian possessions by signing a definitive peace with the Lombards.[1]

The Empire had saved Constantinople, and retained Rome and the Exarchate of Ravenna, but was henceforth confined—after the loss of Spain and Africa—to the Eastern Mediterranean. And it seemed at this moment that the Roman Church, which had itself lost Africa and Spain through the advance of Islam, was very far from turning toward the West. The Council of 680 seemed to link its destinies very definitely with those of the Empire, which had become purely Greek. Of thirteen Popes who had filled the Papal throne between 678 and 752, only two were of Roman origin—Benedict II (684–685) and Gregory II (715–731). All the rest were Syrians, Greeks, or at least Sicilians. Now Sicily, where the Greek element had been considerably increased by the Syrian immigration which followed the conquest of Syria by the Musulmans, was almost completely Hellenized by the end of the 7th century.[2]

The new orientation of the Church toward Byzantium was not in any sense due to the increasing intervention of the Byzantine power in the affairs of the Pontificate. The intervention of the Exarch, who, since Heraclius, had to ratify the Papal elections, was little more than a formality. The Papal elections, entirely free from any interference, took place in the Roman *milieu*, so that it is strange that Greeks were so constantly chosen to occupy the throne of Saint Peter.

Since the peace with the Lombards the only troops in Byzantine Italy were those levied locally, the others being employed against Islam. Byzantium, therefore, was powerless to enforce her authority at the Papal elections. But in these elections the troops, like the clergy of Rome, played a preponderant part. Now, the majority of the military officers were Hellenized, and so were very many of the priests, which explains these Syrian nominations.

[1] VASILIEV, *op. cit.*, vol. I, p. 283.   [2] GAY, *op. cit.*, pp. 9–10.

These troops, however, were not obedient to orders received from Byzantium. Isolated from the seat of power, and without any contact with it, they did not obey the Exarch of Ravenna, or even the Emperor. In 692, when Pope Sergius refused to affix his signature at the foot of the instruments of the Council *in Trullo*, which contained clauses that were opposed to the usages of Rome, Justinian II gave orders that he was to be arrested and brought to Constantinople. But the Roman militia rebelled, and it was only thanks to the Pope's intercession that the Imperial delegate was not put to death.

Thus, although Rome was included in the Empire, the Pope enjoyed a *de facto* independence. He was at once the religious and military and civil head of the city. But he acknowledged the Imperial connection; and as a matter of fact it very greatly increased his authority, since the Emperor regarded him as the first personage in the Church; while he, on the other hand, did not renounce his headship of the universal Church, of which the greater part, since the conquest of Africa and Spain, consisted of the Oriental provinces.

Thus the momentary rupture which followed the incident of 692 was desired neither by the Pope nor the Emperor. The last Pope to be received in the capital of the Empire had the greatest honour shown to him: it is recorded that the Emperor prostrated himself before him and kissed his feet,[1] and once more an arrangement was entered into which satisfied both parties. Peace was restored.

However, the old quarrel between the Orthodox and the Monothelists was revived from time to time. In 711 the advent of the Monothelist Emperor Philippicus provoked riots in Rome. And, on the other hand, the temporal authority of the Emperor in Italy was becoming weaker and weaker. In 710 the troops at Ravenna revolted; the Exarch was killed, and replaced by a leader elected by the troops themselves.[2] This called for vigorous intervention on the part of the Empire. But the death of Justinian II (711) marked the

---

[1] VASILIEV, *op. cit.*, vol. I, p. 297.
[2] HARTMANN, *op. cit.*, vol. II, pp. 77–78.

opening of a period of anarchy (711–717), which enabled the Bulgars to advance as far as Constantinople, while the Arabs marched through Asia Minor, and their fleets, commanding the Aegean and the Propontis, attacked the capital by sea (717).[1]

It may be said that Europe was then saved by the energy of the soldier who had just assumed the crown—Leo III the Isaurian. What with his superiority over the Arab fleet, thanks to the terrible Greek fire, and the alliance which he was able to conclude with the Bulgars, he compelled the decimated enemy to withdraw after a siege of more than a year (718).

This is a historical fact of far greater importance than the battle of Poitiers, for this was the last attack ever made by the Arabs upon the city "protected by God." It was, in the words of Bury, an oecumenical date.[2] From this time forward, until the reign of the Empress Irene (782–803), the Arabs were held in check and even driven back into Asia Minor. Under Leo and his son Constantine the Empire made a recovery, and an administrative reorganization gave it the cohesion which it had lacked by extending to all parts the régime of the themes.[3]

But Leo wished to complete his work by a religious reform: Iconoclasty. Perhaps this may be in some degree explained by the desire to diminish the opposition between Christianity and Islam, and to conciliate the Eastern provinces of Asia Minor, where the Paulicians were numerous.[4]

In Rome the promulgation of the new doctrine had the most serious consequences: Leo published his first edict against images in 725–726.[5] It was immediately anathematized by Pope Gregory II. The conflict that followed assumed from the beginning an acute character. To the Emperor's assertion of his claim to impose his authority upon the Church the Pope replied by declaring the separation of the two powers, in a tone that none of his predecessors

---

[1] VASILIEV, *op. cit.*, vol. I, p. 313.   [2] *Ibid.*, p. 314.
[3] The theme was an administrative division of the Byzantine Empire (Tr.). VASILIEV, *op. cit.*, vol. I, p. 331.
[4] VASILIEV, *op. cit.*, vol. I, p. 339.   [5] *Ibid.*, p. 342.

had ever yet employed.[1] He even defied the Emperor, by requesting the faithful to refrain from the heresy which Leo had proclaimed. And while flatly denying his authority, he reproached the Emperor with his inability to defend Italy, threatening to turn toward the Western nations, and forbidding the Romans to pay taxes to the Emperor. The Imperial troops cantoned in Italy immediately mutinied, deposed their officers, and appointed others; the Exarch Paul was killed in a riot; and the Romans expelled their duke. The whole of Byzantine Italy was in a state of rebellion, ready, no doubt, to elect an anti-Emperor if the Pope had advised it to do so. But he did nothing of the kind. Was this perhaps due to a last scruple of loyalty, or was the Pope unwilling to instal an emperor beside him in Italy?[2]

The Emperor, however, did not give way. A new Exarch was sent to Ravenna, but he was powerless to act, having no troops at his disposal. The situation was all the more serious inasmuch as the Lombard dukes of Spoleto and Benevento, who had rebelled against their king, were supporting the Pope. There was only one thing for the Emperor to do: to ally himself with the King of the Lombards, Luitprand, who took this opportunity of reducing the rebellious dukes.

Thanks to Luitprand, the Exarch entered Rome, and although the Pope still continued to oppose iconoclasty, he capitulated politically. He agreed to acknowledge the temporal authority of the Emperor, but he claimed the right of independence in the spiritual domain. In 730 he protested once more against the new iconoclastic edict promulgated by the Emperor, and declared that the Patriarch of Constantinople had forfeited his office.

Politically, however, the Pope now acted in agreement with the Exarch, whose authority was re-established without contest. An anti-Emperor who had been proclaimed in Tuscany was killed, and his head was sent to Byzantium; Ravenna, after repelling a Byzantine fleet, once more fell into the Exarch's hands.

---

[1] JAFFÉ-WATTENBACH, *Regeste*, No. 2180. Cf. HARTMANN, *op. cit.*, vol. II², p. 94.　　[2] HARTMANN, *op. cit.*, vol. II², p. 95.

Gregory II died in 729. His successor was the Syrian Gregory III, the last Pope to require the Emperor to ratify his election.[1]

But he was no sooner enthroned than he resumed the struggle against iconoclasty. In 731 he convoked a synod which excommunicated the destroyers of images. The Emperor replied to this frontal attack by detaching from the jurisdiction of Rome all the dioceses on the east of the Adriatic (Illyria), Sicily, Bruttium, and Calabria, which he placed under the authority of the Patriarch of Constantinople.[2] He also deprived the Church of its domains in Sicily, Calabria and Bruttium, which brought in a yearly revenue of 350 pounds of gold. Thus the Pope, from the Byzantine standpoint of the Emperor, was henceforth little more than an Italian bishop. His hierarchic and dogmatic influence would no longer be exercised in the Orient, from which he was excluded. The Latin Church was expelled from the Byzantine world by the Emperor himself.

And yet the Pope did not break with the Emperor. His loyalty may perhaps be explained by a change of attitude on the part of Luitprand, who, breaking with the Exarch, seized Ravenna, and thereby betrayed his intention of conquering the whole of Italy. As a result of this conquest, if Rome had fallen, the Pope would have been degraded to the rank of a Lombard bishop. Thus, in spite of all that had happened, he supported the Greek cause. He exhorted the Bishop of Grado to induce the people of the lagoons—that is, the Venetians—to employ their ships against the Lombards of Ravenna, who possessed no fleet. Thanks to these hardy sailors, the city was captured, and was once more occupied by the Exarch in 735. But Luitprand was still formidable.[3] In 738 the Pope entered into an alliance against him with the Dukes of Spoleto and Benevento, who were attempting to assert their independence.[4] But in 739 Luitprand attacked the Duke of Spoleto,

---

[1] JAFFÉ-WATTENBACH, *Regesta*, p. 257.
[2] HARTMANN, *op. cit.*, vol. II[2], pp. 111–112.
[3] *Ibid.*, p. 134.
[4] JAFFÉ-WATTENBACH, *Regesta*, No. 2244.

forced him to take refuge in Rome, and proceeded to pillage the Roman Campagna.[1]

In the midst of these constant dangers the Pope, with the help of the Anglo-Saxon Church, proceeded to undertake the conversion of the pagan regions of Germany. The Anglo-Saxon Church, organized by the Greek monk Theodore, whom Pope Vitalianus, in 669, had created Archbishop of Canterbury,[2] was a true outpost of the Papacy in the North.

From the Anglo-Saxon Church proceeded the great evangelizers of Germany: Wynfrith (Saint Boniface), who entered the country in 678, and Willibrord, who arrived on the continent in 690. Before entering upon his mission he proceeded to Rome, and asked the blessing of Pope Sergius, who entrusted him officially with the task of evangelizing Germany and establishing churches there, for which he gave him certain relics.

Willibrord began by preaching in Frisia. He was supported in his task by Pippin; for religious reasons, of course, yet mainly for political reasons, since the Franks would find it easier to penetrate into Frisia if the Frisians were Christianized. In 696 Willibrord returned to Rome, received the name of Clement, and the *pallium*, and was consecrated Bishop of Utrecht by Pope Sergius.[3]

On May 15th, 719, Gregory II gave a mandate to Boniface (Wynfrith) to continue the evangelizing of Frisia, in conformity with the Roman doctrine. It was then that he received the name of Boniface, that being the name of the patron of the day.[4] During the whole of his apostolate in Frisia, where he laboured beside Willibrord, Boniface enjoyed the protection of Charles Martel. Returning to Rome in 722, he was appointed bishop by Gregory II, and given the mission of preaching the faith in Germany on the right bank of the Rhine.[5] The letters which Gregory gave him made him a veritable Roman missionary. In 724 the Pope recom-

[1] HARTMANN, *op. cit.*, vol. II², p. 138.
[2] SCHUBERT, *Geschichte der Christlichen Kirche im Frühmittelalter*, p. 269.
[3] JAFFÉ-WATTENBACH, *Regesta*, p. 244.
[4] SCHUBERT, *op. cit.*, p. 300.
[5] JAFFÉ-WATTENBACH, *Regesta*, Nos. 2159–2162.

mended him to Charles Martel,[1] and finally, in 732, Gregory III consecrated him archbishop, authorizing him to appoint bishops himself in the regions which he conquered for Christ.

Thus, while the Emperor was shutting Rome off from the East, the mission of Boniface afforded her the prospect of advancing into those *extremas occidentis regiones* whose conversion had already been envisaged by Gregory II. This great missionary, who extended over Germany the authority of the Pope of Rome, was at the same time, by the force of circumstances, the protégé of that very Charles Martel who plundered and despoiled the Church and confiscated its estates in order to provide fiefs for his vassals. How could the Pope, whose position in Italy was so distressing, avoid appealing to this all-powerful protector of Saint Boniface? In 738 Boniface returned once more to Rome, where he remained for about a year. We may be sure that he discussed other matters with Gregory III besides the organization of the German Church, and we must suppose that he advised the Pope to seek support from Charles Martel, for in 739 the Pope entered into communication with the omnipotent master of the Occident. He sent Charles his great "decoration," the keys of the sepulchre of Saint Peter, and offered, in return for his protection against the Lombards, to abandon the Emperor.[2]

But Charles was in no position to quarrel with the King of the Lombards, who had just undertaken on his behalf an expedition against the Saracens in Provence. He therefore confined himself to sending Gregory an embassy, which had instructions to promise the Pope assistance; but this help never arrived.[3]

In 741 Gregory III, Charles Martel, and the Emperor Leo III died about the same time. The first was succeeded by Zaccharias, the second by Pippin, and the third by Constantine V Copronymus (741–775), who was a fanatical Iconoclast.

Fleeing from religious persecution, 50,000 Greek monks took refuge in Rome, infuriated with the Emperor who had banished

[1] JAFFÉ-WATTENBACH, *Regesta*, No. 2168. Cf. SCHUBERT, *op. cit.*, p. 301.
[2] *Ibid.*, No. 2249.   [3] HARTMANN, *op. cit.*, vol. II², pp. 170–171.

them. Zacharias did not apply to the Emperor for ratification of his election. But almost immediately after this election he concluded a truce of twenty years with Luitprand, who profited by the truce to make another attack on the Exarchate in 743. Then, in spite of everything, the Pope took the Emperor's part, and at the Exarch's request he persuaded Luitprand, at Ravenna, to sign a truce with the Empire.[1]

However, through the intermediary of Boniface the Pope's relations with Pippin, who was much more favourably inclined to the Church than his father had been, had become increasingly intimate. Meanwhile Pippin, being rid of Carloman, was preparing his *coup d'état*. Of course, he had only to wish it, and the thing was done. But he did not want to leave anything to chance, and knowing that he could count on the favour of Zacharias he made his celebrated application to the Pope.

In 751 Berchard, Bishop of Wurtzburg, one of the bishops recently created in Germany, and the Abbot Fulrad, went to Rome to ask the Pope the famous question: Who should wear the crown—he who bore the title of king, or he who actually exercised the sovereign power? The Pope's reply, which was in favour of Pippin, signified the end of the Merovingian dynasty.

The poor Merovingian king, who was awaiting his fate, was despatched to a monastery, and no one troubled further about him.

From this moment the great change of orientation was realized. The North had definitely prevailed. It was there that the temporal power resided, since Islam had ruined Southern Gaul, and this was the only power that could now support the Papacy, since the Greek Empire had cut it off from the Orient.[2]

[1] HARTMANN, *op. cit.*, vol. II², p. 144.

[2] SCHUBERT, *op. cit.*, p. 287, has very justly described this reversal in the following terms: "The home of Western Christendom, the theatre of its history, was displaced towards the North; it was represented by the line Rome–Metz–York. Rome, the mistress, lay no longer at the centre, but on the periphery. The unitary culture of the Mediterranean countries was shattered. New peoples were surging forward into the light, and striving after a new unity. A new age was beginning; the age of transition was over."

The year 751 saw the alliance of the Carolingians with the Papacy. It was planned under Zacharias and completed under Stephen II. Before the situation could be completely reversed the last thread that connected the Pope with the Empire had to be broken, for so long as it existed the Papacy was forced to remain, in defiance of its nature, a Mediterranean power. It doubtless would have remained a Mediterranean power if Islam had not robbed it of Africa and Spain. But Germany, in the North, was now of greater significance.

Still, tradition was so powerful that if by some impossibility the Emperor could have driven out the Lombards, the Pope would have remained faithful to him. But in 749, with the appearance of Aistulf, the Lombards resumed their policy of conquest.

In 751 they seized Ravenna, and this time they remained permanently in possession of the city. Rome could no longer evade her fate. In 752 Aistulf's army was before the walls. Only immediate assistance could save the city. Stephen began by imploring help of the Iconoclast. He begged him to come with an army and save the city of Rome.[1] But Constantine V contented himself with sending an embassy to the Lombards. Aistulf received it, but refused to make any concession. Pope Stephen II then appealed to Pippin for assistance, but before taking this decisive step he himself went to Pavia, where he besought Aistulf to renounce his conquests. Having suffered a rebuff, he left for the court of Pippin, where he arrived in January 754.

The inevitable had come to pass at last. The tradition which Pippin had broken in 751 was abandoned three years later by the Pope himself.

4. The New Empire

Thus, in 754, Stephen II found himself in those *extremae occidentis regiones* to which Gregory II had pointed the way in 729. What had he come to do there? To implore protection for Rome, since

---

[1] JAFFÉ-WATTENBACH, *Regesta*, No. 2308.

Aistulf would not listen to him, and since the Emperor's envoy had failed to obtain any concessions. Of course, if his overtures in Pavia had been successful he would not have crossed the Alps. He was doubtless fully aware of the gravity of the step, but he was at his wits' end. Pippin awaited him at Ponthion, on January 6th, 754. Stephen implored him to intervene against the Lombards. And Pippin swore to the Pope *exarchatum Ravennae et reipublicae jura sue loca reddere*.[1]

To judge from the texts, there was something equivocal about this. That was to be restored to the *respublica* which the Lombard had taken from it. But the *respublica* was either the Empire or it was Rome, which was in the Empire. And Pippin, who doubtless had no desire to make war, sent an embassy to Aistulf. But Aistulf refused to listen to Pippin; what is more, he incited Carloman to oppose him, for he had managed to persuade the latter to leave the Abbey of Montekassino. But on entering France Carloman was apprehended, and died at Vienne.[2]

By this maladroit policy the Lombard king had embroiled himself with Pippin. It would seem, therefore, that this time he had really made up his mind to seize Rome and conquer the whole of Italy. It was for Pippin to decide whom he should support, Aistulf or the Pope. Before opening his campaign, Pippin assembled his *grandi* at Quiersy-sur-Oise. He gave the Pope a diploma containing his promises (April 14th). Three months later, at Saint Denis, before proceeding to make war, the Pope solemnly renewed the consecration which Boniface had already bestowed upon Pippin, and, on penalty of excommunication, forbade the Franks ever to choose a king who was not descended from Pippin. Thus the alliance was concluded between the dynasty and the head of the Church. And in order to confirm it, Stephen conferred upon Pippin and his two sons the title of *patricius Romanorum*. In so doing, of course, he was usurping the rights of the Emperor. The Exarch had borne the title of patrician. Pippin thus became, like the Exarch,

[1] BÖHMER-MUHLBACHER, *Die Regesten des Kaiserreichs*, vol. I, 2nd ed., p. 36.
[2] LOT, PFISTER and GANSHOF, *op. cit.*, p. 410.

the protector of Rome, but this office was delegated by the Pope, not by the Emperor.[1] It seems, however, that the Pope was acting on his own initiative, without considering Pippin's feelings in the matter, for Pippin never used the title and probably never wanted it.

Aistulf, being defeated, restored to the Romans, by treaty, the conquests which he had made; that is to say, the *patrimonia* of Narni and Ceccano, together with the territories of the Exarchate. As soon as the Emperor was advised of this, in 756, he demanded that Pippin should deliver up Ravenna and the Exarchate. Pippin naturally refused, despite the great sum which the Emperor promised him in exchange. What he had done was done only out of reverence for Saint Peter, and nothing could induce him to go back upon his promises.[2] However, by the time the Imperial embassy arrived Pippin and Aistulf were at war again, the latter having immediately violated his promises. He even laid siege to Rome, on January 1st, 756. Blockaded in Pavia a second time, for the second time the Lombard sued for peace. Again he restored the conquered territories, and Pippin returned them to the Pope. Henceforth the Pope was master of Rome and her territory.[3] Nevertheless, he continued to acknowledge the theoretical sovereignty of the Emperor.

It is characteristic of Pippin that he did not enter Rome on either of his two expeditions. Nor did he ever again appear in Italy, although Aistulf's successor, Didier, who had become king partly through Pippin's influence, caused him further difficulty. Didier had promised to surrender to the Pope various Lombard conquests of Luitprand's. But he would not consent to restore more than a portion of them.

Stephen's successor, Paul I (757–767) protested in vain. It seems that the Emperor then endeavoured to profit by the situation. His ambassador George, who had already negotiated with Pippin

---

[1] LOT, PFISTER and GANSHOF, *op. cit.*, p. 411.

[2] L. OELSNER, *Jahrbücher des Fränkischen Reiches unter König Pippin*, 1871, p. 267. [3] BÖHMER-MUHLBACHER, *op. cit.*, pp. 42–43.

in 756, arrived in Naples in 758, and negotiated with Didier a plan of coalition with a view to retaking Rome and Ravenna. Then he repaired to the court of Pippin, but obtained no satisfaction, Pippin remaining loyal to the Pope.[1] In 760 it was rumoured in Rome that the Emperor was sending a fleet of 300 ships against Rome and France.[2] Doubtless the Pope was hoping, by this rumour, to induce Pippin to march into Italy; and later, he spoke of attacks which the *nefandissimi Greci* were preparing against Ravenna,[3] contrasting these heretics with the *vere orthodoxus* Pippin.[4]

He knew that the Emperor was still negotiating with Pippin. In 762 ambassadors from Pippin and from the Pope repaired to Constantinople. It was evident that after all the Emperor was seeking a *rapprochement*. About 765 the Emperor sent to Pippin the spatharius Anthi and the eunuch Sinesius, to discuss the question of the images, and the betrothal of Gisla, Pippin's daughter, to the son of the Emperor.[5] There was another great discussion respecting the images in 767 at Gentilly.[6]

But Pippin remained immovable, acting in all things in agreement with the Pope. As for the Pope's dispute with Didier, Pippin settled this in 763 by an agreement in virtue of which the Pope renounced his territorial claims, and also his attempt to declare a protectorate over Spoleto and Benevento.[7] In short, thanks to Pippin, the Pope felt that he was protected from his enemies, and that the orthodox faith was safe, but also that he was obliged to rely absolutely upon Pippin's protection.

Charlemagne's reign was in all respects the completion of that

---

[1] OELSNER, *op. cit.*, pp. 320-321.

[2] OELSNER, *op. cit.*, p. 346. Cf. *Codex Carolinus*, ed. GUNDLACH, M.G.H. EPIST., vol. III, p. 521.

[3] *Codex Carolinus*, ed. GUNDLACH, M.G.H. EPIST., vol. III, p. 536.

[4] He wrote to him: *post Deum in vestra excellentia et fortissimi regni vestri brachio existit fiducia.* And, further on, paraphrasing a Biblical text: *Salvum fac, Domine, Christianissimum Pippinum regem, quem oleo sancto per manus apostoli tui ungui praecepisti, et exaudi eum, in quacumque die invocaverit te. Codex Carolinus, loc. cit.*, p. 539.   [5] OELSNER, *op. cit.*, p.p. 396-397.

[6] BÖHMER-MUHLBACHER, *op. cit.*, p. 53.

[7] LOT, PFISTER, and GANSHOF, *op. cit.*, p. 413.

of Pippin. His father bequeathed to him his Italian policy; that is
to say, his Lombard and his Roman policy. He ascended the throne
October 16th (768) with the title of patrician, like his brother
Carloman. It was only after Carloman's death that he was really
able to take action (December 771).

The King of the Lombards, Didier, still cherished the ambition
of becoming the master of Rome. In January 773 Pope Adrian
had to appeal to Charlemagne for assistance against Didier. Charlemagne immediately marched into Italy, and while his army laid
siege to Pavia, where Didier was blockaded, he proceeded to
Rome, in order to be present at the Easter festival (774). On this
occasion he intervened as the great benefactor of the Holy See.
He not only renewed, but enormously increased, the donations
made to the Pope by his father, to the point of including among
them the duchies of Spoleto and Benevento as well as Venetia and
Istria.[1] Then, returning to Pavia, which, with Didier, surrendered
in June 774, he himself assumed the title of King of the Lombards.

Hitherto he had been content to call himself *Carolus, gratia Dei,
rex Francorum vir inluster*. His title was now: *Rex Francorum et
Longobardorum atque patricius Romanorum*.[2]

This innovation makes it clear that for him his Roman patriciate—
though this was certainly not what the Pope would have wished—
was of secondary importance to his Lombard monarchy. The King
of the Franks had become an Italian potentate. His power, which
had its origin in Germanic Austrasia, was extended to the Mediterranean. But he did not settle in Rome; he did not become a
Mediterranean; he remained a Northerner. Italy and the Papacy
henceforth gravitated in his orbit. He left the Lombard kingdom a
certain autonomy, but he sent Frankish counts thither, and he distributed some of its domains among the great churches of *Francia*.

As for the Pope, he naturally tried to regard this patrician, who
after all had received his power from Stephen II at Quiersy, as

[1] BÖHMER-MUHLBACHER, *op. cit.*, p. 73. Cf. LOT, PFISTER, and GANSHOF,
op. cit., p. 422.

[2] LOT, PFISTER, and GANSHOF, *op. cit.*, p. 423.

merely the protector of the Papacy. But here there was a fatal contradiction. To begin with, a protector readily becomes a master. Pippin was never that, for he had loyally modelled his Italian policy on that of the Pope; but Charles was to become the master. The fact that he assumed the title of patrician only when he had conquered the Lombard kingdom shows plainly that he regarded this title also as a conquest; as one that he held in his own right. As for the Pope, who from the year 772 no longer dated his Bulls from the year of the Emperor's accession—and who from the year 781 dated them from the beginning of his pontificate[1]—he was evidently attempting to extend his power. But he encountered the opposition of the Lombard prince of Benevento and the patrician of Sicily, who governed, or professed to govern, in the name of the Emperor, Sicily, Calabria, and the Duchy of Naples.

Charles had no intention of surrendering Italy to the Pope. He was King of the Lombards, and as such he fully intended to become the master of the whole Peninsula. Thus, when he went to Rome for the second time, at Easter 780, going back on his first declarations, made when he had not yet conquered the Lombard crown, he prevented the Pope from extending his authority to Spoleto, whose duke acknowledged his sovereignty.

On the other hand, the Byzantine Empire, where, after the death of Leo IV, the Empress Irene had renounced Iconoclasty, was suggesting a *rapprochement*. In 781 an embassy came from Constantinople to ask Charles for the hand of his daughter Rothrude for the young Emperor, and they were accordingly betrothed.[2] This was obviously not the moment for embroiling himself with the Emperor, so that Charles was unable to support the enterprises of the Pope against the Imperial territories.

At the close of the year 786 Charles was once more in Rome, having been called thither by the conspiracies of the Duke of Benevento, whom he was obliged to reduce to obedience. But almost immediately upon his departure Duke Arichis concocted

---

[1] JAFFÉ-WATTENBACH, *Regesta*, p. 289.
[2] LOT, PFISTER, and GANSHOF, *op. cit.*, p. 425.

an alliance with Byzantium, according to which he was to receive the title of patrician and represent the Emperor in Italy, and even in Rome. The Pope and Charles were thus suddenly threatened with a Byzantine offensive. The clash which occurred in 788 ended in reinforcing Charles's hold on Benevento, while in the North he conquered Istria.[1] Nevertheless, Charles was never really able to impose his sovereignty upon Benevento, despite his unsuccessful expeditions against the Duke in 791, 792–793, 800, 801–802.[2]

Charles protected the Pope because of his veneration for Saint Peter, but he did not subordinate himself to the pontiff, as Pippin had done. He even attempted to dictate to him in a matter of dogma. After the reprobation of Iconoclasty by the Council of Nicaea in 787, which, from the dogmatic standpoint, reconciled Rome and Constantinople, Charles refused to accept all the decisions of the Council. He had a series of treatises against the Council composed by theologians—the Libri Carolini—and he sent an ambassador to Rome, who presented to the sovereign pontiff a capitulary containing eighty-five remonstrances addressed to the Pope; and finally, in 794, he assembled all the bishops of the West at Frankfort, in a Council which abandoned several of the conclusions of the Council of Nicaea, and condemned the doctrines of the worshippers of images.[3]

In 796, after the death of Adrian, Charles wrote to his successor, Leo III, that he was "lord and father, king and priest, chief and guide of all Christians."[4] And he laid down the lines which the Pope was to follow, defining very exactly the limits of his own temporal power and those of the spiritual power of the Pope.[5]

---

[1] LOT, PFISTER, and GANSHOF, op. cit., p. 427.   [2] Ibid., p. 427.

[3] DAWSON, Les origines de l'Europe, French translation, p. 227.

[4] DAWSON, op. cit., p. 226.

[5] Nostrum est: secundum auxilium divinae pietatis sanctam undique Christi ecclesiam ab incursu paganorum et ab infidelium devastatione armis defendere foris, et intus catholicae fidei agnitione munire. Vestrum est, sanctissime pater: elevatis ad Deum cum Moyse manibus nostram adjuvare militiam, quatenus vobis intercedentibus Deo ductore et datore populus Christianus super inimicos sui sancti nominis ubique semper habeat victoriam, et nomen domini nostri Jesu Christi toto clarificetur in orbe. Alcuini Epistolae, No. 93, ed. DÜMMLER, M.G.H. EPIST., vol. IV, pp. 137–138.

Meanwhile, on succeeding to Adrian, Leo III sent him the banner of the city of Rome[1] and introduced the new fashion of inserting in the date of his bulls the year of Charles's reign, *a quo cepit Italiam.*

It is obvious that Charles no longer regarded himself as a *patricius Romanorum.* He was acting as the protector of Christianity. At this period he had triumphed over Saxony and the Lombards, and had subdued the Avars or driven them across the Theiss (796), and in the plenitude of his power he could claim to assume this rôle. Apart from the petty princes of England and Spain he was the only sovereign in the West. His situation was superior to that enjoyed by any king in history, and although the remnants of Byzantine supremacy still lingered in "Romania," there was no such influence in the North, nor in the Anglo-Saxon and Germanic environment which Charles inhabited; Alcuin, in addressing himself to Charles, might well call him Emperor.[2]

In Rome itself, the Pope, although he did not deny the sovereignty of the Emperor of Byzantium, was in fact no longer his subject. Was it not inevitable that the idea should occur to him, recognizing as he did the power and the prestige of the King of the Franks, of reconstituting, for the benefit of Charles, that Empire which since the 5th century had no longer existed in the West? But it is evident that what he had in mind was not merely to reconstitute the Empire *in partibus Occidentis*, and to create, so to speak, a successor to Romulus Augustulus. To do this would be to bring the Emperor back to Rome, and then he would be in his power. But he wished to remain independent of him. This is clearly proved by the mosaic which he had placed in the *triclinium* of the Lateran, in which we see Saint Peter presenting the *pallium* to Leo III and the standard to Charles. It was not Imperial Rome, but the Rome of Saint Peter that the Pope wished to exalt by reconstituting the Empire; Rome, the head of the *ecclesia*, that *ecclesia* of which Charles

---

[1] BÖHMER-MUHLBACHER, *op. cit.*, p. 145.

[2] *Ad decorem imperialis regni vestri.* LOT, PFISTER, and GANSHOF, *op. cit.*, p. 457, n. 10.

proclaimed himself the soldier. Did not Charles himself declare, in speaking to Leo III, that his people was the *populus Christianus?*

Charles, of course, could have conferred upon himself the dignity of Emperor, or he could have had it conferred upon him by a synod of his Church. But how much more legitimate it would appear to all Christendom if it were bestowed upon him by the initiative of the Pope! The disproportion between the title of *patricius* which Charles bore and the power which he possessed would disappear. He would be the military representative of Saint Peter as the Pope was his religious representative. They would both be bound together in the same system, that of the *ecclesia.*

By the year 800 Charles had conquered Saxony and Bavaria, annihilated the Avars, and attacked Spain. Almost the whole of Western Christendom was in his hands.

And on December 25th, 800, by placing on his head the Imperial crown, the Pope consecrated this Christian Empire. Charlemagne received his title in accordance with the usage of Byzantium; that is to say, by *acclamatio.* The Pope then placed the crown upon his head and adored him.[1]

As regards its form, then, Charles's accession to the Empire was in conformity with legality.[2] He was acclaimed by the people, as in Byzantium. In reality, however, there was one essential difference between the accession of Charles and that of a Byzantine Emperor. As a matter of fact, the Romans who acclaimed him were not, like the people of Constantinople, the representatives of an Empire, but the inhabitants of a city of which the Emperor elect was the patrician. Their acclamations could not bind the subjects of Charles from the Elbe to the Pyrenees. As a matter of fact, these acclamations were simply drama. In reality it was the Pope, the head of the *ecclesia,* and therefore the *ecclesia* itself, that gave Charles the Empire; and thereby he became its appointed defender. Unlike

[1] HARTMANN, *op. cit.,* vol. II², p. 348, does not credit Eginhard when the latter claims that Charles was surprised by the initiative of Leo III. According to him the whole ceremony was agreed upon beforehand.

[2] *Ibid.,* vol. II², p. 350.

the title of the old Roman Emperor, his Imperial title had no secular significance. The accession of Charles to the Empire did not correspond with any kind of Imperial institution. But by a sort of *coup d'état* the patrician who had protected Rome became the Emperor who protected the Church.

The power which had been conferred upon him made him not an Emperor, but *the* Emperor. There could no more be two Emperors than there could be two Popes. Charles was the Emperor of the *ecclesia* as the Pope conceived it, of the Roman Church, regarded as the universal Church.[1] He was *serenissimus Augustus, a Deo coronatus, magnus, pacificus, imperator.* Note that he did not call himself *Romanorum imperator*, nor *semper Augustus*, titles borne by the Roman Emperors. He added only *Romanorum gubernans imperium*, a somewhat vague expression to which reality was given by the titles *rex Francorum* and *Longobardorum*. The Pope himself called him in his Bulls *imperante domino nostro Carolo piissimo perpetuo Augusto a Deo coronato magno et pacifico imperatore.*[2]

The centre of the effective power of this defender of the Church, this holy and pious Emperor, was not in Rome, where he had received the Imperial power, but in the north of Europe. The ancient Mediterranean Empire had logically been centred upon Rome. The new Empire was logically centred upon Austrasia. The Emperor of Byzantium was an impotent witness of the accession of this new Emperor. All he could do was to refuse to acknowledge Charles. But on January 13th, 812, the two Empires concluded peace. The Emperor of Byzantium accepted the new condition of things. Charles surrendered Venice and Southern Italy, which

---

[1] Charles's position as the head of Christendom found further expression on his coins, which were impressed with the legend: *Christiana religio* (HARTMANN, *op. cit.*, vol. II², p. 334). According to PROU, *Cat. des monnaies carol.*, p. xi, these coins were struck after the coronation. They show the bust of the Emperor, looking to the right, with the legend: D. N. Karlus Imp. Aug. Rex F. et L. The head is crowned with a classic wreath of laurel and the shoulders are covered with the *paludamentum*, like those of the Roman Emperors of the Early Empire.

[2] A. GIRY, *Manuel de Diplomatique*, p. 671. Under Justinian the Pope wrote: *imperante domino nostro Justiniano perpetuo augusto* (GIRY, *op. cit.*, p. 668).

he restored to the Byzantine Empire.[1] On the whole, Charles's policy in Italy had failed; he had not become a Mediterranean power.

Nothing reveals more clearly the upheavals of the ancient and Mediterranean order which had prevailed for so many centuries. The Empire of Charlemagne was the critical point of the rupture by Islam of the European equilibrium. That he was able to realize this Empire was due, on the one hand, to the fact that the separation of East from West had limited the authority of the Pope to Western Europe; and, on the other hand, to the fact that the conquest of Spain and Africa by Islam had made the king of the Franks the master of the Christian Occident.

It is therefore strictly correct to say that without Mohammed Charlemagne would have been inconceivable.

In the 7th century the ancient Roman Empire had actually become an Empire of the East; the Empire of Charles was an Empire of the West.

In reality, each of the two Empires ignored the other.[2]

And in conformity with the direction followed by history, the centre of this Empire was in the North, to which the new centre of gravity of Europe had shifted. With the Frankish kingdom—but it was the Austrasian-Germanic Frankish kingdom—the Middle Ages had their beginning. After the period during which the Mediterranean unity subsisted—from the 5th to the 8th century—the rupture of that unity had displaced the axis of the world.[3]

Germanism began to play its part in history. Hitherto the Roman tradition had been uninterrupted. Now an original Romano-Germanic civilization was about to develop.

[1] HARTMANN, op. cit., vol. III[1], p. 64.

[2] The coronation of Charles was not in any sense explained by the fact that at this moment a woman was reigning in Constantinople.

[3] HARTMANN, op. cit., vol. II[2], p. 353, perceived this very clearly when he wrote: "Geographically and economically, politically and culturally, there had been a rearrangement in the grouping of the Christian peoples which gave the mediaeval epoch its peculiar stamp."

Cf. also DAWSON, op. cit., p. 147: *It is in the seventh century, and not in the fifth, that we must place the end of the last phase of ancient Mediterranean civilization, the age of the Christian Empire, and the beginnings of the Middle Ages.*

THE CAROLINGIANS AND THE VOLTE-FACE OF THE PAPACY

The Carolingian Empire, or rather, the Empire of Charlemagne, was the scaffolding of the Middle Ages. The State upon which it was founded was extremely weak and would presently crumble. But the Empire would survive as the higher unity of Western Christendom.

CHAPTER III

THE BEGINNINGS OF THE MIDDLE AGES

1. *Economic and Social Organization*

It is quite usual to regard the reign of Charlemagne as a period of economic restoration. Some have even gone so far as to suggest that in the economic domain, as in that of letters, there was an actual renaissance. But this is an obvious mistake, explained not merely by a bias in favour of the great Emperor, but also by what may be called an incorrect perspective.

The historians have always compared the last phase of the Merovingian epoch with the reign of Charlemagne; and if this is done it is not difficult to perceive a recovery. In Gaul, anarchy was followed by order; while in Germany, conquered and evangelized, the social progress is plainly visible. But if we wish to arrive at a correct appreciation of the actual state of affairs, we must compare the whole of the ages which proceeded the Carolingian epoch with that epoch itself. We see then that we are confronted with two different and indeed contrasting economies.

Before the 8th century what existed was the continuation of the ancient Mediterranean economy. After the 8th century there was a complete break with this economy. The sea was closed. Commerce had disappeared. We perceive an Empire whose only wealth was the soil, and in which the circulation of merchandise was reduced to the minimum. So far from perceiving any progress, we see that there was a regression. Those parts of Gaul which had been the busiest were now the poorest. The South had been the bustling and progressive region; now it was the North which impressed its character upon the period.

In this anti-commercial civilization, however, there was one exception, which seems to contradict all that has just been said.

It is undoubtedly the fact that in the first half of the 9th century the extreme north of the Empire—later to become the Low

Countries—was a centre of the busiest navigation, which formed a striking contrast with the atony of the rest of the Empire.

In this, however, there was nothing absolutely new. Even under the Roman Empire this region, where the Scheldt, the Meuse, and the Rhine mingle their waters, had carried on a maritime trade with Britain. It exported corn for the garrisons of the Rhine, and imported spices and other products which had come by way of the Mediterranean. Such commerce, however, was merely a prolongation of the commercial current of the Tyrrhenean Sea. The trade of this region constituted part of the general commercial activity of "Romania," and the region itself was the extreme tip of the Empire. The monument of the goddess Nehalennia, the Celtic patroness of navigation, still serves to remind us of the importance of this traffic.[1] The vessels engaged in it sailed as far afield as the mouths of the Elbe and the Weser. Later on, at the time of the invasions of the 3rd century, it was necessary to organize a battle fleet to ward off the raids of the Saxons. The principal port in which the seagoing vessels met those from the interior was Fectio (Vechten), near Utrecht.

This navigation, which suffered greatly from the invasions of the 5th century and the conquest of Britain by the Saxons, recovered itself, and was continued in the Merovingian epoch. It is possible that in the 8th century this traffic was extended as far as Scandinavia.[2] Fectio was replaced by the ports of Duurstede on the Rhine and Quentovic at the mouth of the Canche. At Quentovic many Merovingian coins have been found[3]; we have also many from Maastricht,[4] and these are far more numerous than those from Cologne, Cambrai, etc. We have also coins found in Antwerp, and many from Huy,[5] Dinon, and Namur.[6] Finally, many coins were struck at Duurstede[7] in Frisia.[8]

[1] CUMONT, *Comment la Belgique fut romanisée*, pp. 26 and 28.
[2] VOGEL, *Die Normannen*, pp. 44 et seq.
[3] PROU, *Catalogue des monnaies mérovingiennes*, pp. 245–249.
[4] *Ibid.*, pp. 257–261.   [5] *Ibid.*, pp. 261–264.
[6] *Ibid.*, pp. 265–266.   [7] *Ibid.*, pp. 267–269.
[8] *Ibid.*, pp. 269–270. For the trade of Duurstede, see VOGEL, *Die Normannen*, pp. 66 et seq.

Why had this commerce, which flourished in the Northern provinces, disappeared in the Carolingian epoch? The seas on the Northern coast were still free. Moreover, the Flemish cloth industry, which had fed the navigation of the region since the Roman epoch, had not disappeared.[1] There were even fresh reasons which should have favoured the continuation of this commercial activity. In the first place, the presence of the court at Aix-la-Chapelle, and, secondly, the pacification and annexation of Frisia. We know that the Frisian boats were very busy on all the rivers of this region, and on the Upper Rhine, until the catastrophe of the Norman invasions.[2] Gold coins have been found in Frisia.[3] Finally, the principal *tonlieux* of the Carolingian epoch—that is to say, Rouen, Quentovic, Amiens, Maastricht, Duurstede, and Pont-Saint-Maxence—were all situated in the North.[4] Commerce was therefore very active in this northern corner of the Empire; indeed, it seems to have been even more active than before.

This commerce, however, was oriented toward the North, and had no longer any connection with the Mediterranean. It seems to have included in its domain, in addition to the rivers of the Low Countries, Britain, and the seas of the North. Here, then, we have a characteristic proof of the closing of the Mediterranean. In this

---

[1] H. PIRENNE, *Draps de Frise ou draps de Flandre?* VIERTELJAHRSCHRIFT FUR SOZIAL UND WIRTSCHAFTSGESCHICHTE, vol. VII, 1909, pp. 309-310.

[2] PROU mentions numerous deniers which were struck at Duurstede under Charlemagne, Louis the Pious, and Lothair I. PROU, *Catalogues de monnaies carolingiennes*, pp. 9-12. There are also deniers from Maastricht, Visé, Dinant, Huy, Namur, Cambrai, Verdun (very numerous), Ardenburg, Bruges, Gand, Cassel, Courtrai, Thérouanne, Quentovic (very numerous), Tournai, Valenciennes, Arras, Amiens, Corbie, Peronne. *Ibid.*, pp. 14-38.

[3] PROU, *op. cit.*, p. xxxiii.

[4] VERCAUTEREN, *Etude sur les Civitates*, p. 453. In 790, Gervoldus is: *super regni negotia procurator constituitur per multos annos, per diversos portus ac civitates exigens tributa atque vectigalia, maxime in Quentawich. Gesta abbatum Fontanellensium*, ed. M.G.H. SS. *in usum scholarum*, p. 46. In 831 Louis the Pious granted the Church of Strasbourg exemption from the *tonlieu* throughout his kingdom, except at Quentovic, Duurstede and the *Clusae*. Cf. G. G. DEPT, *Le mot "Clusa" dans les diplômes carolingiens*, MELANGES H. PIRENNE, vol. I, p. 89.

Northern commerce the Frisians played the part which the Syrians had played in the Mediterranean.

The hinterland of Amiens and Quentovic extended as far as the threshold of Burgundy, but not farther.[1] The trade of Tournai seems to have been fairly important in the 9th century.[2]

But in the second half of the 9th century the Norman invasions put an end to this commerce.[3]

Nevertheless, it had been extremely active, and it had been able to preserve a superior kind of economic activity. To a great extent, moreover, this commerce must have become increasingly dependent on the commerce of the Scandinavians, who, in the 9th century, exported French wines to Ireland.[4] The relations which the Scandinavians maintained with Islam by way of Russia must have given their trade a powerful impetus. In the 9th century there were important ports in the Baltic, or perhaps we should rather say maritime *étapes*.[5] We know, thanks to the archaeologists, that the trade of Haithabu extended, between 850 and 1000, to Byzantium and Baghdad, along the Rhine, and into England and the north of France.

The Viking civilization developed very considerably in the 9th century, as is shown by the funeral furnishings found in the ship of Oseberg, which is to-day in the museum at Oslo.[6] The oldest Arab *dirhems* found in Scandinavia date from the end of the 7th

---

[1] VERCAUTEREN, *L'interprétation économique d'une trouvaille de monnaies carolingiennes faite près d'Amiens*, REVUE BELGE DE PHIL. ET D'HIST., vol. XIII, 1934, p. 750–759, shows that there were no coins in this treasure originating from the south of the Loire, and that 90 per cent of them were struck in the region between the Meuse and the Seine.

[2] VERCAUTEREN, *Etude sur les Civitates*, pp. 246–247.

[3] Concerning BUGGE's exaggerations in respect of the trade of the Normans with France, see VOGEL, *Die Normannen*, pp. 417–418.

[4] BUGGE, *Die Nordeuropäischen Verkehrswege im frühen Mittelalter*, VIERTELJAHRSCHRIFT FUR SOZIAL UND WIRTSCHAFTSGESCHICHTE, vol. IV, 1906, p. 271.

[5] In 808–809 the port of Reric was destroyed by the King of Denmark, who compelled the merchants to settle at Haithabu in order to facilitate the collection of the *tonlieu*. Annales regum Franc., ed. KURZE, a_7^0 808, p. 126.

[6] E. DE MOREAU, *Saint Anschaire*, 1930, p. 16.

century (698). But the greatest expansion of the Vikings dates from the close of the 9th century and the middle of the 10th century. At Birka, in Sweden, objects of Arab origin have been found, and others originating in Duurstede and Frisia. In the 9th century the Scandinavians of Birka exported wine from Duurstede.[1]

The coins of Birka, of the 9th and 10th centuries, have been found in Norway, Schleswig, Pomerania and Denmark. They were imitations of the deniers of Duurstede, struck under Charlemagne and Louis the Pious.

The Carolingian Empire had therefore two sensitive economic points: one in northern Italy, thanks to the commerce of Venice, and one in the Low Countries, thanks to the Frisian and Scandinavian trade. And in these two regions the economic renaissance of the 11th century had its beginnings. But neither was able to reach its full development before the 11th century: the first was very soon crushed by the Normans, and the other hampered by the Arabs and the turmoil in Italy.

One cannot too strongly insist on the importance of the Scandinavians after the close of the 8th century.[2] They took possession of Frisia and held all the river valleys to ransom, very much as the Arabs were doing in the Mediterranean at this same period. But here there was no Byzantium, Venice, or Amalfi to resist them. They crushed all those whom they encountered, until the moment came when they resumed peaceful negotiations.

In 834 the Normans made their first attack upon Duurstede and burned part of the town.[3] During the next three years Duurstede was attacked every year. Its decline, and that of the whole of Frisia, dates from this period, although some traces of activity survived until the close of the 9th century.

In 842 Quentovic was attacked in its turn,[4] and in 844 the town was given over to the most terrible pillage, from which it did

[1] Concerning Birka see the *Vita Anskarii*, ed. G. WAITZ, M.G.H. SS. *in us. schol.*, p. 41.

[2] H. PIRENNE, *Les villes du Moyen Age*, pp. 46 et seq.

[3] VOGEL, *Die Normannen*, pp. 68 and 72. According to HOLWERDA Duurstede must have disappeared in 864.　　　　[4] VOGEL, *op. cit.*, p. 88.

not recover. Its trade was removed, seventy years later, when the incursions of the Northmen had ceased, to Étaples.[1]

This flourishing commerce, for which Duurstede and Quentovic were the harbours of export, was absolutely different from the trade carried on by the Scandinavians. While the latter was undergoing continual development, on account of its contact, by way of Byzantium, with the Oriental world, the commerce of the Frisians was not in touch with the South. It was strictly confined to the North. And in this it is very clearly distinguished from the commerce of Gaul in the Merovingian epoch, which enabled the Mediterranean civilization to penetrate everywhere, with the wine, spices, papyrus, silk, and other products of the Orient.

In the Carolingian Empire there were hardly any other commercial centres besides Quentovic and Duurstede.

A certain importance may be attributed to Nantes, which was burned in 843, and whose boatmen carried on a certain amount of trade with the region of the Loire,[2] but we must not take it for granted that the existence of a *tonlieu* is sufficient proof of commercial transit.[3]

Of course, it is not difficult to glean from Theodulf, Ermoldus, Nigellus, the lives of the saints, and the poems of the time, to say nothing of the too famous monk of Saint Gall, sporadic mentions of merchants and merchandise. And it is quite possible to construct, with these scattered elements, an edifice which is merely a fantasy of the imagination. It is enough for a poet to say that there were boats upon a river, and we immediately conclude, from this commonplace detail, that a great commercial traffic existed; while the presence of a few pilgrims in Jerusalem, or of some Oriental artist or scholar at the Carolingian court, is enough foundation for the statement that there was constant navigation between the West and the East.

[1] VOGEL, *op. cit.*, p. 100.　　　　　　　　　　　　　　[2] *Ibid.*, p. 90.
[3] There is a good example in VOGEL, *op. cit.*, p. 138, n. 2. In 856 the Duke of Brittany, Erispoë, gave the bishop the *tonlieu* of the boats at Nantes. Now at this time the commerce of this city had been destroyed by the Normans.

Certain writers have even gone so far as to invoke the maritime commerce of Venice and the cities of Southern Italy, which belonged to the economic system of Byzantium, on behalf of the Carolingian economy.

And what does it signify if a few pieces of gold were still struck in the 9th century ?[1] The important thing is not to discover in the texts a few references to commerce and exchange; for commerce and exchange have existed in all ages. What does matter is the importance and the character of this commerce and this exchange. In order to appreciate the nature of an economic movement we need general and comprehensive data; something better than miscellaneous details, than exceptions and singularities. The presence of an isolated pedlar or boatman is no proof of the existence of a system of exchange. If we consider that in the Carolingian epoch the minting of gold had ceased, that lending money at interest was prohibited, that there was no longer a class of professional merchants, that Oriental products (papyrus, spices, silk) were no longer imported, that the circulation of money was reduced to the minimum, that laymen could no longer read or write, that the taxes were no longer organized, and that the towns were merely fortresses, we can say without hesitation that we are confronted with a civilization which had retrogressed to the purely agricultural stage; which no longer needed commerce, credit, and regular exchange for the maintenance of the social fabric.

We have already seen that the essential cause of this transformation was the closing of the Western Mediterranean by Islam. The Carolingians were able to check the Saracen advance towards the North; they were not able to reopen the sea, and for that matter, they did not attempt to do so.

Their attitude toward the Musulmans was purely defensive. The first Carolingians, and even Charles Martel himself, still further increased the disorder in placing the kingdom, attacked

---

[1] F. VERCAUTEREN, in LOT, PFISTER, and GANSHOF, *Histoire du Moyen Age*, vol. I, p. 608. Cf. Offa, King of Mercia, who was still minting a few pieces of gold, *ibid.*, p. 693.

on every side, in a state of defence. Under Charles Martel everything was mercilessly sacrificed to military necessity. The Church was plundered. There were profound disturbances everywhere, provoked by the substitution of Germanic vassals for the Roman aristocrats, the partisans of Ebroin or Eudes of Aquitaine. It seems indeed that the reign of Charles saw the recurrence of disturbances analogous to those of the Germanic invasions. We must not forget that he burned the cities of the Midi, and by so doing definitely destroyed what still remained of the commercial and municipal organization. And it was the same with the great ecclesiastical fabric on which public charity was dependent, the hospitals, and the education which the schools henceforth ceased to provide.

When Pippin succeeded to his father, the entire aristocracy, and consequently the entire people, must have been as illiterate as himself. The merchants of the cities were dispersed. The clergy itself had lapsed into a state of barbarism, ignorance, and immorality of which we may obtain some idea by reading the letters of Saint Boniface. "At this lamentable period," says Hincmer,[1] "not only did they carry off from the Church of Reims all the precious things that it possessed, but the houses of the religious were destroyed and dilapidated by the bishop. The few unhappy clerics who remained sought a means of livelihood in trade, and they hid the deniers which they gained thereby in the charters and manuscripts."

If this was the condition of one of the richest churches of the kingdom we may judge what must have happened elsewhere.

Leidrad's report on Lyons tells us that matters were no better elsewhere. Saint Boniface was receiving incense only in small parcels, which were sent him by his friends in Rome.

As for the currency, this was in a terrible state of confusion. There was practically no gold in circulation. In the contracts of the 8th century there are frequent mentions of prices paid in grain or cattle.[2] The minters of base coins profited by this state of affairs.

[1] *Vita S. Remigii*, M.G.H. SS. RER. MEROV., vol. III, p. 251.
[2] PROU, *Catalogue des monnaies mérovingiennes*, p. vii.

There were no longer any standards of monetary weight or purity.

Pippin attempted without much success to reform the monetary system. His twofold initiative in this domain constituted a complete rupture with the Mediterranean monetary system of the Merovingians. Henceforth only silver coins were minted, and the *solidus* was equivalent to twelve deniers, the denier being now the only real coin. The livre of 327 grammes of silver (the Roman *libra*) was equivalent, after Pippin's reform, to 22 *solidi* or 264 deniers; and by Charlemagne it was reduced to 20 *solidi* or 240 deniers.[1]

Charlemagne completed the monetary reform of his father. He was the founder of the medieval monetary system. This system was therefore established at a period when the circulation of money had sunk lower than it had ever sunk before. Charlemagne adapted the system to a period when wholesale trade had disappeared. In the Merovingian epoch, on the contrary, gold was still minted in consequence of the prevailing commercial activity, and we cannot doubt that this was an epoch of active trade when we see the use of gold perpetuated in the form of the *hyperper*, the successor to the gold *solidus*, in the commercial world of Byzantium, and installing itself in that of Islam. It is characteristic of the period that in the Carolingian Empire itself gold was still minted here and there, wherever there was still some commercial activity; for example, at the foot of the Pyrenees, where there was some traffic with Musulman Spain, and in Frisia, where a certain amount of commercial activity was maintained by the Scandinavian trade.

Charlemagne also struck a few gold *solidi* in the Lombard kingdom before he enforced his monetary system[2] there, which proves that normally he did not mint gold. We have a few gold *solidi* from the mint of Uzès, which were struck during Charlemagne's reign. And we have also a few fine gold coins which

---

[1] LUSCHIN VON EBENGREUTH, *Allgemeine Münzkunde*, 2nd ed., 1926, p. 161.
[2] PROU, *Catalogue des monnaies carolingiennes*, p. xxxii.

were minted under Louis the Pious,[1] bearing the inscription *munus divinum*. These coins must have been fairly widely distributed, since they were imitated by the commercial peoples of the North, probably by the Frisians.[2] The majority of the known examples come from Frisia, but they have been found also in Norway.

"To sum up, while it is true that we find a few gold coins, of a quite exceptional character, struck in the name of Charles and of Louis the Pious, we are none the less justified in saying that these coins were not comprised in the monetary system of the Carolingians. This system comprised only silver coins; it was essentially monometallic,"[3] for we cannot regard this occasional coining of gold as constituting proof of a bimetallist system.[4]

What we have to remember is that under the Carolingians there was a complete break in the monetary system. This break meant the end, not only of gold, but of the *solidus*, the monetary

---

[1] King Offa of Mercia (757–796) minted gold coins, but they were imitated from the Arab coins. LOT, PFISTER, and GANSHOF, *Histoire du Moyen Age*, vol. I, p. 693. This gold was doubtless furnished by the Scandinavian trade, like the gold of the Frisian coins. In any case, this proves the necessity of gold currency for trading over great distances, and confirms the fact that commerce had disappeared where gold coins were replaced by silver.

[2] PROU, *op. cit.*, p. xxxiii.   [3] *Ibid.*, p. xxxv.

[4] DOPSCH, *Naturalwirtschaft und Geldwirtschaft*, 1930, p. 120, is here completely mistaken. He repeats what he said in vol. II, 2nd ed., 1922, of his *Wirtschaftsentwicklung der Karolingerzeit*, p. 306. He attempts, to begin with, to prove, in contradiction to the current theory, which concludes—wrongly, according to him—that silver was minted because there was no more gold, that this latter metal had not disappeared in the 8th century. He tries to prove this by citing the fines in gold which Charlemagne and Louis imposed on the Duke of Benevento (*ibid.*, p. 319), the booty captured from the Avars, and the gold brought into the South of France by the Musulmans of Spain (*ibid.*, p. 319). He alludes to the sum of 900 gold *solidi* given by the mayor of the palace to Saint Corbinian (*ibid.*, p. 319), the finding at Ilanz (Coire, Switzerland) of a few pieces of gold (*ibid.*, p. 320), and also the Frisian gold coins; and lastly, he adduces the great luxury of the epoch! According to him, *loc. cit.*, vol. II, pp. 309 *et seq.*, if the Carolingians minted silver coins it was because they were confronted with a formidable monetary crisis, and that they wished to abolish the prevailing lack of confidence in the base gold coins by replacing these with good, solid silver deniers. In my opinion, this historian is entirely mistaken in comparing this reform with that of the heavy deniers of the 13th century.

basis. And further, the Roman *libra* was abandoned for a much heavier livre: of 491 grammes instead of 327. It was divided into 240 coins of pure silver, which bore or retained the name of deniers. These deniers, and the oboli, in value a demi-denier, were the only real money. But there were also accountants' coins, which were merely numerical expressions, corresponding to a definite number of deniers. These were the sou, which, probably by reason of the duodecimal notation of the Germans, corresponded to 12 deniers, and the livre, which contained 20 sous. Obviously these small coins were not intended for wholesale commerce; their principal function was to serve the convenience of the customers in the small local markets so frequently mentioned in the capitularies, where sales and purchases were made *per denaratas*. The capitularies, by the way, never mention any other coins than these silver deniers.

Thus, the monetary system of Charles constituted a complete break with the Mediterranean economy which had continued until the invasion of Islam, and which after this was no longer applicable, as is clearly proved by the monetary crisis of the 8th century. It is explained by the desire to meet the actual state of affairs, to adapt legislation to the new conditions which were imposing themselves upon society, to accept the facts and comply with them, to replace disorder by order. The new system of silver monometallism corresponded with the state of economic regression.

Where it was still necessary to make large payments, gold was utilized: either the gold of those countries in which it was still being minted, or Arabic or Byzantine coins.[1]

We should also note the paucity of the monetary stock and the restricted diffusion of money. It seemed, as it were, to be tied to those small local markets of which we shall speak presently. It will be readily understood that henceforth it played quite a secondary part in a society from which the impost was no longer collected. We arrive at the same conclusion when we note the

[1] PROU, *Catalogue des monnaies carolingiennes*, pp. xxxi–xxxii; M. BLOCH, *Le problème de l'or au Moyen Age*, ANNALES D'HISTOIRE ÉCONOMIQUE ET SOCIALE, 1933, p. 14.

insignificance of the royal treasury, which was formerly of such material importance. Its liquid property was infinitesmal compared with its real estate.

Charlemagne also introduced new weights and measures, the standards of which were deposited in the palace. Here again there was a break with the ancient tradition. But no later than 829 the bishops notified Louis the Pious of the fact that different measures were employed in the different provinces. Evidently here, as in so many other respects, Charlemagne had attempted more than he could perform.

The Carolingians restored the royal character of the coinage. They caused it to be supervised by the counts and the *missi*, and regulated the number of mints.[1] In 805, however, they attempted to centralize the minting of money in Paris,[2] but in this they were not successful. From the reign of Louis the Pious coins were struck in most of the cities.[3] But in the reign of Charles the Bald the counts usurped the right of minting money. In 827 Louis the Pious granted the right of mintage to a church, but the coins which were struck by the church were still royal. In 920 some of the churches obtained the right to mint coins with their own superscription. This was a complete usurpation, the natural consequence of the king's abandonment of his proper rights.[4]

We may therefore say that until the Carolingian reform there was only a single monetary system for the whole of Christian Europe: Roman and Mediterranean. There were now two, each corresponding to a special economic domain: the Byzantine and the Carolingian, the Oriental and the Occidental. The coinage was affected by the economic disorder of Europe. The Carolingians did not continue the Merovingian monarchy. The contrast between them was as complete as that between gold and silver. That wholesale commerce had disappeared, and that this fact explains the disappearance of gold, must now be demonstrated in some detail, since the matter has been disputed.

This commerce, as we have seen, and as is generally admitted,

[1] PROU, *op. cit.*, p. lxxiv. [2] *Ibid.*, p. lxlix.
[3] *Ibid*, p. li. [4] *Ibid.*, p. lxi.

247

was maintained by means of the navigation of the Western Mediterranean. Now, we have already seen that Islam, in the course of the 8th century, closed the sea to Christian navigation wherever the Byzantine fleet was unable to protect it. The Arab invasions of Provence in the 8th century, and the burning of the cities by Charles Martel, did the rest. It is true that Pippin regained a footing on the shores of the Gulf of Lyons, re-establishing, in 752, his sovereignty over Nîmes, Maguelonne, Agde and Béziers, which were surrendered to him by the Goth Ansimundus;[1] but there were Saracen garrisons in these Visigothic cities, and the population had to take up arms against these garrisons. Narbonne held out the longest. It was only in 759 that the inhabitants massacred the garrison, and consented to receive a Frankish garrison on condition of retaining their national rights.[2]

The foundation of the Omayyad Caliphate in Spain, in 765, resulted in more peaceful relations between the Carolingian State and Islam. But neither this lull, nor the recovery of the coast of the Gulf of Lyons, had the effect of reviving maritime commerce.[3] This was because the Carolingians had no fleet, and therefore could not clear the sea of the pirates who infested it.

They did, however, attempt to obtain security at sea; in 797 they occupied Barcelona,[4] and in 799 the Balearics, which the Saracens had lately devastated, and which yielded themselves to Charles.[5] In 807 Pippin drove the Moors out of Corsica with an Italian fleet.[6] At one moment it seemed as though Charles intended to undertake a naval war; in 810 he commanded that a fleet should be built,[7] but nothing came of it, and he could not prevent the Moors, in 813, from ravaging Corsica, Sardinia, Nice, and Civita Vecchia.

The expedition against the African coast[8] organized in 828 by

---

[1] RICHTER and KOHL, *Annalen des Fränkischen Reichs im Zeitalter der Karolinger*, vol. II, part I, p. 1. L. OELSNER, *Jahrbücher des Fränkischen Reiches unter König Pippin*, p. 340.

[2] RICHTER and KOHL, *op. cit.*, vol. II, part I, 1885, p. 16.

[3] Charles was on excellent terms with Haroun from 797 to 809. KLEINCLAUSZ, *Charlemagne*, p. 342.   [4] RICHTER and KOHL, *op. cit.*, p. 116.

[5] *Ibid.*, p. 144.   [6] *Ibid.*, p. 173. Cf. *ibid.*, p. 184, a° 810.   [7] *Ibid.*, p. 186.

[8] KOHL, *Annalen des Fränkischen Reichs im Zeitalter der Karolinger*, vol. II, part II, 1887, p. 260.

Boniface of Tuscany was no more effectual. Incapable of assuring the safety of the seas, Charles had to confine himself to protecting the coast against the Moors, who were making piratical descents upon it.[1] The Pope also was compelled to put the coast in a state of defence in order to protect it against the expeditions of the Saracens.[2]

After Charles, who had at least an effective defensive policy, the State was helpless. In 838 Marseilles was invaded. In 842 and 850 the Arabs penetrated as far as Arles. In 852 they took Barcelona. The coast was now defenceless against attack. In 848 it was actually infested by Greek pirates, and in 958 the Danes, who had circumnavigated Spain, appeared in Camargue.

About 890 some Saracens from Spain installed themselves between Hyères and Fréjus and established a fortified position at Fraxniétum (La Garde-Frainet) in the Chaîne des Maures.[3] From this they dominated Provence and Dauphine, which they subjected to continual *razzias*.[4] In 931 they were defeated—an extraordinary incident—by a Greek fleet.

Not until 973 was Count Guillaume of Arles able to expel them. Until then they not only retained the mastery of the coast, but they even controlled the passes of the Alps.[5]

The situation was no better on the Italian coast. In 935 Genoa was pillaged.[6]

It will be understood that under these conditions the ports were closed to all traffic. For those who wished to enter Italy from the North the only possible route henceforth was through the passes of the Alps, where they ran the risk of being robbed or massacred by the men of Fraxinetum. We find, on the other hand, that the passes leading to Provence were now deserted.

And it would be a mistake to imagine that there was any trade

---

[1] ABEL and SIMSON, *Jahrbücher des Fränkischen Reiches unter Karl dem Grossen*, vol. II, p. 427. [2] *Ibid.*, vol. II, pp. 488–489.

[3] In August 890, a text informs us: *Sarrazeni Provinciam depopulantes terram in solitudinem redigebant.* M.G.H. CAPIT,. ed. BORETIUS-KRAUSE, vol. II, p. 377.

[4] A. SCHAUBE, *Handelsgeschichte der Romanischen Völker*, p. 98.

[5] *Ibid.*, p. 99.

[6] In 979 the archbishop of this city declared that *res nostrae ecclesiae vastatae et depopulatae et sine habitatore relicte.*

between "Francia" and Spain.[1] Yet Spain was extremely prosperous. It is said that the port of Almeria was provided with hostelries in the year 970. The only imports from Gaul of which we have mention were those of slaves; brought, no doubt, by pirates, and also by the Jews of Verdun.

In this direction, then, international trade was dead after the beginning of the 8th century. The only trade that had managed to survive was the hawking of articles of value of Eastern origin, and this was carried on by the Jews. It is doubtless to this that Theodulf alludes.

There may perhaps have been a certain amount of traffic between Bordeaux and Great Britain,[2] but this in any case was of little importance. Thus all the sources are in agreement.

We have already seen that the importation of papyrus, spices, and silks into "Francia" had ceased. There was no commercial intercourse between "Francia" and Islam. What Lippmann says concerning the manufacture of sugar, which was spreading through the south of Italy, but did not reach the north of the peninsula before the 12th century, is conclusive.[3] The Greeks of Italy might have served as intermediaries, but they did not do so; why, is only too comprehensible.[4]

The class of wealthy merchants had disappeared. Here and there we find mention of a *mercator*[5] or a *negotiator*, but there were no such professional merchants as existed in the Merovingian epoch; no men of affairs who gave land to the churches and succoured the poor; no capitalists who farmed the taxes and lent money to

---

[1] LEVI-PROVENÇAL, *L'Espagne musulmane au Xᵉ siècle*, 1932, p. 183, observes that Languedoc was doubtless tributary to the Musulman industries of Spain in the 10th century, "but the absolute lack of documents on the subject unhappily forbids us to do more than conjecture."

[2] THOMPSON, *An Economic and Social History of the Middle Ages*, 1928, p. 334.

[3] LIPPMANN, *Geschichte des Zuckers*, 2nd ed., 1929, p. 283.

[4] The Monk of Saint-Gall records that Louis the Pious used to give *preciosissima vestimenta* to the great officers of his palace on the occasion of great festivals. Were they of silk? Cf. R. HARPKE, *Die Herkunft der friesischen Gewebe*, HANSISCHE GESCHICHTSBLAETTER, vol. XII, 1906, p. 309.

[5] E. SABBE, *Quelques types de marchands des IXᵉ et Xᵉ siècles*, REVUE BELGE DE PHIL. ET D'HIST., vol. XIII, 1934, pp. 176-187.

officials. We find no further mention of a commercial class in the cities. There were still occasional merchants; there have been such in all ages; but they did not constitute a class of merchants. There were doubtless men who would take advantage of a famine to sell corn outside their own province, or who even sold their own possessions.[1] Above all, there were men who followed the armies in search of profit. Some ventured to the frontiers, where they sold arms to the enemy, or they engaged in barter with the Barbarians. But this was the trafficking of adventurers, not to be regarded as a normal economic activity. The revictualling of the palace at Aix gave rise to a regular service. But this was not a commercial affair; the purveyors were subject to the control of the palace.[2] We find a further proof of the great diminution of fluid capital in the fact that the lending of money at interest was prohibited. Here, no doubt, we see the influence of the Church, which had at an early date forbidden its members to lend money at interest; but the fact that this prohibition was imposed upon commerce, upon which the interdict rested during the whole of the Middle Ages, certainly tends to prove that commerce on a large scale had disappeared. As early as 789 a capitulary prohibited the taking of any profit on money or any other form of loan.[3] And the State adopted the interdict issued by the Church.[4]

---

[1] M.G.H. CAPIT., ed. BORETTUS-KRAUSE, vol. I, p. 131: Order to bishops to inspect the treasuries of churches *quia dictum est nobis, quod negotiatores Judaei necnon et alii gloriantur, quod quicquid eis placeat possint ab eis emere.*

[2] WAITZ, *Deutsche Verfassungsgeschichte*, vol. IV, 2nd ed., 1885, p. 45.

[3] *Ibid.*, p. 51. M.G.H. CAPIT., vol. I, pp. 53 ff. and 132: *Usura est ubi amplius requiritur quam datur; verbi gratia si dederis solidos 10 et amplius requisieris; vel si dederis modium unum frumenti et iterum super aliud exigeris.* M. DOPSCH endeavours in vain to prove that the Carolingians did not oppose interest; he contrives to do so only by an evasion; laymen, he says, *op. cit.*, vol. II, p. 278, were not forbidden to charge interest.

[4] According to M. DOPSCH, Charles made no innovations in respect of anti-usurious legislation, but confined himself to continuing the Merovingian tradition, which forbade clerics to charge interest, *op. cit.*, vol. II, p. 281. The same author gives a few somewhat unconvincing examples to prove that the taking of interest was practised in the Carolingian epoch. It obviously was; since the practice was prohibited it must have existed. That it was

As a general thing, then, there were no merchants by profession in the Carolingian epoch. At most we have evidence, more especially in time of famine, of occasional merchants and abbatial serfs who sold the products of the estates, or bought them in the event of dearth. That commerce was extinct was due to the fact that there were no longer any outlets for it, since the urban population had disappeared; or more precisely, the only commerce was that which supplied the palace in the reigns of Charlemagne and Louis the Pious, when the palace was at Aix. The court was supplied by merchants, but they were merchants of a special category, who were in some degree agents of the revictualling service, amenable to the jurisdiction of the palace and subject to the orders of *magistri*.[1]

They were exempted from the payment of the *tonlieux* at *Clusae*, Duurstede and Quentovic. But they seem to have done business on their own account while attending to the business of the Emperor.[2]

In some cities, and certainly in Strasbourg in 775,[3] the bishop organized a revictualling service with the help of his own people, whom Charles exempted from the payment of the *tonlieux* throughout the kingdom, except at Duurstede, Quentovic, and Clusae.

It was the same, as we know, with the great abbeys.[4] But it is

prohibited is the interesting fact, *op. cit.*, vol. II, pp. 282–284. He concludes, vol. II, p. 286, with this improbable assertion: *Von einer verkehrsfeindlichen Tendenz der Karolinger oder ihrer Gesetzgebung kann also wohl doch nicht die Rede sein.*

[1] The capitulary *de disciplina palatii* (about 820), M.G.H. CAPIT., vol. I, p. 298, entrusts a certain Ernaldus with the supervision of the *mansiones omnium negotiatorum, sive in mercuto sivi aliubi negotientur, tam christianorum quam et judaeorum.* This seems to refer to permanent shops. *Ernaldus seniscalcus* (?) at table, say BORETIUS-KRAUSE. One of the *Formulae Imperiales* of 828, ed. ZEUMER, *Formulae*, p. 314, adds that the merchants are to present their accounts at the palace in May.

[2] *Et si vehicula infra regna . . . pro nostris suorumque utilitatibus negotiandi gratia augere voluerint.* M.G.H. FORMULAE, ed. ZEUMER, p. 315.

[3] G. G. DEPT, *op. cit.*, MELANGES PIRENNE, vol. I, p. 89.

[4] Concerning the circulation of the boats belonging to the abbeys, see LEVILLAIN, *Receuil des actes de Pépin Ier et de Pépin II, rois d'Aqnitaine*, 1926, p. 19, n° VI, p. 59, n° XXI, p. 170, n° XLI. Cf. IMBART DE LA TOUR, *Des immunités commerciales accordées aux églises du VIIe au IXe siècle*, ETUDES D'HISTOIRE DU MOYEN AGE DEDIÉES A. G. MONOD, 1896, p. 71.

only too evident that such services did not, properly speaking, constitute commerce, but rather a privileged revictualling service. On the other hand, this method of revictualling had a very comprehensive radius, since it extended from the North Sea to the Alps.

The very large and constantly increasing number of markets which were established in all parts of the Empire might be regarded as contradicting this theory. We can assume that there was always a market in each *civitas*, and even that there were markets in many of the fortresses, in the vicinity of the abbeys, etc. But we must beware of confounding these markets with fairs. As a matter of fact, we find mention of only a single fair in the Carolingian epoch, that of Saint Denis.

All the data which have come to our knowledge show that these small markets were frequented only by the peasants of the neighbourhood, pedlars, and boatmen. Goods were sold "par deniers"—that is to say, retail. They were places of assembly as well as places where goods were bought and sold.[1] The capitularies which refer to them show that they were frequented mainly by serfs, that is, by peasants. They were visited by unlicensed hawkers, like that *negotiator* who went from market to market offering for sale a sword which he had stolen from the Count of Burgundy, and which, as he could not find a purchaser, he returned to the owner.[2] They were also frequented by Jews. Agobart even complains that in order to facilitate their access to the

[1] M.G.H. CAPIT., vol. I, p. 88: *Ut ... familia nostra ad eorum opus bene laboret et per mercata vacando non eat.* Charles prohibited the holding of markets on Sunday, but only *in diebus in quibus homines ad opus dominorum suorum debent operari* (M.G.H. CAPIT., vol. I, p. 150, §18). Cf. also the priest who *per diversos mercatus indiscrete discurrunt.* M.G.H. CAPIT., vol. II, p. 33. Concerning the infinitesimal character of the transactions, and the ruses of the women who offered base coin, see also M.G.H.CAPIT., vol. II, p. 301, *sub anno* 861. And, further, for mention of the small retail trade: *ibid.*, vol. II, p. 319, a° 864: *illi, qui panem coctum aut carnem per deneratas aut vinum per sextaria vendunt.*

[2] FLODOARD, *Historia Remensis*, IV, 12, M.G.H. SS., vol. XIII, p. 576. Another pedlar is the *mercator* mentioned in the *Vita S. Germani*, who, mounted on his ass *quidquid in una villa emebat, carius vendere satagebat in altera.* HUVELIN, *Essai historique sur le droit des marchés et des foires*, p. 151, n. 4.

markets the day of the market was changed when this was a Saturday.[1]

When the monasteries celebrated a saint's day there was an afflux of the *familia*, coming from long distances, and transactions were effected between its members.[2] The Miracles of Saint Remaclius relate that the serf whose duty it was to look after the vines of the monastery at Remagen, having attended the market, bought two oxen there, which he lost on the road on account of the copious libations in which he had indulged.[3] The date of the religious festival therefore coincided with that of a fair. According to Waitz, the royal authorization was not required for the foundation of the market, unless there was question of an exemption from or a donation of the *tonlieu*. Later, a mint was sometimes erected beside the market, and in this case there was a royal concession. The Edict of Pitres[4] shows that the number of markets was constantly increasing, since it speaks of those that existed under Charlemagne, those which were established under Louis, and those which were opened in the reign of Charles the Bald. Now, the economic decadence of the country was continually aggravated by the Norman incursions, which clearly proved that the number of markets was explained not by an alleged development of commerce, but rather by the fact that the trade of the country was turned back upon itself.

As early as 744 the capitulary of Soissons instructed the bishops to open in each city a *legitimus forus*.[5] None of these little markets was much frequented.[6] On most occasions eggs, fowls, etc. were sold there. But it was doubtless possible to procure manufactured

---

[1] WAITZ, *op. cit.*, vol. IV, 2nd ed., p. 47, n. 3.

[2] *Ibid.*, p. 52. This is called *forum anniversarium* or *mercata annuale* as distinguished from *forum hebdomadarium*.

[3] *Miracula S. Remacli Stabulenses*, M.G.H. SS., vol. XV[1], p. 426.

[4] WAITZ, *op. cit.*, vol. IV, 2nd ed., p. 53 and p. 54 n.

[5] M.G.H. CAPIT, vol. I, p. 30.

[6] VERCAUTEREN *Études sur les civitates*, p. 334 shows that M. DOPSCH, in order to emphasize the importance of the market of Laon, made use of texts which actually do not mention this market.

articles in a few more favoured markets. For example, it is probable that textiles were sold in the Flemish region. A formulary of the *Codex Laudunensis*, originating from Gand, gives the text of a letter in which a clerk sends five sous to a friend, asking him to buy for him a hood (*cucullum spissum*).[1] But we cannot possibly conclude from this that there were wholesale markets, or anything resembling a circulation of goods.

These little markets, which were very numerous, must have been supplied by the domestic industry of the rural potters, blacksmiths and weavers, who supplied the needs of the local population, as in all primitive civilizations. But there was certainly nothing more; we find no trace of resident merchants or artisans. The fact that a small mint was very often established in a market is yet another proof that there was no circulation of money. Moreover, in 865 Charles the Bald granted the Bishop of Chalons permission to open a mint because he could not obtain the deniers which were struck in the royal mints.[2]

No products of distant origin could be obtained in these markets. Thus, Alcuin had a *negotiator* whom he sent to make purchases in Italy.[3] In the 8th century the fair of Saint Denis was almost the only one at which Saxons and Frisians might be encountered.[4]

The more important transactions, as far as there were any, were not concluded in the markets. They took place as occasion offered. They related to valuables, pearls, horses, cattle. The text of a capitulary shows that it was of such transactions that the trade of the *negotiatores* properly so called consisted;[5] and these, "the specialists, the professionals," were almost exclusively Jews.

These Jews were men who actually lived by commerce, and apart from a few Venetians they were almost the only people who did so. To convince ourselves of this we have only to read the capitularies, in which the word *Judaeus* is constantly coupled with

[1] VERCAUTEREN, *op. cit.*, p. 334.
[2] PROU, *Catalogue des monnaies carolingiennes*, p. lxii.
[3] WAITZ, *op. cit.*, vol. IV, 2nd ed., p. 42, n. 3.
[4] HUVELIN, *op. cit.*, p. 149.
[5] M.G.H. CAPIT., vol. I, p. 129, c. 11.

the word *mercator*.[1] These Jews evidently continued to engage in the activities of their co-religionists, who, as we have seen, were dispersed throughout the whole of the Mediterranean basin before the invasion of Islam.[2] But they carried them on under somewhat different conditions.

The persecution of which they had been the victims in Spain at the close of the Visigothic period, when Egica (687–702) went to the length of forbidding them to trade with foreigners or Christians, had not spread to the Frankish Empire. On the contrary, they enjoyed the protection of the sovereign, who granted them exemption from the *tonlieu*. Louis the Pious promulgated a capitulary in their favour (it has not been preserved), which declared that they must be prosecuted only *secundum legem eorum*.[3] The murder of a Jew was punished by a fine to be paid to the *camera* of the king. These were very important privileges, which they had not enjoyed formerly, and which show that the king regarded them as indispensable.

The Carolingians, for that matter, very frequently made use of them. The ambassadors whom they sent to Haroun-al-Raschid were Jews, and we have already seen that there were Jews among the merchants of the palace established at Aix-la-Chapelle.

Louis the Pious took into his service the Jew Abraham of Saragossa, to whom he accorded special protection, and who served him faithfully in his palace.[4] We do not find that any Christian merchant was so favoured.

[1] HOPSCH himself declares: *Die Handelsleute und Juden, was ja vielfach dasselbe war, op. cit.,* vol. I, 2nd ed., p. 168.

[2] We find that in the 9th century there were Jews in Narbonne and Vienne, and above all in Lyons, and perhaps elsewhere in the Midi.

[3] DOPSCH, *op. cit.,* vol. II, 2nd ed., p. 345. M.G.H. FORMULAE, ed. ZEUMER, *Formulae Imperiales,* p. 311, No. 32, p. 314, No. 37, p. 309, No. 30, p. 310, No. 31, p. 325, No. 52. All these formulae date from the reign of Louis the Pious, probably from before 836. See COVILLE, *Recherches sur l'histoire de Lyon,* p. 540.

[4] *Ibid.,* vol. I, 2nd ed., p. 68, M.G.H. FORMULAE, ed. ZEUMER, *Formulae Imperiales,* p. 325, No. 52, *liceat illi sub mundeburdo et defensione nostra quiete vivere et partibus palatii nostri fideliter deservire.*

About 825 Louis the Pious granted a privilege to David Davitis, and Joseph, and their co-religionists, resident in Lyons.[1] They were exempted from the *tonlieu* and other dues imposed on traffic, and placed under the protection of the Emperor (*sub mundeburdo et defensione*). They were allowed to live in accordance with their faith, to perform their religious offices in the palace, to engage Christians *ad opera sua facienda*, to buy foreign slaves and to sell them within the Empire, and to exchange goods and otherwise trade with whom they pleased, and therefore, if the need arose, with foreigners.[2]

What we have learned of the Jews from the *Formulae* is confirmed by what Agobard says of them in his opuscules, which were written between 822 and 830. He angrily emphasizes the wealth of the Jews, the credit which they enjoyed at the palace, the charters which the Emperor sent to Lyons by the hands of his *missi*, and the clemency of these *missi* toward the Jews. The Jews, he says, were supplying wine to the councillors of the Emperor; the relatives of the princes and the wives of the palatines sent presents and clothing to the Jewish women; and new synagogues were being built.[3] This is almost the voice of an anti-Semite speaking of the Jewish "barons." Here, incontestably, we are dealing with great merchants who were indispensable. They were even allowed to employ Christian servants. They could own land; we have proof of this in respect of the "pays de Narbonne," where they owned estates which were cultivated by Christians, for the Jews did not live in the country. As early as 768–772 we find the Pope complaining of this state of affairs.[4] They also possessed estates and vineyards at Lyons, at Vienne in Provence, and in the suburbs of the cities. These they doubtless acquired in order to invest their profits.

The commerce in which they were engaged was generally

---

[1] M.G.H. FORMULAE, ed. ZEUMER, p. 310.
[2] COVILLE, *op. cit.*, p. 540.
[3] At Lyons. Cf. COVILLE, *op. cit.*, p. 541.
[4] JAFFÉ-WATTENBACH, *Regesta pontificum Romanorum*, No. 2389.

wholesale trade; what is more, it was foreign trade. It was through them that the Occidental world still kept in touch with the Orient. The intermediary was no longer the sea but Spain; and through Spain the Jews were in touch with the powers of Musulman Africa and Baghdad. Ibn-Kordadbeh, in the *Book of Routes* (857–874), mentions the Radamite Jews, who "speak Persian, Roman, Arab, and the Frankish, Spanish, and Slav languages. They voyage from the Occident to the Orient, and from the Orient to the Occident, now by land and now by sea. They bring from the Occident eunuchs, women slaves, boys, silk, furs, and swords. They embark in the country of the Franks, on the Western sea, and sail to Farama (Pelustum)[1]. . . . They proceed to Sind, India and China. On returning they are laden with musk, aloes, camphor, cinnamon, and other products of the Eastern lands. Some set sail for Constantinople, in order to sell their merchandise there; others repair to the country of the Franks."[2] It is possible that some may have come by way of the Danube, but undoubtedly the majority travelled through Spain. Theodulf's verses relating to the wealth of the Orient doubtless referred to the goods imported by the Jews.[3] Spain is further mentioned in the text of a *Formula* of Louis the Pious, with reference to the Jew Abraham of Saragossa, and what we know of the merchants of Verdun[4] shows us that they too were in communication with Spain. Also we know that Jews imported textiles from Byzantium and the East into the kingdom of Leon.[5] The Jews, therefore, were the purveyors of spices and costly fabrics. But we see from Agobard's texts that they also dealt in wine.[6] And on the banks of the Danube they traded in

[1] A city "destroyed" near Port Said.

[2] *Le livre des routes et des voyages*, edited and translated from the French by C. BARBIER DE MAYNARD in the JOURNAL ASIATIQUE, 6th series, vol. V, 1865, p. 512.

[3] Ed. DUMMLER, M.G.H. POETAE LATINI AEVI CAROLINI, vol. I, p. 460–461, p. 499, etc.

[4] ROUSSEAU, *La Meuse et le pays mosan en Belgique*, 1930, p. 72.

[5] SANCHEZ-ALBORNOZ, *Estampas de la Vida en Leon durante el siglo* X, 1926, p. 55.

[6] AGOBARD, *Epistolae*, ed. DUMMLER, M.G.H. EPIST., vol. V, p. 183.

salt.[1] In the 10th century the Jews possessed salt works near Nuremberg.[2] They also traded in arms, and exploited the treasuries of the churches.[3]

But their great speciality, as we have already seen, was their trade in slaves. Some of these slaves were sold in the country, but the majority were exported to Spain. We know that at the close of the 9th century the centre of the trade in slaves and eunuchs was Verdun.[4] Our information as to the sale of eunuchs dates from the 10th century, but between 891 and 900 the *Miracula S. Bertini* speak of *Verdunenses negotiatores* going to Spain. According to Luitprand this trade was enormously profitable. The trade in slaves was strictly prohibited in 779 and 781,[5] and again in 845.[6] Nevertheless, it continued. Agobard shows that this trade has existed for a long time, and was doubtless the continuation of the trade of the Merovingian epoch. He mentions that at the beginning of the 9th century a man came to Lyons after escaping from Cordova, where he had been sold as a slave by a Jew of Lyons. And in this connection he asserts that people had told him of children whom the Jews had stolen or bought in order to sell them.[7]

Lastly, it must be added that the Jews also traded in silver, concerning which branch of commerce we have little information.

In addition to these wealthy Jews, who were travelling merchants, there were probably small brokers or pedlars who frequented the markets. But it was the Jews who continued to carry on the wholesale trade. And the goods in which they traded were precisely those which a text of 806 mentions as constituting the speciality of the *mercatores*: gold, silver, slaves, and spices.[8]

[1] M.G.H. CAPIT., vol. II, p. 250.

[2] ARONIUS, *Regesten zur Geschichte der Juden*, p. 56.

[3] *Dictum est nobis, quod negotiatores Judaei necnon et alii gloriantur, quod quicquid eis placeat possint ab eis emere.* M.G.H. CAPIT., vol. I, p. 131, a° 806.

[4] AGOBARD, *Epistolae,* M.G.H. EPIST., vol. V, p. 183, and ROUSSEAU, *op. cit.*, p. 72.

[5] M.G.H. CAPIT., vol. I, p. 51 and p. 190.   [6] *Ibid.*, vol. II, p. 419.

[7] *Epist., loc. cit.*, p. 185, and COVILLE, *op. cit.*, pp. 541–542.

[8] *Auro, argento et gemmis, armis ac vestibus nec non et mancipiis non casatis et his speciebus quae proprie ad negotiatores pertinere noscuntur.* M.G.H. CAPIT., vol. I, p. 129.

Apart from the Jews and the Frisians, there were hardly any merchants properly so called at this period. (I am not here speaking of occasional merchants.) This might well be deduced from the favour which the Jews enjoyed; if they had not been indispensable they would not have been protected as they were. On the other hand, since the Jews were allowed to employ Christians, many of their agents must have passed for *mercatores christiani*. Moreover, the language of the time proves as much: "Jew" and "merchant" became synonymous terms.[1]

Besides the Jews, there may have been here and there a Venetian who had crossed the Alps, but such cases must have been very rare.

In short, the Jew was the professional merchant of the Carolingian age. But it goes without saying that he could not have maintained a large import trade. This is obvious, from the rarity of spices and the decline of luxury. The very fact that goods had to travel overland instead of by sea was bound to result in a great reduction of the import trade. But it was for that reason all the more profitable.

One proof of the unimportance of commerce is found in the fact that neither in the *Formulae* nor in the various records of the period is there any allusion to it. While there is mention in one capitulary of 840 of *cautiones* and of silver confided *ad negociandum*,[2] and in another, of 880, of *scriptum fiduciationis*,[3] the references are to Venice. Commercial law continued as long as the Mediterranean trade continued. It disappeared when the sea was closed.

From all this, then, we may conclude that there was a commercial regression which resulted in making the soil more than ever the essential basis of economic life. It was so already in the Merovingian epoch, although the circulation of merchandise still played an important part. Before the closing of the sea there was

[1] *Mercatores, id est Judaei et ceteri mercatores*, M.G.H. CAPIT., vol. II, p. 252; *mercatores hujus regni, christiani sive Judei, ibid.*, vol. II, p.. 419; *mansiones omnium negotiatorum . . . tam christianorum quam et Judaeorum, ibid.*, vol. I, p. 298; *de cappis et aliis negotiatoribus, videlicet ut Judaei dent decimam et negotiatores christiani undecimam, ibid.*, vol. II, p. 361.

[2] M.G.H. CAPIT., vol, II, p. 134.   [3] *Ibid.*, p. 140.

also, as we have seen, some trade in the products of the soil; we have very little information on the subject, but the trade undoubtedly existed. This may be deduced from the fact that the great landowners paid the impost in money, and that their *conductores* remitted the revenues of their domains in silver. This, of course, implies that the products of the soil were sold. But to whom were they sold? Undoubtedly to the inhabitants of the cities, which were still numerous. And also, perhaps, to traders. Now, under the Carolingians we no longer find any trace of this normal circulation of the products of the soil. The best proof of this is found in the disappearance of oil as a source of light in the churches, and also of incense. No more oil was arriving, even from Provence. Hence the appearance of the *cerarii*, who were unknown before the end of the Merovingian period. Eginhard, at Seligenstadt, could not obtain any wax, and was obliged to have it sent from his domains near Gand.

It was the same with wine, but here the decline was still more striking. It could no longer be obtained in the ordinary way of trade, except here and there through the intermediary of a Jew. Consequently, as it was indispensable, if only for the purposes of religion, every effort was made to secure estates which produced wine. This was especially noticeable in the case of the abbeys of the Low Countries. And it is all the more significant in that these abbeys were situated in the country traversed by the rivers on which the Frisians circulated. It is evident, therefore, that the small amount of traffic on these rivers was not sufficient to supply the abbeys with wine; nevertheless, until the incursions of the Normans a certain amount of wine was exported from France to Scandinavia.

The only way of making sure of obtaining wine was to produce it oneself, for even when it was possible to obtain it through commercial channels one might not always have enough silver to buy it. The only expedient was to purchase vineyards. The abbeys in the valley of the Meuse obtained vineyards on the banks of the Rhine and the Moselle, while those in the valley of the

Scheldt bought vineyards on the banks of the Seine.[1] This wine, one's own property, was brought by serfs, who conveyed it to the monastery under the most profitable conditions, since it was exempted from the *tónlieu*. Thus every abbey had its own means and organs of replenishment. It had no need of outside assistance. It constituted a little self-sufficing commonwealth. We need not regard these abbeys, as did Imbart de la Tour, as privileged merchants, but we must agree with him that "it was by a combination of *corvées* that the church organized their transport by road or river."[2] And the goods which they had brought to them in this way were those which they required as consumers.[3]

Of course, in time of famine the domainal proprietors who had any corn or wine to dispose of were implored to sell it, and they put up the prices. This, however, led to intervention on the part of the Emperor, who wished to prevent the making of unjust profits. But we cannot regard this, as Dopsch has done, as proving the existence of a regular trade in these commodities, any more than we can find such proof in the prohibition to sell outside the Empire.[4]

If we read the correspondence of Lupus of Ferrières, we see that he regarded the necessity of buying and selling as deplorable; and as far as possible people tried to avoid it.

---

[1] VAN WERVEKE, *Comment les etablissements religieux belges se procuraient-ils du vin au haut Moyen Age?* REVUE BELGE DE PHIL. ET D'HIST., vol. II, 1923, p. 643. A clear proof that these domains served to supplement the insufficiencies of commerce is the fact that they were sold when trade revived.

[2] IMBART DE LA TOUR, *Des immunités commerciales accordées aux églises du VIIe au IXe siècle*, ÉTUDES D'HISTOIRE DU MOYEN AGE DÉDIÉES A. G. MONOD, 1896, p. 77.

[3] DOPSCH, *op. cit.*, vol. I, 2nd ed., pp. 324 *et seq.*, endeavours to prove that they produced commodities for the markets. I cannot see that they did this anywhere. But it is true that people who found their vintage insufficient endeavoured to procure *vinum peculiare*, M.G.H. CAPIT., vol. I, p. 83, *Capit. de Villis*, c. 8, in order to supply the *villae dominicae*. This, I suppose, was bought during a superabundant vintage; but we cannot deduce from this, with DOPSCH, *ibid.*, p. 324, the existence of a considerable wine trade. Other texts which he cites in order to prove that the domains produced commodities for the markets are without relevance.   [4] *Ibid.*, pp. 324 *et seq.*

The fact that King Charles the Bald deprived the monastery of Ferrières of the "cell" of Saint Josse[1] had the result that the monks received no further clothing and hardly any fish or cheese, so that they had to live on purchased vegetables;[2] but this was an exceptional case.

The domain of the abbey of Saint Riquier was organized in such a way as to produce all that was necessary to the subsistence of the monks.[3]

In 858 the bishops addressed a letter to the king in which they advised him to govern his *villae* in such a manner that they would be self-sufficing.[4]

In the statutes of Adalhard of Corbie, which date from the first half of the 9th century, we have a lifelike description of an entirely closed domainal administration. There is nowhere any mention of such a thing as sale. The prestations to be furnished to the monastery, whose maximum population was 400 persons, were settled in detail, week by week, for the whole year, from January 1st to January 1st. There were within the monastery, and working for it, *matricularii* and *laici*; in particular, shoemakers, fullers, goldsmiths, carpenters, workers who prepared parchment, blacksmiths, physicians, etc.[5] The monastery lived on the prestations—generally in kind—of the serfs, and by means of their *corvées*. Hence the organization of the *curtes*, which seems to me a creation of the period.[6]

---

[1] Saint Josse, department of Pas-de-Calais, arrondissement and canton of Montreuil-sur-Mer.

[2] LOUP DE FERRIÈRES, *Correspondance*, ed. L. LEVILLAIN, vol. I, 1927, p. 176, n°. 42, a° 845.

[3] *Ut omnis ars, omneque opus necessarium intra loci ambitum exerceretur.* HARIULF, *Chronique de Saint-Riquier*, ed. F. LOT, 1894, p. 56.

[4] *Sufficienter et honeste cum domestica corte vestra possitis vivere.* M.G.H. CAPIT., vol. II, p. 438.

[5] L. LEVILLAIN, *Les statuts d'Adalhard*, LE MOYEN AGE, 1900, p. 352. See also HARIULF, *Chronique de Saint-Riquier*, ed. F. LOT, p. 306.

[6] According to J. HAVET, *Œuvres*, vol. I, p. 31, the word *mansus* is a Carolingian word. BRUNNER, however, *Deutsche Rechtsgeschichte*, vol. I, 2nd ed., p. 370, mentions the existence of *servi mansionarii* from the second half of the 7th century.

Now, we must imagine the society of this epoch as interspersed with monasteries and ecclesiastical foundations, which were its characteristic organs. It was only there that the existence of an economy was possible, thanks to the art of writing.

The ecclesiastical estates were the only domains which were increasing, thanks to the pious donations of the faithful. The royal domain was constantly diminishing, as it was continually creating fresh benefices. These benefices passed into the possession of the military aristocracy, than which nothing could have been less productive, whether it consisted of great officers or of petty vassals (*milites*). We cannot possibly suppose that it engaged in any sort of commerce. Moreover, the *grandi* endeavoured to exploit the estates of the Church by imposing themselves upon them as advowees and devouring their resources. Strictly speaking, the freeholders could, in theory, produce commodities for sale, but they were increasingly burdened with *corveés* and fines.[1]

There were among them many unfortunate wretches who lived on alms, or hired themselves out at harvest-time. We cannot discover that any of them produced commodities for the market. The most fervent desire of all those who possessed a little land was to place themselves under the protection of the monasteries in order to escape the exactions of the justiciary seigneurs.

In short, the whole of society was in a state of dependency on the owners of the soil and the dispensers of justice, while the public power had assumed, or was more and more assuming, a private character. Economic independence, like the circulation of money, had reached its lowest point.

It is true that the capitularies still contained frequent references to *pauperes liberi homines*, but in a great many cases it is evident that each of these *homines* had a seigneur.

The royal power intervened, as long as it still had any prestige, in the cause of Christian morality, in order to prevent the oppression of the poor and helpless. The economic legislation of Charles and

[1] See the picture that the bishops drew of the king's tenants in 858. M.G.H. CAPIT., vol. II, p. 437, § 14.

Louis, so far from seeking to facilitate profit, condemned it as unlawful (*turpe lucrum*).

But all such intervention disappeared in the anarchy of the feudal system, above which still hovered the mirage of the Christian Empire. The Middle Ages had arrived.

2. *Political Organization*

Many historians regard what they call the Frankish epoch as constituting an unbroken whole, so that they describe the Carolingian period as the continuation and development of the Merovingian. But in this they are obviously mistaken, and for several reasons.

1st. The Merovingian period belongs to a *milieu* entirely different from that of the Carolingian period. In the 6th and 7th centuries there was still a Mediterranean with which the Merovingians were constantly in touch, and the Imperial tradition still survived in many domains of life.

2nd. The Germanic influence, confined to the vicinity of the Northern frontier, was very feeble, and made itself felt only in certain branches of the law and of procedure.

3rd. Between the more glorious Merovingian period, which lasted until nearly the middle of the 7th century, and the Carolingian period, there was a full century of turbid decadence, in the course of which many of the features of the ancient civilizations disappeared, while others were further elaborated; and it was in this decadence that the Carolingian period had its origin. The ancestors of the Carolingians were not Merovingian kings, but the mayors of the palace. Charlemagne was not in any sense the successor of Dagobert, but of Charles Martel and Pippin.

4th. We must not be confused by the identity of the name *regnum Francorum*. The new kingdom stretched as far as the Elbe and included part of Italy. It contained almost as many Germanic as Romanic populations.

5th. Lastly, its relations with the Church were completely modified. The Merovingian State, like the Roman Empire, was secular. The Merovingian king was *rex Francorum*. The Carolingian king was *Dei gratia rex Francorum*,[1] and this little addition indicates a profound transformation. So great was this transformation that later generations did not realize the significance of the Merovingian usage. Later copyists and forgers embellished what seemed to them the inadmissible title of the Merovingian kings with a *Dei gratia*.

Thus, the two monarchies—the second of which, as I have endeavoured to show in these pages, was due in some sort to the submersion of the European world by Islam—were far from being continuous, but were mutually opposed.

In the great crisis which led to the collapse of the State founded by Clovis, the Roman foundations crumbled away to nothing.

The first to go was the very conception of the royal power. This, of course, in the form which it assumed under the Merovingians, was not a mere transposition of the Imperial absolutism. I am quite willing to admit that the royal power was, to a great extent, merely a *de facto* despotism. Nevertheless, for the king, as for his subjects, the whole power of the State was concentrated in the monarch.

All that belonged to him was sacred; he could put himself above the law, and no one could gainsay him; he could blind his enemies and confiscate their estates under the pretext that they were guilty of *lèse-majesté*.[2] There was nothing, there was no one that he need consider. The power most resembling his own was that of the Byzantine Emperor, if we take into account the enormous differences due to the unequal levels of the two civilizations.

All the Merovingian administrations preserved, for good or ill, the bureaucratic character of the Roman administration. The

---

[1] This had not yet become the regulation formula under Pippin, but it was always employed from the beginning of Charlemagne's reign. GIRY, *Manuel de Diplomatique*, p. 318.

[2] In the Carolingian period the crime of *lèse-majesté* became synonymous with *Herisliz* and *infidelitas*. WAITZ, *op. cit.*, vol. III, 2nd ed., pp. 308–309. The name of the offence was no longer merely imitated from antiquity. WAITZ, *op. cit.*, vol. IV, 2nd ed., p. 704.

Merovingian chancellery, with its lay referendars, was modelled upon that of Rome; the king picked his agents where he chose, even from among his slaves;[1] his bodyguard of *antrustions* was reminiscent of the Pretorian guard. And to tell the truth, the populations over whom he reigned had no conception of any other form of government. It was the government of all the kings of the period, Ostrogothic, Visigothic, Vandal. It should be noted that even when the kings assassinated one another the peoples did not revolt. Ambitious men committed murder, but there were no popular risings.

The cause of the Merovingian decadence was the increasing weakness of the royal power. And this weakness, by which the Carolingians profited, was due to the disorder of the financial administration, and this again was completely Roman. For, as we have seen, the king's treasury was nourished mainly by the impost. And with the disappearance of the gold currency, during the great crisis of the 8th century, this impost also disappeared. The very notion of the public impost was forgotten when the *curiales* of the cities disappeared.

The *monetarii* who forwarded this impost to the treasury in the form of gold *solidi* no longer existed. I think the last mention of them refers to the reign of Pippin. Thus the mayors of the palace no longer received the impost. The monarchy which they established by their *coup d'état* was a monarchy in which the Roman conception of the public impost was abolished.

The kings of the new dynasty, like the kings of the Middle Ages long after them, had no regular resources apart from the revenues of their domains.[2] There were still prestations, of course (*paraveredi, mansiones*), which dated from the Roman epoch, and in particular the *tonlieu*. But all these were diminishing. The *droit de gîte* was exercised by the functionaries rather than by the king. As for the *tonlieu*, which brought in less and less as the circulation

[1] See the characteristic example of the Count Leudastes, the enemy of Gregory of Tours.

[2] All that remained of the Roman impost was the *justiciae*.

of goods diminished, the kings made donations of it to the abbeys and the *grandi*.

Some writers have attempted to prove the existence of an impost under the Carolingians. As a matter of fact, there was a custom of annual "gifts" in the Germanic portion of the Empire. And, further, the kings decreed collections and levies of silver at the time of the Norman invasions. But these were expedients which were not continued. In reality, it must be repeated, the basis of the king's financial power was his domain, his fisc, if you will. To this, at least, in the case of Charlemagne, we must add the booty taken in time of war. The ordinary basis of the royal power was purely rural. This was why the mayors of the palace confiscated so many ecclesiastical estates. The king was, and had to remain, if he was to maintain his power, the greatest landowner in the kingdom. No more surveys of lands, no more registers of taxes, no more financial functionaries; hence no more archives, no more offices, no more accounts. The kings no longer had any finances; this, it will be realized, was something new. The Merovingian king bought or paid men with gold; the Carolingian king had to give them fragments of his domain. This was a serious cause of weakness, which was offset by booty as long as the country was at war under Charlemagne, but soon after his reign the consequences made themselves felt. And here, let it be repeated, there was a definite break with the financial tradition of the Romans.

To this first essential difference between the Merovingians and the Carolingians another must be added. The new king, as we have seen, was king by the grace of God. The rite of consecration, introduced under Pippin, made him in some sort a sacerdotal personage.[1] The Merovingian was in every sense a secular king. The Carolingian was crowned only by the intervention of the Church, and the king, by virtue of his consecration, entered into the Church. He had now a religious ideal, and there were limits to his power—the limits imposed by Christian morality. We see

[1] There was no unction in Byzantium at this period. M. BLOCH, *Les rois thaumaturges*, 1924, p. 65.

that the kings no longer indulged in the arbitrary assassinations and the excesses of personal power which were everyday things in the Merovingian epoch. For proof we have only to read the *De rectoribus Christianis* of Sedulius of Liège, or the *De via regia* of Smaragdus, written, according to Ebert, between 806 and 813.

Through the rite of consecration the Church obtained a hold over the king. Henceforth the secular character of the State was kept in the background. Here two texts of Hincmar may be cited:[1] "It is to the unction, an episcopal and a spiritual act," he wrote to Charles the Bald in 868; "it is to this benediction, far more than to your earthly power, that you owe the royal dignity." We read further, in the Acts of the Council of Sainte-Macre: "The dignity of the pontiffs is above that of the kings: for the kings are consecrated by the pontiffs, while the pontiffs cannot be consecrated by the kings." After consecration the king owed certain duties to the Church. According to Smaragdus, he had to endeavour with all his might to remedy any defects that had crept into it. But he had also to protect it and to see that the tithe was paid to it.[2]

It will be understood that under these conditions the monarchy acted in association with the Church. We have only to read the Capitularies to realize that these were as much concerned with ecclesiastical discipline and morality as with secular administration.

In the eyes of the Carolingian kings to administer their subjects meant to imbue them with ecclesiastical morality. We have already seen that their economic conceptions were dominated by the Church. The bishops were their councillors and officials. The kings entrusted them with the functions of *missi* and filled their chancellery with clerics. Here is a striking contrast with the Merovingians, who rewarded their lay referendaries by making them bishops. From the time of Hitherius, the first ecclesiastic to enter

[1] Cited by BLOCH, *op. cit.*, p. 71.

[2] EBERT, *Histoire de la littérature du Moyen Age*, French translation by AYMERIC and CONDAMIN, vol. II, p. 127.

the chancellery under Charlemagne, no more laymen were employed there for centuries.[1] Bresslau is mistaken in his belief that the invasion of the palace offices by the Church is explained by the fact that the first Carolingians wished to replace the Roman personnel of the Merovingians by an Austrasian personnel, and that they had to engage Austrasian clerics as being the only Austrasians who could read and write. No: they wanted to make sure of the collaboration of the Church.

However, it is true that they had to seek men of education among the clerics. During the crisis the education of laymen was discontinued. The mayors themselves were unable to write. The platonic efforts of Charlemagne to spread education among the people came to nothing, and the palace academy had only a few pupils. A period was commencing in which "cleric" and "scholar" were synonymous; hence the importance of the Church, which, in a kingdom where hardly anyone had retained any knowledge of Latin, was able for centuries to impose its language on the administration. We have to make an effort to understand the true significance of this fact: it was tremendous. Here we perceive the appearance of a new medieval characteristic: here was a religious caste which imposed its influence upon the State.

And in addition to this religious caste, the king had to reckon with the military class, which comprised the whole of the lay aristocracy, and all such freemen as had remained independent. Of course, we have glimpses of the rise of this military class under the Merovingian kings. But the aristocracy of the Merovingian epoch was strangely unlike that of the Carolingian era. The great Roman landowners, the *senatores*, whether they resided in the cities or in the country, do not give one the impression that they were primarily soldiers. They were educated. Above all things, they sought employment in the palace or the Church. It is probable that the king recruited his army leaders and the soldiers of his bodyguard more particularly among his Germanic *antrustions*. It is

[1] BRESSLAU, *Handbuch der Urkundenlehre*, vol. I, 2nd ed., pp. 373 and 374.

certain that the landowning aristocracy lost no time in attempting to dominate him. But it never succeeded in doing so.[1]

We do not find that the king governed by means of this aristocracy, nor that he allowed it any share in the government as long as he remained powerful. And even though he conferred immunity upon it, he did not surrender either to the aristocracy or to the churches any of the rights of the crown. As a matter of fact, he had at his disposal two terrible weapons against it: prosecution for *lèse-majesté* and confiscation.

But in order to hold his own against this aristocracy it is obvious that the king had to remain extremely powerful: in other words, extremely wealthy. For the aristocracy—like the Church, for that matter—was constantly increasing its authority over the people. This social development, which began in the days of the late Empire, was continuing. The *grandi* had their private soldiers, numerous *vassi* who had recommended themselves to them (had applied to them for protection), and who constituted a formidable following.

In the Merovingian period the seigneurial authority of the landowners was manifested only within the limits of their private rights. But in the period of anarchy and decadence, when war broke out between the mayors of the palace, who were backed by factions of aristocrats, the institution of vassalage underwent a transformation. It assumed an increasing importance, and its military character became plainly apparent when the Carolingian triumphed over his rivals. From the time of Charles Martel the power exercised by the king was essentially based on his military vassals in the North.[2]

He gave them benefices—that is to say, estates—in exchange for military service, and these estates he confiscated from the churches. "Now," says Guilhiermoz,[3] "owing to their importance,

[1] See the references in an earlier chapter to Ebroin and Brunehaut.

[2] Charlemagne's Empire was based on vassalage. Charles had hoped to govern by means of his vassals, and urged men to become vassals of these vassals. LOT, PFISTER, and GANSHOF, *Histoire du Moyen Age*, vol. I, p. 668.

[3] GUILHIERMOZ, *Essai sur les origines de la noblesse*, p. 125.

these concessions to vassals were henceforth found to tempt, not only persons of mean or moderate condition, but the *great*."

And this was entirely in the interest of the grantor, who henceforth gave large benefices "on the condition that the concessionaire served him, not only with his own person, but with a number of vassals in proportion to the importance of the benefice conceded."[1] It was undoubtedly by such means that Charles Martel was able to recruit the powerful Austrasian following with which he went to war. And the system was continued after his time.

In the 9th century the kings exacted an oath of vassalage from all the magnates of the kingdom, and even from the bishops.[2] It became increasingly apparent that only those were truly submissive to the king who had paid homage to him. Thus the subject was disappearing behind the vassal, and Hincmar went so far as to warn Charles the Bald of the consequent danger to the royal authority.[3] The necessity in which the first mayors of the palace found themselves, of providing themselves with loyal troops, consisting of sworn beneficiaries, led to a profound transformation of the State. For henceforth the king would be compelled to reckon with his vassals, who constituted the military strength of the State. The organization of the counties fell into disorder, since the vassals were not amenable to the jurisdiction of the count. In the field they commanded their own vassals themselves; the count led only the freemen to battle. It is possible that their domains were exempt from taxation.[4] They were known as *optimates regeis*.

The chronicle of Moissac, in 813, called them *senatus* or *majores natu Francorum*, and together with the high ecclesiastics and the counts they did indeed form the king's council.[5] The king, therefore, allowed them to partake of his political power. The State was becoming dependent on the contractual bonds established between the king and his vassals.

This was the beginning of the feudal period.

---

[1] GUILHIERMOZ, *Essai sur les origines de la noblesse*, p. 123.
[2] *Ibid.*, p. 128.   [3] *Ibid.*, p. 129, n. 13.
[4] *Ibid.*, p. 134.   [5] *Ibid.*, p. 139, n. 4.

All might still have been well if the king could have retained his vassals. But at the close of the 9th century, apart from those of his own domain, they had become subject to the suzerainty of the counts. For as the royal power declined, from the time of the civil wars which marked the end of the reign of Louis the Pious, the counts became more and more independent. The only relation which existed between them and the king was that of the vassal to his suzerain. They collected the *regalia* for the king; and sometimes they combined several counties into one.[1] The monarchy lost its administrative character, becoming transformed into a *bloc* of independent principalities, attached to the king by a bond of vassalage which he could no longer force his vassals to respect. The kings allowed the royal power to slip through their fingers.

And it was inevitable that it should be so. We must not be misled by the prestige of Charlemagne. He was still able to rule the State by virtue of his military power, his wealth, which was derived from booty, and his *de facto* pre-eminence in the Church. These things enabled him to reign without systematic finances, and to exact obedience from functionaries who, being one and all great landowners, could very well have existed in independence. But what is the value of an administration which is no longer salaried? How can it be prevented from administering the country, if it chooses, for its own benefit, and not for the king's? Of what real use were such inspectors as the *missi*? Charles undoubtedly intended to administer the kingdom, but was unable to do so. When we read the capitularies, we are struck by the difference between what they decreed and what was actually effected. Charles decreed that everyone should send his sons to school; that there should be only one mint; that usurious prices should be abolished in time of famine. He established maximum prices. But it was impossible to realize all these things, because to do so would have presupposed the obedience—which could not be assured—of the *grandi*, who were conscious of their independence, or of the bishops,

[1] In this connection the history of the formation of the country of Flanders is highly characteristic.

who, when Charlemagne was dead, proclaimed the superiority of the spiritual over the temporal power.

The economic basis of the State did not correspond with the administrative character which Charlemagne had endeavoured to preserve. The economy of the State was based upon the great domain without commercial outlets.

The landowners had no need of security, since they did not engage in commerce. Such a form of property is perfectly consistent with anarchy. Those who owned the soil had no need of the king.

Was this why Charles had endeavoured to preserve the class of humble freemen? He made the attempt, but he was unsuccessful. The great domain continued to expand, and liberty to disappear.

When the Normans began to invade the country, the State was already powerless. It was incapable of taking systematic measures of defence, and of assembling armies which could have held their own against the invaders. There was no agreement between the defenders. One may say with Hartmann: *Heer und Staat werden durch die Grundherrschaft und das Lehnwesen zersetzt.*[1]

What was left of the king's *regalia* he misused. He relinquished the *tonlieu*, and the right of the mint. Of its own accord the monarchy divested itself of its remaining inheritance, which was little enough. In the end, royalty became no more than a form. Its evolution was completed when in France, with Hugh Capet, it became elective.

3. *Intellectual Civilization*

As we have seen, the Germanic invasions had not the effect of abolishing Latin as the language of "Romania," except in those territories where Salic and Ripuarian Franks, Alamans, and Bavarians had established themselves *en masse.* Elsewhere the German immigrants became Romanized with surprising rapidity.[2]

---

[1] *Op. cit.,* vol. III[1], p. 22.

[2] According to GAMILLSCHEG, *Romania Germanica,* vol. I, p. 294, their Romanization must have made great progress as early as 600, and was complete by 800.

The conquerors, dispersed about the country, and married to native wives who continued to speak their own language, all learned the Latin tongue. They did not modify it in any way, apart from introducing a good many terms relating to law, the chase, war, and agriculture,[1] which made their way southwards from the Belgian regions, where the Germans were numerous.

Even more rapid was the Romanization of the Burgundi, Visigoths, Ostrogoths, Vandals and Lombards. According to Gamillscheg,[2] nothing was left of the Gothic language when the Moors conquered Spain but the names of persons and places.

On the other hand, the confusion into which the Mediterranean world was thrown by the invasion of Islam resulted in a profound transformation where language was concerned. In Africa Latin was replaced by Arabic. In Spain, on the other hand, it survived, but was deprived of its foundations: there were no more schools or monasteries, and there was no longer an educated clergy. The conquered people made use of a Roman patois which was not a written language. Latin, which had survived so successfully in the Peninsula until the eve of the conquest, disappeared; people were beginning to speak Spanish.

In Italy, on the other hand, it resisted more successfully; and a few isolated schools survived in Rome and Milan.

But it is in Gaul that we can best observe the extent of the confusion, and its causes.

The Latin of the Merovingian epoch was, of course, barbarously incorrect; but it was still a living Latin.[3] It seems that it was even taught in the schools where a practical education was given, while here and there the bishops and senators still read and sometimes even tried to write the classic Latin.

The Merovingian Latin was by no means a vulgar language. It showed few signs of Germanic influence. Those who spoke it

---

[1] GUILHIERMOZ, *op. cit.*, pp. 152 *et seq.*

[2] *Op. cit.*, vol. I, pp. 397–398.

[3] LOT, *A quelle époque a-t-on cessé de parler latin?* BULLETIN DUCANGE, vol. VI, 1931, pp. 97 *et seq.*

could make themselves understood, and understand others, in any part of "Romania." It was perhaps more incorrect in the North of France than elsewhere, but nevertheless, it was a spoken and written language. The Church did not hesitate to employ it for the purposes of propaganda, administration, and justice.[1]

This language was taught in the schools. Laymen learned and wrote it. Its relation to the Latin of the Empire was like that of the cursive in which it was written to the writing of the Roman epoch. And since it was still written and extensively employed for the purposes of administration and commerce, it became stabilized.

But it was destined to disappear in the course of the great disorders of the 8th century. The political anarchy, the reorganization of the Church, the disappearance of the cities and of commerce and administration, especially the financial administration, and of the secular schools, made its survival, with its Latin soul, impossible. It became debased, and was transformed, according to the region, into various Romanic dialects. The details of the process are lost, but it is certain that Latin ceased to be spoken about the year 800, except by the clergy.[2]

Now, it was precisely at this moment, when Latin ceased to be a living language, and was replaced by the rustic idioms from which the national languages are derived, that it became what it was to remain through the centuries: a learned language: a novel mediaeval feature which dates from the Carolingian epoch.

It is curious to note that the origin of this phenomenon must be sought in the only Romanic country in which the Germanic invasion had completely extirpated Romanism: in Britain, among the Anglo-Saxons.

The conversion of this country was organized, as we have seen,

---

[1] H. PIRENNE, *De l'état de l'instruction des laïques a l'époque mérovingienne,* REVUE BENEDICTINE, vol. XLVI, 1934, pp. 165–177.

[2] In 813 a provincial synod assembled at Tours enacted: *Ut easdem homilias quisque aperte transferre studeat in rusticam Romanam linguam, aut Theotiscam, quo facilius cuncti possint intelligere quae dicuntur.* Cf. GAMILLSCHEG, *Romania Germanica,* vol. I, p. 295. The text is in MANSI, *Sacrorum Conciliorum . . . Collectio,* vol. XIV, col. 85.

on the shores of the Mediterranean, and not in the neighbouring country of Gaul. It was the monks of Augustine, despatched by Gregory the Great in 596, who promoted the movement already commenced by the Celtic monks of Ireland.[1]

In the 7th century Saint Theodore of Tarsus and his companion Adrian enriched the religion which they brought with them by the Graeco-Roman traditions. A new culture immediately began to evolve in the island, a fact which Dawson rightly considers "the most important event which occurred between the epoch of Justinian and that of Charlemagne."[2] Among these purely Germanic Anglo-Saxons the Latin culture was introduced suddenly, together with the Latin religion, and it profited by the enthusiasm felt for the latter. No sooner were they converted, under the influence and guidance of Rome, than the Anglo-Saxons turned their gaze toward the Sacred City. They visited it continually, bringing back relics and manuscripts. They submitted themselves to its suggestive influence, and learned its language, which for them was no vulgar tongue, but a sacred language, invested with an incomparable prestige. As early as the 7th century there were men among the Anglo-Saxons, like the Venerable Bede and the poet Aldhelm, whose learning was truly astonishing as measured by the standards of Western Europe.

The intellectual reawakening which took place under Charlemagne must be attributed to the Anglo-Saxon missionaries. Before them, of course, there were the Irish monks, including the greatest of all, Saint Columban, the founder of Luxeuil and Bobbio, who landed in Gaul about 590. They preached asceticism in a time of religious decadence, but we do not find that they exercised the slightest literary influence.

It was quite otherwise with the Anglo-Saxons; their purpose was to propagate Christianity in Germany, a country for which the Merovingian Church had done little or nothing. And this purpose coincided with the policy of the Carolingians; hence the

---

[1] DAWSON, *Les origines de l'Europe*, French translation, p. 208.
[2] *Ibid.*, p. 213.

enormous influence of Boniface, the organizer of the Germanic Church, and, by virtue of this fact, the intermediary between the Pope and Pippin the Short.

Charlemagne devoted himself to the task of literary revival simultaneously with that of the restoration of the Church. The principal representative of Anglo-Saxon culture, Alcuin, the head of the school of York, entered Charlemagne's service in 782, as director of the palace school, and henceforth exercised a decisive influence over the literary movement of the time.

Thus, by the most curious reversal of affairs, which affords the most striking proof of the rupture effected by Islam, the North in Europe replaced the South both as a literary and as a political centre.

It was the North that now proceeded to diffuse the culture which it had received from the Mediterranean. Latin, which had been a living language on the further side of the Channel, was for the Anglo-Saxons, from the beginning, merely the language of the Church. The Latin which was taught to the Anglo-Saxons was not the incorrect business and administrative language, adapted to the needs of secular life, but the language which was still spoken in the Mediterranean schools. Theodore came from Tarsus in Cilicia, and had studied at Athens before coming to Rome. Adrian, an African by birth, was the abbot of a monastery near Naples, and was equally learned in Greek and in Latin.[1]

It was the classic tradition that they propagated among their neophytes, and a correct Latin, which had no need, as on the continent, to make concessions to common usage in order to be understood, since the people did not speak Latin, but Anglo-Saxon. Thus, the English monasteries received the heritage of the ancient culture without intermediary. It was the same in the 15th century, when the Byzantine scholars brought to Italy, not the vulgar Greek, the living language of the street, but the classical Greek of the schools.

[1] *Graecae pariter et latinae linguae peritissimus.* BEDE, *Hist. Ecclesiastica*, IV, 1, ed. MIGNE, *Patr. Lat.*, vol. XCV, *circa* 171.

In this way the Anglo-Saxons became simultaneously the reformers of the language[1] and also the reformers of the Church. The barbarism into which the Church had lapsed was manifested at once by its bad morals, its bad Latin, its bad singing, and its bad writing. To reform it at all meant to reform all these things. Hence questions of grammar and of writing immediately assumed all the significance of an apostolate. Purity of dogma and purity of language went together. Like the Anglo-Saxons, who had immediately adopted it,[2] the Roman rite made its way into all parts of the Empire, together with the Latin culture. This latter was the instrument *par excellence* of what is known as the Carolingian Renaissance, although this had other agents in such men as Paulus Diaconus, Peter of Pisa, and Theodulf. But it is important to note that this Renaissance was purely clerical. It did not affect the people, who had no understanding of it. It was at once a revival of the antique tradition and a break with the Roman tradition, which was interrupted by the seizure of the Mediterranean regions by Islam. The lay society of the period, being purely agricultural and military, no longer made use of Latin. This was now merely the language of the priestly caste, which monopolized all learning, and which was constantly becoming more divorced from the people whose divinely appointed guide it considered itself. For centuries there had been no learning save in the Church. The consequence was that learning and intellectual culture, while they became more assertive, were also becoming more exceptional. The Carolingian Renaissance coincided with the general illiteracy of the laity. Under the Merovingians laymen were still able to read and write; but not so under the Carolingians. The sovereign who instigated and supported this movement, Charlemagne, could not write; nor could his father, Pippin the Short. We must not attach any real importance to his ineffectual attempts to bestow this culture upon his court and his family. To please him, a few

[1] We owe a treatise on grammar to Boniface himself. DAWSON, *op. cit.*, p. 229.

[2] DAWSON, *op. cit.*, p. 231.

courtiers learnt Latin. Men like Eginhard, Nithard and Angilbert were passing luminaries. Generally speaking, the immense majority of the lay aristocracy were unaffected by a movement which interested only those of its members who wished to make a career in the Church.

In the Merovingian epoch the royal administration called for a certain culture on the part of those laymen who wished to enter it. But now, in so far as it still required literate recruits—as it did, for example, for the chancellery—it obtained them from the Church. For the rest, since it no longer had a bureaucracy, it had no further need of men of education. The immense majority of the counts were no doubt illiterate. The type of the Merovingian senator had disappeared. The aristocracy no longer spoke Latin, and apart from a very few exceptions, which prove the rule, it could neither read nor write.[1]

A final characteristic of the Carolingian Renaissance was the reformed handwriting which was introduced at this period. This reform consisted in the substitution of the minuscule for the cursive script: that is to say, a deliberate calligraphy for a current hand. As long as the Roman tradition survived, the Roman cursive was written by all the peoples of the Mediterranean basin. It was, in a certain sense, a business hand, or, at all events, the writing of a period when writing was an everyday necessity. And the diffusion of papyrus was simultaneous with this constant need of corresponding and recording. The great crisis of the 8th century inevitably restricted the practice of writing. It was hardly required any longer except for making copies of books. Now, for this purpose the majuscule and the uncial were employed. These scripts were introduced into Ireland when the country was converted to Christianity.[2] And in Ireland, not later than the close of the 7th

[1] BRUNNER, *Deutsche Rechtsgeschichte*, vol. II, 2nd ed., p. 250, confirms this, observing that after Charlemagne the scribes of the judiciary whose appointment he had decreed could no longer be recruited, on account of the repugnance of the (German) laity for *Urkundenbeweis*.

[2] Ireland was converted by the Britons of England (St. Patrick) in the 5th century, shortly before the arrival of the Saxons. DAWSON, *op. cit.*, p. 103.

century, the uncial (semi-uncial) gave rise to the minuscule, which was already employed in the antiphonary of Bangor (680–690).[1] The Anglo-Saxons took these manuscripts, together with those which were brought by the missionaries deriving from Rome, as their example and pattern.[2] It was from the insular minuscule and the Roman *scriptoria*, in which the semi-uncial was much employed, that the perfected or Caroline minuscule was derived at the beginning of the 9th century.[3]

The first dated example of this minuscule is found in the evangelary written by Godescalc in 781, at the request of Charlemagne, who was himself unable to write.[4] Alcuin made the monastery of Tours a centre of diffusion for this new writing, which was to determine the whole subsequent graphological evolution of the Middle Ages.[5]

A number of monasteries, which might be compared to the printing-offices of the Renaissance, provided for the increasing demand for books and the diffusion of these new characters. In addition to Tours, there were Corbie, Orleans, Saint Denis, Saint Wandrille, Fulda, Corvey, Saint Gall, Reichenau, and Lorsch. In most of them, and above all in Fulda, there were Anglo-Saxon monks.[6] It will be noted that nearly all these monasteries were situated in the North, between the Seine and the Weser. It was in this region, of which the original Carolingian domains formed the centre, that the new ecclesiastical culture, or, shall we say, the Carolingian Renaissance, attained its greatest efflorescence.

Thus we observe the same phenomenon in every domain of life. The culture which had hitherto flourished in the Mediter-

---

[1] PROU, *Manuel de paléographie*, 4th ed., 1924, p. 99.
[2] *Ibid.*, p. 102.   [3] *Ibid.*, p. 105.
[4] *Ibid.*, p. 169. M. RAND believes that he has discovered an example of pre-Carolingian minuscule in the Eugippius of the B.N. of Paris, which he places about 725–750. Cf. SPECULUM, April 1935, p. 224.
[5] Tours was also a centre of painting. See W. KOHLER, *Die Karolingischen Miniaturen. Die Schule von Tours*, vol. I²: *Die Bilder*, Berlin, 1933.
[6] DAWSON, *op. cit.*, p. 231.

ranean countries had migrated to the North. It was in the North that the civilization of the Middle Ages was elaborated. And it is a striking fact that the majority of the writers of this period were of Irish, Anglo-Saxon or Frankish origin: that is, they came from regions which lay to the north of the Seine. This was the case, for example, with Alcuin, Nason, Ethelwulf, Hibernicus exul, Sedulius Scotus, Angilbert, Eginhard, Raban Maur, Walahfrid Strabon, Gottschalc, Ermenrich, Wandalbert, Agius, Thegan of Trèves, Nithard, Smaragdus, Ermoldus Nigellus, Agobard, Archbishop of Lyons, Paschase Radvert, Ratram, Hincmar, Milon of Saint-Amand. From the Southern or Mediterranean regions came: Paulus Diaconus, Theodulf of Orleans, Paulinus of Aquiliea, Jonas, Prudentius, Bishop of Troyes, Bertharius, Abbot of Monte Cassino, Audradus, Florus of Lyons, Heric of Auxerre, Servatus Lupus of Sens.

Thus we see that Germany, being converted, immediately began to play an essential part in the civilization to which she had hitherto been a stranger. The culture which had been entirely Roman was now becoming Romano-Germanic, but if truth be told it was localized in the bosom of the Church.

Nevertheless, it is evident that a new orientation was unconsciously effected in Europe, and that in this development Germanism collaborated. Charlemagne's court, and Charlemagne himself, were certainly much less Latinized than were the Merovingians. Under the new dispensation many functionaries were recruited from Germany, and Austrasian vassals were settled in the South. Charlemagne's wives were all German women. Certain judicial reforms, such as that of the sheriffs, had their origin in the regions which gave birth to the dynasty. Under Pippin the clergy became Germanized,[1] and under Charlemagne there were many German bishops in Romanic regions. Angelelmus and Heribald, at Auxerre, were both Bavarians; Bernold, at Stras-

[1] H. WIERUZOWSKI, *Die Zusammensetzung des gallischen und fränkischen Episkopats bis zum Vertrag von Verdun.* BONNER JAHRBÜCHER, vol. 127, 1922, pp. 1-83.

bourg, was a Saxon; at Mans there were three Westphalians in succession; Hilduin, at Verdun, was a German; Herulfus and Ariolfus, at Langres, came from Augsburg; Wulferius, at Vienne, and Leidrad, at Lyons, were Bavarians. And I do not think there is any evidence of a contrary migration. To appreciate the difference we have only to compare Chilperic, a Latin poet, with Charlemagne, at whose instance a collection was made of the ancient Germanic songs!

All this was bound to result in a break with the Roman and Mediterranean traditions. And while it made the West more and more self-sufficing, it produced an aristocracy of mixed descent and inheritance. Was it not then that many terms found their way into the vocabulary to which an earlier origin has often been attributed? There were no longer any Barbarians. There was one great Christian community, coterminous with the *ecclesia*. This *ecclesia*, of course, looked toward Rome, but Rome had broken away from Byzantium and was bound to look toward the North. The Occident was now living its own life. It was preparing to unfold its possibilities, its virtualities, taking no orders from the outer world, except in the matter of religion.

There was now a community of civilization, of which the Carolingian Empire was the symbol and the instrument. For while the Germanic element collaborated in this civilization, it was a Germanic element which had been Romanized by the Church. There were, of course, differences within this community. The Empire would be dismembered, but each of its portions would survive, since the feudality would respect the monarchy. In short, the culture which was to be that of the period extending from the early Middle Ages to the Renaissance of the 12th century—and this was a true renaissance—bore, and would continue to bear, the Carolingian imprint. There was an end of political unity, but an international unity of culture survived. Just as the States founded in the West in the 5th century by the Barbarian kings retained the Roman imprint, so France, Germany, and Italy retained the Carolingian imprint.

CONCLUSION

From the foregoing data, it seems, we may draw two essential conclusions:

1. The Germanic invasions destroyed neither the Mediterranean unity of the ancient world, nor what may be regarded as the truly essential features of the Roman culture as it still existed in the 5th century, at a time when there was no longer an Emperor in the West.

Despite the resulting turmoil and destruction, no new principles made their appearance; neither in the economic or social order, nor in the linguistic situation, nor in the existing institutions. What civilization survived was Mediterranean. It was in the regions by the sea that culture was preserved, and it was from them that the innovations of the age proceeded: monasticism, the conversion of the Anglo-Saxons, the *ars Barbarica*, etc.

The Orient was the fertilizing factor: Constantinople, the centre of the world. In 600 the physiognomy of the world was not different in quality from that which it had revealed in 400.

2. The cause of the break with the tradition of antiquity was the rapid and unexpected advance of Islam. The result of this advance was the final separation of East from West, and the end of the Mediterranean unity. Countries like Africa and Spain, which had always been parts of the Western community, gravitated henceforth in the orbit of Baghdad. In these countries another religion made its appearance, and an entirely different culture. The Western Mediterranean, having become a Musulman lake, was no longer the thoroughfare of commerce and of thought which it had always been.

The West was blockaded and forced to live upon its own resources. For the first time in history the axis of life was shifted northwards from the Mediterranean. The decadence into which the Merovingian monarchy lapsed as a result of this change gave birth to a new dynasty, the Carolingian, whose original home was in the Germanic North.

With this new dynasty the Pope allied himself, breaking with the Emperor, who, engrossed in his struggle against the Musulmans, could no longer protect him. And so the Church allied itself with the new order of things. In Rome, and in the Empire which it founded, it had no rival. And its power was all the greater inasmuch as the State, being incapable of maintaining its administration, allowed itself to be absorbed by the feudality, the inevitable sequel of the economic regression. All the consequences of this change became glaringly apparent after Charlemagne. Europe, dominated by the Church and the feudality, assumed a new physiognomy, differing slightly in different regions. The Middle Ages—to retain the traditional term—were beginning. The transitional phase was protracted. One may say that it lasted a whole century—from 650 to 750. It was during this period of anarchy that the tradition of antiquity disappeared, while the new elements came to the surface.

This development was completed in 800 by the constitution of the new Empire, which consecrated the break between the West and the East, inasmuch as it gave to the West a new Roman Empire—the manifest proof that it had broken with the old Empire, which continued to exist in Constantinople.

UCCLE,
    May 4th, 1935, 10.30 a.m.

                                        HENRI PIRENNE

INDEX

INDEX

MERIDIAN BOOKS

7 Union Square West, New York 3, New York

If you have enjoyed this book, you will want these titles of related interest. Ask your bookseller for them.

Titles listed here are not necessarily available in the British Empire.

MERIDIAN BOOKS

17 Union Square West, New York 3, New York

If you have enjoyed this book, you will want these titles of related interest. Ask your bookseller for them.

ANTHROPOLOGY

M15 SEX AND REPRESSION IN SAVAGE SOCIETY
by Bronislaw Malinowski

ART AND ART HISTORY

M7 THE PHILOSOPHY OF MODERN ART *by Herbert Read*
M8 CREATIVE INTUITION IN ART AND POETRY
by Jacques Maritain
M18 NEW DIRECTIONS 15: An anthology of new directions in prose and poetry. International issue
M33 VISION AND DESIGN *by Roger Fry*. Illustrations
M38 THE ESSENCE OF LAUGHTER AND OTHER ESSAYS ON ART AND LITERATURE *by Charles Baudelaire. Edited, selected, and introduced by Peter Quennell*. Meridian Original
ML2 A DICTIONARY OF CLASSICAL ANTIQUITIES *by Oskar Seyffert*. Revised and edited by Henry Nettleship and J. E. Sandys. More than 450 illustrations. Meridian Library

CLASSICS

M9 OUTLINES OF THE HISTORY OF GREEK PHILOSOPHY
by Edward Zeller
M23 BYZANTINE CIVILIZATION *by Steven Runciman*
MG3 PROLEGOMENA TO THE STUDY OF GREEK RELIGION
by Jane Harrison. Meridian Giant
MG7 PLATO: The Man and His Work *by A. E. Taylor*.
Meridian Giant
ML1 ROMAN SOCIETY FROM NERO TO MARCUS AURELIUS *by Samuel Dill*. Meridian Library
ML2 A DICTIONARY OF CLASSICAL ANTIQUITIES *by Oskar Seyffert*. Revised and edited by Henry Nettleship and J. E. Sandys. More than 450 illustrations. Meridian Library

DRAMA AND THEATER

M6 THE PLAYWRIGHT AS THINKER *by Eric Bentley*
MG4 MY LIFE IN ART *by Constantin Stanislavski*.
Meridian Giant
MG5 THE ROMANTIC AGONY *by Mario Praz*. Meridian Giant

EDUCATION

M31 FREEDOM, EDUCATION AND THE FUND: Essays and Addresses, 1946–1956 *by Robert M. Hutchins*. Meridian Original
MG4 MY LIFE IN ART *by Constantin Stanislavski*.
Meridian Giant

Titles listed here are not necessarily available in the British Empire.